Morphing MAGIC

Morphing Magic

Scott Anderson

PUBLISHING

A Division of Prentice Hall Computer Publishing
201 W. 103rd Street, Indianapolis, Indiana 46290 USA

*This book is dedicated to my wonderful wife, Candyce.
She gave birth to our twins, Brooke Elizabeth and Blake William,
on the same day this book was started: February 4, 1993.*

Copyright © 1993 by Sams Publishing

Trademarks

Overview

Contents

Acknowledgments

This wonderful little project sprouted out of a book I worked on with Dick Oliver, *Tricks of the Graphics Gurus.* He is a great guy and a pretty persuasive person. He cajoled me into writing a chapter on morphing. The nice folks at SAMs thought the time was ripe for a whole book on morphing, and I was recruited for the project. I must thank Dick for his good humor while working with me and the introduction he provided. Buy his book.

Dennis Goodrow helped me enormously. If you can arrange to get a friend like Dennis, I recommend you do it. He looked over all my turgid prose and was the kindest critic I could hope for. He made wonderful suggestions about the code, and I included all that I could. This little acknowledgment does not do justice to the generous help Dennis provided.

Tim Floto was kind enough to look over the software and make many useful suggestions. He also helped me round up some pictures and graphics programs that greatly simplified my life. He did all this in the final, hectic days of the schedule—and personified calm under pressure.

I also want to thank the folks at Sams. Stacy Hiquet hacked through dense legal thickets to get permission to use the pictures I wanted. Wayne Blankenbeckler discovered more bugs in the software than I care to talk about and helped to round up pictures for the computer demos. Dean Miller did a thorough editing job on the text. He approaches his work with a good sense of humor—and for my stuff, he needs it.

And thanks to Richard Swadley, the publisher, for running a tight show where things get done. If you must have a publisher, get one like Richard.

Finally, thanks to all the artists and computer programmers who consented to let me reproduce their work. This story would be impossible to tell without their wonderful illustrations.

About the Author

Scott Anderson received a degree in Physics from Sonoma State University in 1978. Upon graduation, he started a software company called Sonoma Softworks.

In 1980 Anderson wrote *SuperMap*, a United States geography program published by Apple Computer. In 1982, he wrote *Datadex*, one of the first microcomputer database programs, for the Apple. It was published by Information Unlimited Software. Anderson also wrote *Fantavision*, an animation program with morphing and tweening, aimed at kids. The Apple version was published by Brøderbund in 1985. *Fantavision* was subsequently ported to the IBM and Amiga computers, and translated into French, German, Spanish, and Japanese.

In 1991, Anderson and his wife, Candyce, formed a software publishing company called Wild Duck. Having retrieved the rights from Brøderbund, Wild Duck is currently selling *Fantavision* and developing further animation and graphics software.

Introduction

Everywhere I turn these days, it seems people are talking about something called *morphing* that they saw in *Terminator 2*, a Michael Jackson video or some shaving commercial. What *is* morphing and what does it have to do with movies, rock videos, and commercials? And why in the world would teachers, students, artists, marketing people, and researchers be interested in such a thing?

Morphing is a merciful shorthand for metamorphosing. The word is stolen from biology, where it describes nature's wonderful magic trick of turning a caterpillar into a butterfly or a tadpole into a frog. Morphing depicts objects that smoothly change shape, like Michael J. Fox becoming a werewolf or Michael Jackson turning into a panther.

It turns out that the roots of morphing go deep, invading the turfs of both science and art. Mother Nature loves a good metamorphosis, and has many up her sleeve. Educators need the tools to illustrate those transformations. Artists want to automate animation, and morphing is the key to making their lives easier. Movie directors crave the latest morphing effect—at any cost. Even auto makers are using morphing to show you how this year's model has changed. Everyone is morphing!

At least, everyone who can afford to.

Now there is good news for artists and communicators everywhere: PC software for creating animation and special effects such as morphing is already available, and getting better and cheaper every day. This book is your tour guide through some of the visual excitement being created by morphing. We'll explore some of the applications, and some of the commercially available software that lets *you* be the artist.

For the intrepid, this book also explores the math behind the magic of morphing. I look at the programming tricks that make it all possible. Nobody is forcing you to look at the math or the code, however. You can derive plenty of satisfaction from just reading the text and looking at all the pretty pictures, and you are encouraged to do just that. To help you out, I have labeled the tough stuff as separate sections. You don't need to know it to understand the text. However, if you *do* digest the math and code sections, you will learn enough to write your own morphing software. *Bon appétit.*

Thanks to the included disk, you can experiment directly with morphing. You will find software that morphs geometric objects and creates blended colors. In addition, you get a chance to work with programs that morph photographic images, just like the movies. You can warp and morph the images provided, or you can scan in your own pictures—mix and match them.

By the end of the book, you will have seen many faces of morphing, some of them in unlikely places. You will probably have several ideas for things you want to morph, and you will know what tools to use. With the included software, you will be able to express yourself right away.

So the next time it comes up in the conversation, you can impress them all with your own show and tell—about the magic of morphing.

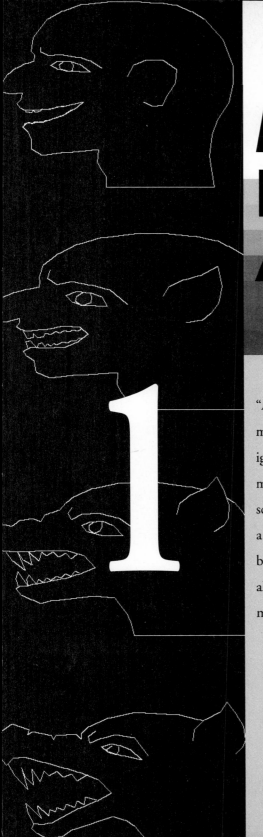

Morphing Helps Animators

1

"Animation, at best, is a costly procedure, in both time and money, and anything that eases its birth process should not be ignored. If audiences only knew all that is involved in any animated production ... a typical team for the production of a large-scale animated film includes a lot of people: a director, a producer, a number of animators and assistant animators, a team of in-betweeners, and special-effects artists ... considering all the personalities involved, it is often a miracle that any animation films get made at all."

Tony White, *The Animator's Workbook*, 1986, Watson-Guptill Publications: New York

Animation is a daunting task. The aspiring animator has to be ready to create a thousand or more drawings for just *one minute* of animation. Of course, most animation studios "cheat" in numerous ways. They might work on twos, meaning they duplicate every other frame, cutting the work in half. Or they might just not animate very often, showing a pan, a zoom or a still shot of a background for several seconds. Or they might animate only small areas, such as the mouth, leaving the rest of the frame completely motionless.

This is because there is very little penetration of computing into animation houses even today. Disney studios and Hanna-Barbera have worked on the problem with notable success, but most animation is still very labor-intensive and expensive.

Software is just in the early stages of dealing with the problem. But some good programs for computer animation do exist and the interfaces are becoming friendlier all the time. Many of these packages support "morphing" and a related concept called "tweening." These powerful tools are becoming more familiar to artists. As a result, animation is becoming an accessible new popular media.

Tweening and morphing are funny words for two powerful animation techniques. At root, these concepts are kissing cousins, yet one yields simple prosaic animation, while the other produces mesmerizing transformations.

Tweening is short for in-betweening, and refers to the computer's ability to calculate and draw frames that are intermediate between the "key" frames hand-drawn by the artist. Because you can have dozens of tweened frames between each pair of key frames, animation can be produced ten to fifty times faster than with manual methods alone. A month of tedious drawing can be squeezed into a day. That gets an animator's attention.

Morphing is short for metamorphosing, and is a similar concept. Like tweening, morphing puts the computer to work doing the hard parts. Whereas tweening is used to fill in the blanks between similar figures, morphing is used between *dissimilar* objects, such as a man and a werewolf, a bat and a vampire, or a rock singer and a panther.

Although these techniques might seem relatively limited, you will be surprised at the wide range of problems they address. Modern movie-making would not be the same without them. As the chapter-opening quote suggests, animation is not for the timid. Tweening and morphing immediately find favor with those artists who have toiled over their celluloid paintings and appreciate the difficulties involved.

As you will discover, this is a perfect niche for a computer—doing a tedious exercise over and over. Rather than putting people out of work, this technology liberates them to pursue their most creative ideas without the hindrance and expense of traditional animation.

Who uses animation software and what is it like? How can it help you get your message across? In this chapter, I look into some of the current software offerings. I discuss what they can do for you, how they work, and their limitations.

Who needs Animation Software?

"The ultimate special effect is far from commonplace and is in fact far from being fully realized. For by creating a visual language in the active medium of computers, image makers have moved us across a human threshold comparable to the moment when some unknown ancestor first created writing by pressing figures into clay."

Joseph Deken, *Computer Images—State of the Art*,
1983 Stewart, Tabori & Chang: New York

In just a few short years, computerized special effects, including tweening and morphing, have made enormous inroads into the Hollywood establishment. These techniques have put new vigor into the cartoons and an amazing new "realism" into feature films.

The most profound impact, however, might be on the small studios and independent film-makers. Without the manpower and gigantic budgets of the large studios, these groups have long been denied the advantages of animation. New computer tools are solving with one stroke the labor and expense sides of this equation. As the entry prices for these tools fall, the medium becomes more democratic, and we should expect completely new and surprising ideas to surface.

Animators aren't the only ones to rejoice at the new software offerings. Educators are happy to find tools that can engage their students, yet cut their overhead. Animation is not only an excellent tool for communicating ideas, it is also an exciting environment for learning about the computer. The first rule of education is to get the student's attention, and nothing does that like animation. Programs such as *Animator* and *Fantavision,* discussed later in the chapter, are wonderful tools for kids to learn about menus, buttons, the mouse, and graphics—not to mention animation!

There was a time when teaching kids animation was an unthinkable project. Now, not only is animation available, it is so simple that it has become a method, not just a goal. Educators are using animation to keep their students' attention while sneaking in lessons about computers, math, science, or English.

Students are excited about animation, too. Almost from the moment they are born, children are bathed in the glow of televised animation. When they get a chance to make their own cartoons, stand back. Kids might not know a lot about art, but they are experts at having fun. And animation is fun—with the computer's help. This generation of children is the first to be exposed to computerized cartooning. Animation will be just another outlet for their self-expression. Only time will tell what the consequences will be.

Another group of people who have recently embraced animation is researchers. Our present knowledge of complicated systems in biology and chemistry is pushing traditional exposition to the limits. Sometimes an animation is the only way to visualize these intricate discoveries. With animation becoming easier, cheaper, and less labor-intensive, more laboratories are adopting it. As scientific journals start to go online for more timely access, it will become natural to include animations along with the more traditional diagrams and charts.

Every little town these days has its own TV station. Without the big city or network budgets, these studios must make do with less. But they are finding that animation is one of the more affordable, quick-payback technologies. Although a distressing number of these applications are just flying logos, some studios are producing striking and novel animated spots. When today's computer-savvy kids graduate and strike the job market, we could witness the flying of some wild and creative sparks.

As animation becomes more ubiquitous, you can expect to see it wherever you currently see print. Brochures, demos and presentations are routinely animated. Even the company newsletter is becoming animated. This has happened because businesses have realized that animation captivates while it educates, and *that* can improve sales. Of course businesses have been animating since Sir Speedy first tap-danced for Alka-Seltzer, and before. Advertisers always have been great customers of the animation studios. But the move to in-house animation had to wait for the recent software solutions.

Painting and Drawing

"Sometimes one has to say difficult things, but one ought to say them as simply as one knows how."

G.H. Hardy

Look closely at your TV screen. You will notice that the apparently smooth picture is really composed of tiny colored dots. These dots are called pixels, which is a twisted shorthand for *picture elements* (programmers are not known for their spelling prowess). These pixels are the basis of the entire computer graphics industry, so we need to digress a bit and discuss them.

In the computer world, there are two ways to create images. All right, there are hundreds of ways, but only two really important ones. One is to color each one of the thousands of pixels on the screen. Software packages that help you do this are called paint programs. So far, so good.

The other major way to create an image is to use graphics primitives such as points, lines, polygons and circles. For no good reason, programs that use this method are called draw programs. Even though these two software species have confusingly similar names, they are very different.

Paint programs provide tools that are comfortable and familiar to artists. They will know how to use the paintbrush, the pencil, the eraser, or the air-brush immediately. These programs support the mouse (which is like drawing with a brick) or any of the various drawing pads. Some of these programs are specially suited to painting over scanned-in photographs. Even though these programs, called retouch programs, have revolutionized the pre-press industry, they are still, at heart, paint programs.

The output of a paint program, which is made up of dots, is usually printed or viewed at its creation size or smaller. If you try to enlarge these images, the dots get bigger as well. Sometimes, pixelation (the name of this effect) is a desired effect, but mostly it is a problem. Figure 1.1 illustrates this irritating artifact.

To get around pixelation, you can use draw programs.

Draw programs produce output that can be enlarged to cover the Astrodome, if you choose, without showing pixels. This is because the primitives, such as lines and polygons, are scalable, mathematical objects. Instead of treating a line as a collection of points, the program re-draws the line for any desired resolution. A typical computer monitor might have 60 dots per inch of resolution. But a draw program routinely creates artwork for the printing press that has a *thousand* dots per inch!

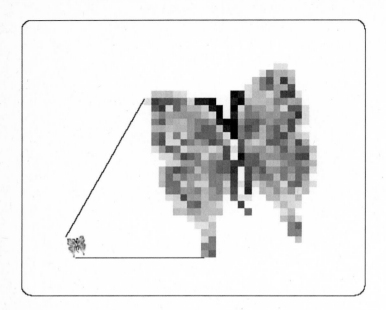

Figure 1.1.
Scaling an image from a paint program scales the pixels as well.

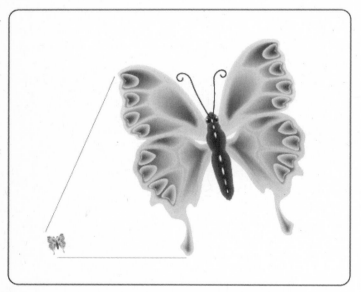

Figure 1.2.
Scaling an image from a draw program works much better.

Contrast Figure 1.2 with Figure 1.1. The draw program produces output that is easily scaled.

With the great power of draw programs, why doesn't everyone use them? The tools aren't as intuitive to the artist. Draw programs offer splines (curved lines) and polygons that are more familiar to the mathematician than the artist. For many applications, however, this is the only choice.

Animation programs come in both paint and draw flavors. The advantages of paint-based animation software, as before, are the simplicity and friendliness of the interface. The advantages of draw-based animation software are more subtle, but one of the most important is the ability to do unassisted tweening and morphing.

While a bit-mapped image needs carefully defined control points to manage morphing (as you shall see), a polygon can unambiguously and automatically metamorphose into another polygon—as long as it has the same number of sides. Even if the number of sides change, there are tricks to automate the animation.

Big deal, you might think. But with enough sides on a polygon, you can make just about any shape you want. A blustery caveman named Fred, for instance, or a wily coyote.

In other words, draw or polygon-based animation programs are perfect for Saturday morning cartoons. In fact, these programs were the first to infiltrate the Hanna-Barbera and Disney studios. Now you can do the same thing on your PC.

Some Animation programs

Animator is a popular paint-based program for the PC from Autodesk. It has a wide range of features—such as fades and dissolves—that allow quick assembly of images for animation. *Animator* supports *positional* tweening, a big time-saver for animators. That means the artist can place an image on the left in the first key frame, on the right in the second key frame, and let the computer smoothly and automatically slide the object across the screen.

Animator images are bitmaps, or pixel images. That means that they have been captured or drawn on a dot-by-dot basis, as discussed earlier. These pictures are rich in detail, and take up large amounts of disk space. *Animator* has a special file format that reduces the storage requirements. Only the things that actually change from frame to frame are recorded. Nevertheless, pixel images are notorious hard-drive hogs.

Fantavision is a draw-based animation package. I wrote the first version of Fantavision about eight years ago, and I've been trying to explain tweening and morphing ever since. At first published by Brøderbund, it is now published by Wild Duck, a company I formed with my wife Candyce in 1991. Wild Duck develops and publishes software primarily for the educational market.

Fantavision features polygon animation and is unusual in that its entire approach is tweening and morphing. Designed specifically for students, *Fantavision* requires only two pictures to start an animation. Even the most jittery student can sit still for the few seconds it takes to metamorphose a bow-tie into a jet-plane.

Because the frames are composed of polygons, they may lack the detail found in painted images. But since only the points, or vertices, of the polygons are saved, these animations are compact. In fact, only the key frames are saved by *Fantavision*, and the tweens are generated on the fly. This is a huge savings, and it is not unusual for an entire *Fantavision* animation to be smaller than a single frame from Animator.

What is Tweening?

"Photography is truth. The cinema is truth twenty-four times per second."

Jean-Luc Godard

So far I've avoided a specific definition of tweening. This rather frivolous name disguises a simple mathematical principle. The mathematical term for tweening from one shape into another is *interpolation*. To interpolate, according to Webster, means to insert between other things or parts, or to estimate values of a function between two known values.

The simplest (although by no means the only) way to interpolate is called *linear*, because the solutions are all on a *line*. Here's an example of how it works. Start with a horizontal line in frame one, and tween to a vertical line in frame two, as in Figure 1.3.

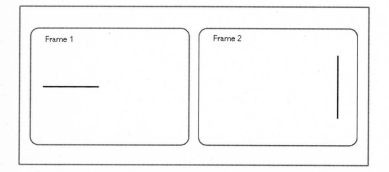

Figure 1.3.
A horizontal and a vertical line, ready to be tweened.

Let the two end-points of the segment take a straight path from frame one to two, as shown by the dotted lines in Figure 1.4. Halfway between the two, at the midpoints of these paths, lies the central tween. As you might have suspected, it is a diagonal line, as you can see in Figure 1.5.

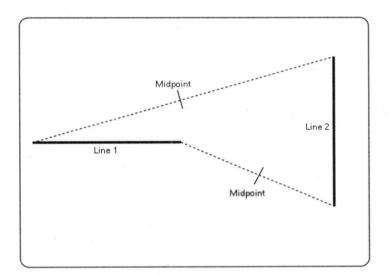

Figure 1.4.
Connect the end-points of these two lines.

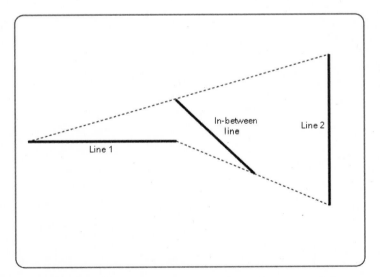

Figure 1.5.
Draw a new line connecting the mid-points. That's the in-between line.

Subdividing the line again in Figure 1.6, you find another tween on each side of the middle tween.

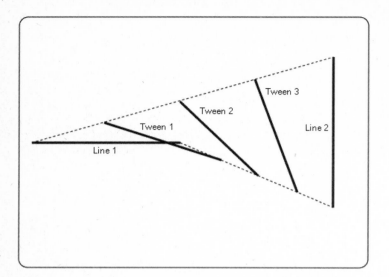

Figure 1.6.
There are two more tweens, on either side of the first tween.

Now there are three tweens between frame one and frame two. You can split the path into as many parts as you need to assure smooth motion. All you need to do is divide the length of the path by the number of tweens, and you have the beginnings of an algorithm.

THE MATH CORNER:

Cartesian coordinates

Before you can get anywhere with the math behind computer graphics, you need to brush up briefly on coordinates and Cartesian space. As you might (or might not) remember from that long math class you took in school, Rene Descarte was a sick little boy. So instead of playing outside, he sat at his desk and toyed around with numbers. Being visually oriented, he wanted a way to graphically represent the equations he was exploring. He came up with a scheme to relate the number he put into an equation (called the input or independent variable) to the number he got out (called the output or dependent variable) on a piece of paper. He put a horizontal line and a vertical line crossing each other in the middle of the sheet. Where the lines crossed was called the origin. He said that the input variable would be represented by the horizontal distance from the origin, and the output variable by the vertical distance.

This simple scheme is so useful that mathematicians call it the Cartesian coordinate system in Descartes' honor. As it is used today, the horizontal line is called the X axis, and the vertical line is called the Y axis.

To locate a point on a piece of paper, you could say it was two inches to the right and three inches up from the center. You could write it as two numbers: (2,3). Two is the X coordinate, and three is the Y coordinate. Negative numbers result when you go left or down from the center: (−3,−1) is the location of a point three inches to the left and one inch down from the center.

On a computer screen, things got a little messed up. Instead of putting the origin at the center, the first computer graphics nerds put it at the upper left corner. Since *negative* numbers result when you go *down* from the origin, all the Y values that show up on the screen would have to be negative. The graphics guys wanted to make them positive—it was their computer—so they did. This messes up three hundred years of math, of course, and we always need to compensate. So if you see some funny sign-switching going on with Y values in a computer graphics program, now you know why.

This adjusted form of the screen value takes the form:

$$Y_{screen} = YMAX - Y$$

where YMAX is the y value at the bottom of the screen. This flips and offsets the screen so that the math matches the machine.

2D Interpolation

Given two points A and B, how can you find the point midway between them? Point A is specified by the coordinates (A_x, A_y) and point B by (B_x, B_y). The midpoint M is halfway between the X values and halfway between the Y values. To go half the way between the X values, take half the distance separating them and add it to the smaller value:

$$M_x = A_x + (B_x - A_x)/2$$

which simplifies to

$$M_x = (A_x + B_x)/2$$

This is also how you compute the average of two numbers. The midpoint is the average of the two end-points. Computers do most things fast, but one thing they do *really* fast is divide by two. That makes this a good algorithm to keep hanging around. You will find a similar algorithm in the chapter on fast lines and ellipses.

The same analysis applies to Y, so you get the coordinates for M:

$$M = \{(A_x+B_x)/2, \ (A_y+B_y)/2\}$$

What if you want to calculate *two* points in between? I will call these tweening points T1 and T2. I can modify the first equation to go one third of the way:

$$T1_x = A_x + (B_x - A_x)/3$$

and

$$T2_x = A_x + 2 * (B_x - A_x)/3$$

for the X coordinates and the same for Y.

In general, for the ith tween of N total tweens, you can write:

$$T_i = \{A_x + i*(B_x - A_x)/N, \ A_y + i*(B_y - A_y)/N\}$$

where i goes from 1 to N. Note that when i=0, the tweening point is just the starting point, and when i=N, it becomes the end-point. If you pre-calculate the interpolation increment D (corresponding to the Delta array), you can avoid the multiplication and just add D. Addition is always faster than multiplication on a PC, so do it when you can. In a loop that tweens from 1 to N, you can repeatedly add to point A the X and Y differences given by D:

$$D_x = (B_x - A_x)/N$$
$$D_y = (B_y - A_y)/N$$

After adding this quantity N times, point A moves to point B. Although substituting repeated addition for multiplication is faster, you must watch out for round-off errors.

What Good is it?

"Computers are useless. They can only give you answers."

Pablo Picasso

So you can move a line around. Who cares? Well, from this admittedly small accomplishment comes some startling results. I think even Picasso would be impressed.

First off, I need to convince you that straight lines can do something worthwhile. Notice that the character in Figure 1.7 is drawn entirely with short straight lines. It might not be high art, but it *is* a passable cartoon. It turns out that computers use this trick everywhere. Even splined curves really consist of short straight lines. On the limited resolution of the computer screen, you can't even tell the difference.

Figure 1.7.
A face, drawn with straight lines only.

What are splines? I've been kicking this word around a lot without really explaining it. The word comes from ship-builders, who use thin strips of bent wood called splines to draw curved shapes. On a computer, splines have a special mathematical meaning, and they have their own user interface to generate them. This usually involves placing the two end-points of the curve on the screen, then adjusting the curvature with little "handles" at those end-points. When several splines are linked together, the algorithm ensures that the curvature changes smoothly as it goes through the points.

Another fun trick with polygons is to squash them. In fact, because polygons are simple mathematical objects, you can squash, stretch, rotate, shrink, or skew them! These active verbs correspond to simple arithmetic transformations, and they can practically do the animation for you. With the click of a mouse, for instance, you could stretch an object by ten percent, without redrawing it. Because squashing and stretching are integral elements in effective animation, they are handy to have as automatic functions.

You can combine these transformations, too. For instance, you could squash and rotate a coyote at the same time. Considering how often it happens, this is a great feature.

THE MATH CORNER:

Polygons

What exactly is a polygon? You might have a good intuitive feeling for triangles, squares, and pentagons. These are just special polygons. A polygon is simply a bunch of points connected by edges. A point in a polygon is called a vertex.

Mathematicians like to refer to a polygon using array syntax:

```
Array(i) = (Xi, Yi)
```

where i is a counter that goes through the vertices of the polygon. Each vertex has an x and a y coordinate—just what you would expect from a string of points. If you write something such as

```
2 * Array
```

it means to multiply the x and y value of every point in the array by two. This doubles the size of the polygon, just as you might suspect. If you want to affect the x and y coordinates separately, you need to specify a function for each variable. For instance:

```
F(xi,yi) = (xi/2,yi*2)
```

This function "squashes" x values and "stretches" y values. This function could turn a square into a tall, skinny box, or turn Oliver Hardy into Stan Laurel.

By applying the interpolation equations discussed earlier to each point in an array, you can transform one array into another—a simple recipe for tweening polygons.

What is Morphing?

As Gregor Samsa awoke one morning from uneasy dreams he found himself transformed in his bed into a gigantic insect.

Franz Kafka, *The Metamorphosis*, 1915

If you tween to a *different* object, it's called morphing. Tweening and morphing are otherwise the same, with the same mathematical underpinnings. Again, the simplest method is linear interpolation. The polygons might be as different as the outlines of a caterpillar and a butterfly. But if the points on the two profiles match up, when they tween, one polygon will metamorphose into the other.

Another example created with *Fantavision* shows the metamorphosis of a man into a werewolf. Figure 1.8 shows the man, Figure 1.9 shows the werewolf, and Figure 1.10 shows some of the intermediate stages of the morphing.

Figure 1.8.
A line-drawing of a man's face before the full moon.

Figure 1.9.
The moon is out, our man has become a werewolf.

Figure 1.10.
Here are some of the tweens from a man to a werewolf, produced by Fantavision.

DISKETTE DEMO: The Werewolf

Enter PLAY WEREWOLF. This is a simple line drawing made with *Fantavision* to illustrate the concept of morphing. Although it looks like there are curves in the image, it is really composed of straight line segments. To create the animation, the man was first drawn and then copied to a new frame. The man was stretched and pulled, point by point, into a werewolf. The polygons have the same number of vertices. Only their positions differ. Therefore, there is a simple one-to-one correspondence of the points. The images have dozens of tweens separating them.

To run the movie faster, press a number from six to nine (fastest). To slow it down, press a number from one (slowest) to four. Press 5 to restore the original speed. The new speed does not take effect until the next key-frame is reached, so you might need to be patient. What these number commands do is to increase or decrease the number of tweens between key-frames. This is useful when compensating for computers that run slower or faster than the original machine the movie was composed on. Press Esc to quit.

What if the points don't match up? If you relax the rules a bit, you can make any shape transform into any other shape. A hexagon can metamorphose into a triangle. The simplest method distributes the point mismatch around the polygon. First determine which polygon of the transforming pair is smaller. Then add enough points to it to match the bigger one. Add the points on top of the existing points. Distribute them around the polygon, so each vertex, or corner, has approximately the same number of duplicate points.

This is the method used in the program *Fantavision*, and it is particularly well suited for novices and students. They can easily put things in motion without sweating the details.

You can't have it all

The marcelled waves of Captain Hook's hair in *Peter Pan* caused much consternation in the Inbetween Department because the contour could not be a straight inbetween of the lines, but had to be a complete drawing of the hair in a new position. However, his hair caused even more consternation in the final film as it faded into the dark shapes in the background in scene after scene. We could have saved ourselves a lot of work and money if we had known that the colors behind him were going to be that dark.

Frank Thomas & Ollie Johnston, *Disney Animation, the Illusion of Life*, 1984 Abbeville Press : New York

For more complicated motion, some other forms of interpolation could be used. For instance, splines and arcs are often more natural for character animation. Your arm pivots around your elbow and takes a circular path as you wave (see Figure 1.11). Your legs rotate around your knees and hip joints as you walk. One of Walt Disney's key observations was that an arcing path created much more realistic animation than the straight line paths I have been discussing.

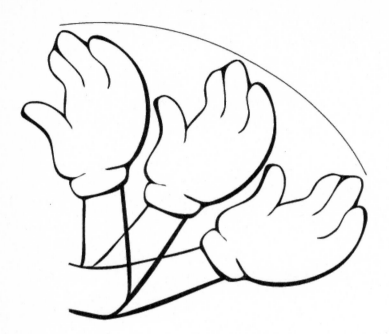

Figure 1.11.
Arcs make the
movement more
realistic - even for
mouse arms.

Unfortunately, none of the available desk-top programs lets the user have that kind of control. Part of the problem is the user interface. Linear paths are obvious and simply specified. All you need are the end-points, and you can uniquely define a line. Splines, as discussed in the earlier sidebar, take more information to specify. Since we are specifying a path that will be taken through time, not just a line on the page, it becomes even more confusing. But it seems likely that software developers will soon be offering some of these advanced features, especially as users start clamoring for them.

Another approach to animation is model-building. In this method you describe, in great detail, the size and degrees of freedom for each part to be animated. For instance, for an animated person, you would state the length and maximum rotation for each joint in the body. A fully articulated cartoon person would have all the necessary information for the ankles, knees, elbows, shoulders, backbone, even fingers and toes!

Needless to say, this is a big job. But when you are done, you still need to specify the equations of motion. And don't forget that animated characters are subject to a lot of squashing and stretching, so many of the constraints you define will have to be broken. Actually, systems like this do exist, but they are expensive, and usually need a physicist to operate them.

Some modified version of model-making will surely be a part of future desktop-animation systems, but for now, you will just have to wait.

Model-building brings up another subject—the third dimension. Successful models are usually created in 3-D and then displayed in 2-D. The third dimension is highly desirable, but artists have managed to indicate the third dimension on a flat painting just fine since the fifteenth century. Disney, Hanna-Barbera, and Warner Brothers have done great work without computerized 3-D modeling.

But that is soon to change, and the stimulus will come from *virtual reality.* In a virtual reality game, you see the computerized world turn in response to the movement of your head. This amazing technology effectively puts you inside the computer. And to do this, you absolutely *must* have three dimensions. As hardware manufacturers recognize this, they have started to create the next generation of graphics chips with 3-D functions built-in.

When this difficult 3-D stuff shows up on chips, you will see a flurry of action as software developers race to create real-time, interactive 3-D animation.

Until these systems become cheap, you will have to be content with 2-D. But don't fret, there is still plenty of territory to cover, even in flat-space.

The last item on the list of things you can't have (yet) is help with your drawing skills. Many people become distressed when they have to draw something. Yet these people shouldn't be denied animation as a creative outlet. What is needed is animated clip-art, and it is just beginning to catch on.

Like clip-art in draw and paint programs, clip-animation includes short animations of everyday or specialized events, people, or places. Produced by professional artists, but provided royalty-free to the user, clip-animation can turn the worst artist into an animation demon.

This is just a short list of some of the limitations still existing in the computer animation field. For every problem, there are dozens of amazing solutions floating around that could be converted from vaporware to software at any minute. In the meantime, let's play with what we have!

DISKETTE DEMO: Dots

On the disk there is a program called DOT that allows you to plot a pixel on the screen. This should be a simple task, yet look at the code it takes to do it. This pretty disgusting situation happened for several reasons, but the most important goes back to the early 1980's when IBM decided that graphics were not relevant to computing. When the first PCs came out, there was only text output. When IBM finally added graphics, they were so pathetic that they weren't useful. And graphics capabilities still weren't built in. Later, other companies came to the rescue and designed graphics cards with greater power. IBM slowly came around to producing a decent graphics card of its own, but by this time, there were dozens of graphics cards on the market, and they all worked differently. Software designers were forced to provide general-purpose solutions that couldn't optimize anything very well.

That is still the situation. Although very few PCs are sold without graphics cards, the computer languages to address those cards are kludgy. The overlords of C haven't really tackled the graphics problem yet. So I have put the non-standard Microsoft graphics routines in CORE.C, to keep them from confusing the issue. If you have a different compiler, this is where you would substitute the graphics primitives specific to its whims. One day, everyone in the computer industry will appreciate the appeal of graphics and will design appropriate hardware and software tools. Until that glorious day, we'll have to hack through a little thicket of code, but we *will* get there.

CORE.C

For our purposes, CORE.C is just to turn on the graphics mode and plot pixels. This file gets linked to the DOT program. All the non-standard graphics calls have been shuffled off to this program.

CORE.C—The Listing

```
/* CORE.C
 *
 * This core file contains the basic routines for tweening as
 * well as the graphics startup routine and a random number
 * routine.
 *
```

```
 * by Scott Anderson, 1/23/1993
 */

/***** Includes *****/

#include <stdio.h>        /* Standard input/output libraries */
#include <stdlib.h>
#include <graph.h>

/***** Globals *****/

int     Wide;
int     Tall;
int     OldMode;

/***** Prototypes *****/

int clearScreen(int back_color);
int setColor(int color);
int setText();
int setVideo();
int startGraphics();
int plotPixel(int x, int y, int color);
int random(int low, int high);

/******************************************************************
* FUNC: int startGraphics()
*
* DESC: Set up the 256 color, 320x200 screen
******************************************************************/

int
startGraphics()
{   /* Make sure we can run in 256 color graphics mode,
     * else quit. */
    struct _videoconfig config;

    _getvideoconfig (&config);  /* Save original video mode */
    OldMode = config.mode;

    if (_setvideomode(_MRES256COLOR) == 0)
    {
        printf("\nUnable to set graphics mode.\n");
        exit(0);
    }
```

continues

CORE.C continued

```
    _getvideoconfig (&config);
    Wide = config.numxpixels;
    Tall = config.numypixels;
    /* clip to entire screen */
    _setcliprgn(0, 0, Wide - 1, Tall - 1);
}

/*****************************************************************
* FUNC: int setVideo()
*
* DESC: Set the video graphics mode
*****************************************************************/

int
setVideo()
{
    _setvideomode (_MRES256COLOR);
}

/*****************************************************************
* FUNC: int setText()
*
* DESC: Reset the original text mode
*****************************************************************/

int
setText()
{
    _setvideomode (OldMode);
}

/*****************************************************************
* FUNC: int setColor(int color)
*
* DESC: Set the color for subsequent pixel drawing
*****************************************************************/

int
setColor(int color)
{
    _setcolor(color);
}
```

```
/***************************************************************
 * FUNC: int clearScreen(int back_color)
 *
 * DESC: Clear screen to the given background color
 ***************************************************************/

int
clearScreen(int back_color)
{
    _setbkcolor(back_color);
    _clearscreen(_GCLEARSCREEN);
}

/***************************************************************
 * FUNC: int plotPixel(int x, int y, int color)
 *
 * DESC: Plot a pixel of the given color at x,y
 ***************************************************************/

int
plotPixel(int x, int y, int color)
{
    int old_color = _getcolor();

    _setcolor(color);
    _setpixel(x, y);
    _setcolor(old_color);
}

/***************************************************************
 * FUNC: int random(int low, int high)
 *
 * DESC: Return a random number between the low and high values
 ***************************************************************/

int
random (int low, int high)
{   /* get a random number between low and high, inclusively */

    /* check limits to avoid divide by zero error */
    if (high <= low) return (low);
    return (low + (rand() % (high-low)));
}
```

DOT.C

DOT.C is the main routine that calls the functions in core to plot a pixel on the screen. It prompts for the x and y coordinates and the color, expressed as an index from 1 to 15:

DOT.C—The Listing

```
/* DOT.C
 *
 * This program draws a dot on the screen at the
 * specified x,y coordinate.
 *
 * by Scott Anderson, 1/23/1993
 */

/***** Includes *****/

#include <stdio.h>              /* Standard input/output libraries */
#include <stdlib.h>
#include <graph.h>

/***** Define the point structure *****/

typedef struct
{   /* for the screen coordinates */
    int x, y;
    int color;
} POINT;

/*****  Globals  *****/

extern int      Wide;
extern int      Tall;

/***** Prototypes *****/

int        getPoint (POINT *thePoint);
int        drawPoint(POINT *thePoint);
int        inputXY(POINT *point);
int        clippedInput (int low, int high);
```

```
/************************************************************
 * FUNC: int main()
 *
 * DESC: Get the coordinates for a point and plot it in color.
 ************************************************************/

int
main()
{
    POINT thePoint;

    startGraphics();           /* check & turn on graphics */
    getPoint (&thePoint);      /* input the point coordinates */
    setVideo();                /* reset graphics mode */
    clearScreen(0);            /* clear to black */
    drawPoint (&thePoint);     /* draw the point on the screen */
    getch();                   /* wait for keypress */
    setText();                 /* reset to text before quitting */
}

/************************************************************
 * FUNC: int getPoint(POINT *thePoint)
 *
 * DESC: Set the text mode and get the x,y coordinates and color
 *       from the user.
 ************************************************************/

int
getPoint (POINT *thePoint)
{
    setText();
    printf ("\n\n");
    printf ("This program plots the point you specify.\n");
    printf ("To quit the program, press ctrl+C during\n");
    printf ("input or Esc during display.\n\n");

    printf ("Please enter the coordinates of the point.\n\n");
    inputXY (thePoint);
}

/************************************************************
 * FUNC: int drawPoint(POINT *thePoint)
 *
 * DESC: Draw an object, in this case, a point.
 ************************************************************/
```

continues

DOT.C continued

```
int
drawPoint(POINT *thePoint)
{
    plotPixel (thePoint->x, thePoint->y, thePoint->color);
}


/*****************************************************************
* FUNC: int inputXY(POINT *point)
*
* DESC: General-purpose routine to input the clipped coordinates
*       and color of a point.
*****************************************************************/

int
inputXY (POINT *point)
{   /* Get clipped coordinates from the user */
    printf ("X: ");
    point->x = clippedInput (0, Wide-1);
    printf ("Y: ");
    point->y = clippedInput (0, Tall-1);
    printf ("Color (1-15): ");
    point->color = clippedInput (1, 15);
}


/*****************************************************************
* FUNC: int clippedInput(int low, int high)
*
* DESC: This function returns a value from the keyboard that has
*       been clipped to the range between the low and high values.
*****************************************************************/

int
clippedInput (int low, int high)
{   /* Get input from the keyboard and clip it to low, high */
    int value;

    scanf ("%i", &value);
    if (value < low) return (low);
    if (value > high) return (high);
    return (value);
}
```

Well, that was the hard part. But now you know something about pixels and how they are related to animation. You even have code to plot a pixel on the PC screen. That first baby step is just the beginning of our stroll through the graphics garden.

In the next chapter you will put these concepts to work. You will see ways of using animation in education. Let's get a move on!

Morphing Goes to School

2

"My students were 'non-science' majors, although 'anti-science' would perhaps be closer to the mark. It didn't take me long to realize that I could not reach them by the kinds of arguments and approaches that appealed to me. The merest whiff of an equation would stampede them to the dean's office to complain about cruel and unusual punishment. Carefully crafted syllogisms moved them about as much as it would have moved a team of sled dogs. What did move them, I discovered, were things they could see and hear and touch.

**Craig F. Bohren, *Clouds in a Glass of Beer*, 1987,
John Wiley & Sons, Inc.: New York**

Kids need to see things to understand and believe them. In fact, most adults need the same thing. The giants of science all learned first by observing. The passage of time and the hindsight of historians have wrung the passion out of those observations and left us with freeze-dried and hermetically sealed equations. Even the original authors couldn't have weaned themselves on that brittle crust.

Children need to see things the way great thinkers do. Then they can understand the importance of observation, of using their eyes, or simply picturing something in their heads. Once visualized, a subject is easier to absorb.

Although this chapter is about *morphing* in education, I can't resist including some simple *tweening* animations. As you remember from the last chapter, tweening and morphing are bound together anyway. In addition, these tweens are polygon animations, which provide a useful backdrop for later chapters (see the About Fantavision section later in the chapter).

Animation tells a story, and everyone likes a good story. Animation seems alive, and can involve the viewer as few other media can. It is only reasonable, then, that animation is often called upon to illustrate topics from natural science.

Many natural phenomena involve one object that slowly changes into another, such as a tadpole developing into a frog or a chimpanzee evolving into a man. Animating these concepts is made easier by computer programs that fill in the many slightly different stages automatically. In such a system, you only need to draw the tadpole and the frog, and all the in-between frames can be generated by the morphing or tweening software. This makes a busy educator happy.

In addition, there are many advanced concepts in biology, chemistry and physics that are difficult to understand without an animation. Researchers often find that they can better appreciate their own discoveries by animating them. Computer software to simplify the preparation of these animated shorts will empower researchers and teachers. Soon there will be electronic journals devoted to disseminating animated diagrams to other researchers and to students around the world.

The people bound to benefit most from this approach include students, teachers, animators, and researchers. In this chapter I explore some of the educational topics that just beg to be morphed, tweened, or just plain animated. I cover a smorgasbord of topics, but feel free to graze at your own speed. Some sections are more obscure than others—you can skip them. Relax. You won't be tested on this.

About Fantavision

The animations for this chapter were created with Fantavision. There are three good reasons for this. First, Fantavision movies are very compact, so I can fit a lot of them on a disk. Second, Fantavision movies are easy to create—they provide a good example of what an interested novice could produce. Finally, I wrote Fantavision, and I gave myself permission to use it in this book.

Before you can approach pixel or image-based morphing, you need some exposure to polygon morphing. This is it. In later chapters, you will see how it all fits together.

Fantavision is really for kids to learn about animation, but it has enough power that I use it professionally to produce the occasional educational video. Although Fantavision is a simple polygon animation tool, it still can get the message across.

I have included the Fantavision movie-player on the disk. It is called PLAY.EXE and it is yours to copy or send to friends, along with any of the movies. To use it, get to the DOS prompt and type:

```
>PLAY <Movie1> [<Movie2>] ...
```

<Movie1> is the name of a Fantavision movie, such as WING.MVE. Optionally, you can enter a list of movies to play in sequence:

```
>PLAY EGG1 EGG2 EGG3 EGG4
```

Notice that you don't have to type ".MVE" after each name; the program will append it automatically.

While the movie is running, you can control it with certain keys:

- Press the SPACE BAR to pause and restart the movie.

- Press a number from 1–9 to change the speed, with 1 being the slowest setting and 9 the fastest. The normal speed is 5.

- Press the left arrow key to reverse the movie, and the right arrow key to go forward again.

- Press ENTER to skip to the next movie in a sequence.

- Press ESC to quit the animation.

Sometimes, especially if you use the direction or speed keys, you might see some unusual animation. Just reset the movie to go forward (right arrow) with normal speed (5). If that doesn't fix things, press ESC and try again.

If you want to create your own Fantavision movies, you need the Fantavision Editor. For that I refer you to the ordering information at the end of this book.

Morphing and Tweening in the Arts

Animation is not often on the arts curricula because it is absurdly consuming of labor and time. But with computerized animation programs, this medium has been tamed. Even the youngest students can create animation. Programs such as Animator, Director, and Fantavision are enthralling both art students and teachers.

Animator makes it easy to string together full-screen images for animated playback. This is a feature-rich program for advanced animators.

Director gives you multimedia control over sound and graphics and includes a sophisticated language to control its many features. This program is also for advanced users.

Fantavision lets even the youngest children create special effects and polygon animation. At its core, Fantavision is a tweening and morphing program. Fantavision is the program used to create and display the animated "movies" included on this disk.

Animation doesn't just mean cartooning. There are new artforms being defined with these software tools. Most of them don't even have names yet, but that doesn't stop the creative artist.

For instance, students can compose a background in a paint program, and then put spot animation on top of it. These are like living landscapes, with birds gliding against the sky, waves washing in, or trees bending in the breeze.

Students can create interactive movies, where the user determines the story flow; or minimalist visual poetry, such as POLRBEAR, one of the movies on the disk.

The barriers to creativity start to crumble as the tools get more powerful. One power tool is morphing. Among other things, morphing can be used to create still frames, not just animation. Given two images, such as a woman and a cat, the artist can mix as much of each as desired to create a unique, realistic cat-woman. This concept is discussed in greater detail in later chapters.

The next generation of students won't know what life was like without computer art, virtual reality, and computerized movie effects. What type of art will appeal to them? Quite likely, it will be some form of computer art. To prepare for that future, students need some exposure today.

When everyone is capable of making animation, the medium will finally become democratic. Get ready for a lot of different ideas when people realize how easy and expressive animation can be.

DISKETTE DEMO: All that Jazz

From the DOS prompt, type:

```
>PLAY JAZZ
```

This animation was created by a group of rock-climbers and animators from Japan called Studio BC (Base Camp). From their tiny office in Tokyo, they create television animation using, among other programs, Fantavision. This is an animated interpretation of American Jazz, their favorite music.

The morphing gives it a free-floating flavor that captures the music beautifully.

DISKETTE DEMO: Animation as Haiku

From the DOS prompt, type:

```
>PLAY POLRBEAR
```

Another movie from Studio BC, this piece is about a denizen of the frozen north. This is an example of a whole new style of animation inspired by the tweening effect. A single frame from this movie is almost unrecognizable, but motion immediately clears up the confusion. Notice how sparing the artist is with lines. There is a lean and intriguing form of poetry in Japan called Haiku. It must have three lines with exactly five, seven and five syllables on those lines. A graphic Haiku, this movie tells a story, limiting the lines.

DISKETTE DEMO: Something Fishy

From the DOS prompt, type:

```
>PLAY FLYFISH
```

This animation of an unusual metamorphosis is based on some sketches from Studio BC. It's a nice example of representing living objects with simple primitives—in this case, triangles. This fish has an odd way of changing direction, and a strange desire to fly.

DISKETTE DEMO: Moon River

From the DOS prompt, type:

```
>PLAY MOONRIVR
```

This is an example of a "living landscape" (see Figure 2.1). The animation is very simple—tweening does most of the work. The main effort is creating the background in a paint program, but that's pretty straightforward. Projects like this are a natural introduction to full-blown animation.

Figure 2.1.
A moonlit scene with just enough animation to give it life.

Evolution Illustrated

"Underlying many scientific theories are 'images' of wide scope: Darwin's vision of the 'tree of life,' Freud's notion of the unconscious as submerged like an iceberg, John Dalton's view of the atom as a tiny solar system, are the productive figures that give rise to, and help to embody, key scientific conceptions."

Howard Gardner, *Frames of Mind*, 1983,
Basic Books, Inc.: New York

It took millions of years for humans to evolve from the apes. The transition involved the accumulation of hundreds of minute changes. Explaining all of this to the average hormonalized high-school student also can seem to take millions of years. What is needed is a way to show the changes graphically—tweened animation!

All that is required is a before and after drawing. For many of these academic expositions, a diagramming style of animation is sufficient and even desirable. Too many details can sidetrack the student's already strained attention. To create proper diagrams, you should look to the draw-style animation programs.

Figure 2.2 shows a chimpanzee skull, and Figure 2.3 shows your garden-variety Homo Sapien skull. Examining just these stills, you can spot many of the areas where changes occurred. The canines are obvious. Man evidently has succeeded based on the sharpness of his wit, not his teeth. Another important change is the increase in cranial capacity. But these features are better appreciated when the two frames are metamorphosed. Then you also can see the change in position of the nose and the brow ridge. Your eye is very sensitive to motion, and can follow the subtlest movement of each feature.

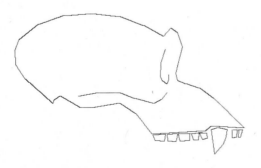

Figure 2.2.
A line drawing of a chimp skull.

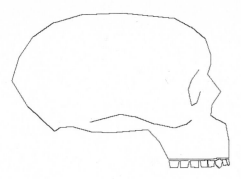

Figure 2.3.
A line drawing of a human skull.

Presumably (but not too literally), you also can see the "missing links" between chimp and man. In fact, to do justice to this morph, it would be nice to add a Neanderthal or Cro-Magnon between the extremes. But the simplicity of making an animation from just two pictures is the charm of this example. Harried educators, take note.

DISKETTE DEMO: The Chimpman

To run the example animation on the disk, get to the DOS prompt and type:

```
>PLAY CHIMPMAN
```

This runs a Fantavision movie on the disk that morphs a man into a chimpanzee. Note that the interpolation, or tweening, is linear, and so the in-between frames are not strictly factual. Nevertheless, this is a fascinating way to visualize evolution.

Animal Development

Perhaps the most exquisitely complicated modern science is developmental biology. Current research reveals that a huge suite of regulatory proteins feed back on each other under the direction of genes to turn a single cell into an entire animal of flesh and blood. Unraveling the mystery of life is not only exciting, it is also marvelously complex.

The complexity boggles the researchers themselves, as discussed later in this chapter. They are always in search of new ways to illustrate this material, both to their students and their peers. The chemistry is dynamic, so animation is the perfect medium for representing it.

Again, animation in a diagramming style is appropriate. Chemicals can be shown as simple figures that indicate their mode of action. Like pac-men or space invaders, the proteins and enzymes move around the screen gobbling up and spitting out other chemicals.

This style is also applicable to animations of large-scale animal development, such as a tadpole changing into a frog, or a caterpillar into a butterfly. In this type of developmental biology, many things are happening at many levels. This adds to its fascination and difficulty. Animation helps convey this dense information in an engaging way.

Alternatively, highly realistic three-dimensional molecular models can be generated and animated by computer. These models show where the binding or catalytic action takes place. These models make chemistry almost like mechanics, and scientists can play with the configuration and orientation of the molecular interactions like tinkertoys. These systems are not yet ready for the desktop, but the wait should not be long.

DISKETTE DEMO: DNA in action

From the DOS prompt, type:

>PLAY DNA

This is a Fantavision movie that suggests the double-helix structure of DNA without actually using a three-dimensional system. The molecule is created from a series of colored dots that represent the bases of DNA. These dots are carefully drawn to indicate the third dimension, then tweening does the rest.

The animation shows the DNA "unzipping" into two complementary strings. Recombination is indicated by the reassembly of the bases onto one of the strings. This sort of thing is going on in your body right now, every time a cell divides.

DISKETTE DEMO: Meiosis in Motion

From the DOS prompt, type:

```
>PLAY EGG1 EGG2 EGG3 EGG4
```

This command plays four Fantavision animations in sequence. If you have a hard disk, I recommend you copy these movies onto it. That way the file-loading intermission won't be so long between acts.

As with the other Fantavision movies on this disk, you can press the space bar to pause the movie. Just press the space bar again to restart it. This can be handy to stop the action while you read the description.

This movie diagrams the most recent research in human embryology. It is a short clip from a longer, narrated video called "Meiosis in Motion," which was commissioned by the Faulkner Center of Reproductive Medicine and the Dana-Farber Cancer Institute, Harvard Medical School. The primary investigators were Dr. G. M. Cooper, Dr. M. M. Seibel, and Dr. A. A. Kiessling. What they have pieced together is the breathtaking story of a human egg, from its creation to its maturity and fertilization. From the anatomical to the molecular level, the major players and their roles have been largely scripted out (OK, there are a few extras yet to be cast). Two new proteins have been given star billing. They are maturation promoting factor (MPF) and a newcomer known simply as cmos. They are cast as antagonists, each gaining a temporary upper hand as the story unfolds.

The following description gets a little bit hairy, so feel free to just watch the movie. On the other hand, there are only a few new words and it *is* an interesting story...

The movie starts with the egg surrounded by a thin blue shell. Around that are a bunch of orange cells called granulosa cells. These cells have sent thin projections through the shell and into the egg. This is how the outside world communicates with the developing egg.

In the cytoplasm, the protein called maturation promoting factor, or MPF, is accumulating. When it is activated, it punches holes in the membrane of the nucleus (green circle). Centromeres (yellow dots) also are activated, causing them to send out microtubules (gray lines) that push into the disintegrating nuclear membrane. In the nucleus,

MPF causes DNA to knot itself up into pairs of chromosomes (blue lines). As the chromosomes condense, the granulosa projections retract. Finally, the nuclear membrane disintegrates. The centromeres migrate to opposite poles of the cell and the microtubules continue to push forward to the chromosomes. The chromosome pairs are neatly lined up. More microtubules form between each pair.

Then MPF is degraded, triggering cell division. The chromosome pairs are torn apart, one half going toward each pole of the cell. As the chromosomes move, the cell membrane starts to constrict. The chromosomes are finally pulled into two separate regions as the cell membrane squeezes off another small cell, called a polar body. Each cell now has half the number of chromosomes it started with. Sometimes this first polar body splits into two more cells, as shown.

MPF levels, which fell and caused the first division, start to rise again. The egg's nucleus does not reform, but the membrane proteins are still hanging around. The activated MPF causes the chromosomes to condense as before. But this time the MPF is not broken down and the cell doesn't get the signal to divide. The egg is stuck at the brink of division. It will stay in that expectant state for years. The protein that stops the division is called cmos.

When its number is up, the egg breaks out of its follicle and travels into a fallopian tube with its contingent of granulosa cells. It is here that it might encounter a sperm (see Figure 2.4). After all these years, what a day! When a sperm penetrates the shell, its nucleus is transformed by the egg. This also triggers cmos to stop holding the cell in limbo. MPF breaks down, and a division is triggered, causing the formation of the second polar body.

Then the nuclear membrane reforms. The sperm and the egg nuclei move toward each other. After a brief embrace, their membranes dissolve and they scramble their genes together. The intermixed DNA is then lined up, and the fertilized egg undergoes its first division (see Figure 2.5).

This animation, which the curious can watch repeatedly, has much greater impact than looking at static pictures of the process. Animation has many charms, but this one shines: the ability to cram tons of information into a few seconds on the screen. And make it seem real.

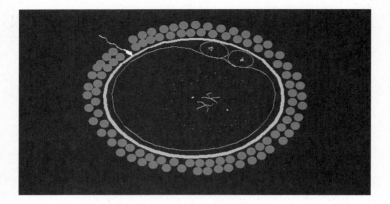

Figure 2.4.
A sperm encounters
an egg.

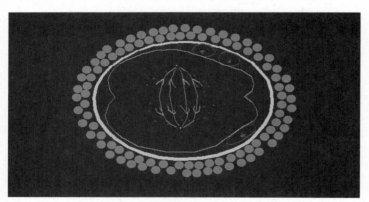

Figure 2.5.
The first division
of the egg.

Weather Patterns

"There is a sumptuous variety about the New England weather that compels the
stranger's admiration—and regret. The weather is always doing something there;
always attending strictly to business, always getting up new designs and trying them
on the people to see how they will go. But it gets through more business in spring
than in any other season. In the spring I have counted one hundred and thirty-six
different kinds of weather inside of four-and-twenty hours."

Mark Twain

A story is told of an anthropologist studying Eskimos in Alaska. A craggy-faced Eskimo hunter scanned the horizon and pronounced, "We'll have clear weather all day—good for the hunt." Impressed with such easy assurance, the anthropologist asked the hunter what clues he had used: the color of the sky, the shape of the clouds, the wind? The Eskimo squinted back. "The satellite pictures on the news last night."

It's no joke that these pictures have changed life for millions. Not just Eskimos, but farmers, golfers and sunbathers. People who can't tell a cumulus cloud from cotton candy can visualize the weather on its way by watching the evening newscast. What has made this possible is not the *pictures*, but the *animation*. When the individual weather "snapshots" are assembled into that little weather movie, every couch potato becomes a climatologist.

This is no accident. The human brain is specially equipped to perceive motion and extrapolate from it. This comes in handy for snagging a pop fly on the baseball field or avoiding a lion on the savanna. The brain instantly computes the trajectory of the ball or the lion and extrapolates the future position based on that information. It's up to you to rush toward or away from that fateful location.

Extrapolation is related to interpolation. Where interpolation gives you the positions *between* two known values, extrapolation carries on *past* the last value, in the same direction. In other words, if a doughnut rolls one foot in one second, you would know it has a speed of one foot per second, and would guess that in the next second it would roll another foot.

That's a linear extrapolation. The brain is capable of non-linear extrapolation as well, but the essence of the argument is the same: humans are good at predicting future motion based on present motion. And motion, of course, is what animation is all about.

So given the general flow of weather, it is no problem to extrapolate to approximately what will happen next. The problem with the weather, however, is that approximations might not be good enough.

DISKETTE DEMO: The Weather

From the DOS prompt, type:

```
>PLAY WEATHER
```

This movie shows weather fronts moving across the United States (see Figure 2.6). There are four "key" frames in this movie. The rest of the action comes from in-betweening. This is just what you need to get smooth motion out of a series of separate stills. Satellite data is not continuous, so this method is perfectly suited to fill in the gaps.

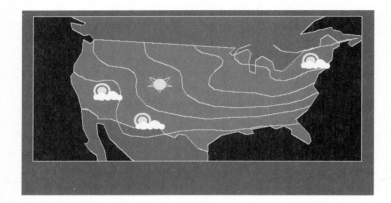

Figure 2.6
Weather fronts moving across the American continent.

The Fortunes of War

"The day of small nations has long passed away. The day of empires has come."

Joseph Chamberlain, 1904

As the Russian empire breaks up and Africa reorganizes, Chamberlain's statement seems pretty silly. How can we keep up with all the new and changing borders? Online systems offer new, updated maps on a regular basis: these are a good start. But even greater impact can be had by animating those wiggling national outlines.

Animation allows the continuity to be followed. Software could be devised that shows the changing property lines through the entire history of nations. Animating the shifting fortunes of countries can entertain the student even while sneaking in a geography lesson.

Interactive software of this kind makes students feel like participants in the history of social events. Sliding the clock through time puts the pupils in charge, granting them king-like powers over the human chronicle. Thus enthroned, they learn and play with vigor.

Someday we will wonder what the world was like before animated maps.

DISKETTE DEMO: The United States

From the DOS prompt, type:

>PLAY ENTRY

This Fantavision movie shows the entry of each state into the Union. On a large scale, you can see the westward expansion of the United States. But there are other interesting things to note. Look how long it took West Virginia to join. Notice that California and Oregon joined before the rest of the western states. For a while, the country was split into two widely separated parts.

You could dredge up this information out of the list of dates, but this animation makes its case simply and effectively—often you can see things in an animation that would be difficult to piece together out of the underlying data.

On Shaky Ground

"In California, everyone loves the earthquakes. That's the only time the traffic moves."

William C. Anderson

The notion of continents floating and drifting like the scum on hot chocolate is not intuitive. The earth is firm under our feet, isn't it? Of course, earthquakes challenge this faith a bit, but we're on solid ground, aren't we? Well actually, no. Not according to the theory of plate tectonics.

Plate tectonics says that there are several large plates (not at all like dinner plates; more like ice floes), that cruise around on the mantle, bumping and grinding into each other. As the sea-floor spreads out, these plates get shoved aside and into each other. All sorts of geologically exciting things happen where they meet, such as volcanoes and earthquakes—not to mention the creation of the mountains and continents, which are like flotsam on the roving plates. According to plate tectonics, mountain ranges are like an auto after a barrier crash—crumpled up from the impact.

This is clearly a prime target for animation. When you watch the continents slide around the globe, it looks almost obvious. For kids, the results are tangible—once they see it, they can understand it.

DISKETTE DEMO: Morphing Moves the Earth

From the DOS prompt, type:

>PLAY EARTH

This quick animation pictured at the start of the chapter has five key frames that correspond to the earth during the Permian, Triassic, Jurassic, Cretaceous and Modern periods, with roughly 50 million years between each frame. Morphing provides continuity between these frames. The animation starts out with a big blob of land called Pangaea. It is basically all the continents mashed together.

First North America and Asia split off from the bunch. Later, the Atlantic ocean starts to form and spread. It pushes Africa and South America apart. Meanwhile, Australia is drifting off and India is cruising north at a good clip. When India crashes into Asia, it forms the Himalayan mountain range. Finally, North America and Eurasia separate as the Atlantic continues to grow.

Morphing Meets Physics

Pick up your average physics book, and you could gag on the cacophony of equations. Certainly animation has no relevance here. Or does it? In fact, most of those equations have *time* as a primary variable. That means that these formulas are actually a description of something that changes through time—like animation. The equations represent the path of a flying missile, the motion of a pendulum, or the genesis of a star. Classical physics is founded on Newton's laws of *motion*, don't forget!

Physics is not on everyone's list of fun things to study, and yet it can be utterly fascinating to watch. The equations of motion describe (among other things) parabolas and ellipses. When we wad up a piece of paper and toss it into the trash can, we admire the parabolic arc. These shapes are far more familiar than the equations that spawn them, and animation is the best way to visualize them.

Once you have been exposed to animated equations and have an intuitive feel for them, you will be ready to explore the real thing. If you visualize enough equations, you start to see the movement hidden within. You join the company of original thinkers who use their "mind's eye" when they tackle a problem.

DISKETTE DEMO: Tweening takes wing

From the DOS prompt, type:

```
>PLAY WING
```

In the mid-1700s, Daniel Bernoulli (of the incredibly prolific Bernoulli family) gave his name to the basic principle underlying flight—the Bernoulli effect. It states that faster-moving fluids or gases have lower pressure. A wing, in cross-section, has a curved surface on top and a flatter surface on the bottom (see Figure 2.7). This forces the air into a pressure difference. The shape causes the air to split into two parts; one part takes the long path over the top, and the other part takes the short path under the bottom. When the air rejoins past the wing, the top part has gone farther in the same time. That means it must have gone faster. Faster air means lower pressure, so the wing is "sucked up." You could read this description anywhere, but now you can see the movie.

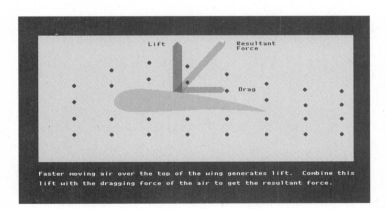

Figure 2.7.
A wing in cross-section, with the force vectors indicated.

DISKETTE DEMO: Morphing Comes into Focus

From the DOS prompt type:

```
>PLAY OPTICS
```

This is a lens Nikon would kill for. This Fantavision movie has only two frames—a convex lens and a concave lens. All the in-between frames are provided by morphing. A rubber lens like this would be invaluable in the classroom. It doesn't exist, so we'll have to be content with this simulation.

Light is not only bent by a lens, it is diffracted. This means the rainbow colors that constitute white light get split up. Every color of light bends to a different degree. The mnemonic is "blue bends best." As you can see from this animation, that puts blue on the inside or outside fringes, depending on the lens. A convex (magnifying—see Figure 2.8) lens bends *blue* toward the center, whereas a concave (reducing—see Figure 2.9) lens bends *red* to the center. Notice that the beam through the center doesn't pass through any curvature at all, so it is not deflected or diffracted.

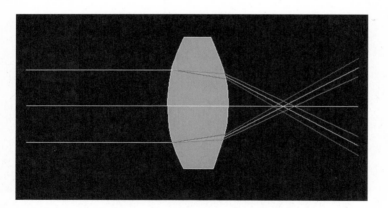

Figure 2.8.
A magnifying, or convex, lens. Notice that the blue is bent best, ending up inside.

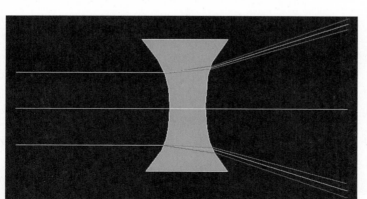

Figure 2.9.
A reducing, or concave, lens. Notice that blue ends up outside—away from the center.

DISKETTE DEMO: Tweening a Tune

From the DOS prompt, type:

```
>PLAY HARMONIC
```

This movie depicts the first two modes of vibration for a plucked string, such as a guitar, harp or piano. The top mode is called the fundamental frequency and does sort of what you would expect a plucked string to do. The bottom mode is called the first harmonic. It has half the wavelength and twice the frequency of the fundamental. These two, plus all the higher overtones, add up to create the sound signature that distinguishes a clavichord from a lute.

DISKETTE DEMO: Morphing Explains Einstein

From the DOS prompt, type:

```
>PLAY SUNSTARS
```

This animation illustrates a bizarre prediction of Einstein's Theory of General Relativity. Einstein said that gravity actually bends space, and that because light travels through that space, it should get bent, too. Since we normally think of light as taking a perfectly straight path, this is counter-intuitive, to say the least. And how would you check it?

Einstein was a theorist, not an experimentalist. He simply turned physics inside out and let others pick up the pieces. Sir Arthur Eddington was left to prove this prediction. He figured that the sun was massive enough to bend any nearby starlight. Close to the edge of the sun, you should see stars that are slightly displaced because of the solar gravity.

The only problem is, you can't *see* stars when the sun's out. But Eddington was not the type to let trifles get in his way. He realized that during a solar eclipse, there would be a brief opportunity to glimpse some nearby stars. Lo and behold, when the experiment was performed, Einstein was vindicated. The stars *did* move under the gravitational influence of the sun.

This animation shows you what it would look like if you could see stars when the sun came out. As the sun goes by, the stars appear to move away. This amazing effect is called gravitational lensing because curved space acts like an optical lens.

Morphing Adds Up

Mathematics is considered dry by non-mathematicians. More than 95 percent of the population don't make a living in the math field, so there aren't many people to rebut that assessment. It's a bum rap. Mathematics can be surprisingly beautiful. What passes for math education in the schools, however, can be painfully boring.

Where did we go wrong? The problem is manyfold. For one thing, subjects are introduced without the slightest explanation of their historical context. There is no insight into the mathematician's motivations. There is no personification at all. It's as if math descended fully formed from heaven. Nothing could be farther from the truth.

Another problem is an insistence on teaching the *mechanics* of problem-solving. With marvelous computer programs such as Mathematica, problem-solving becomes almost automatic. What is needed is problem *stating*, where the student learns how to effectively frame a problem in mathematical terms. It doesn't matter if you know your multiplication tables up to twelve if you don't know when to multiply and when to divide.

Still another problem is visualization. If a picture is worth a thousand words, an animation is worth a million. You can explain something until you're blue in the face and not get anywhere until you can *show* it. Most people, even educators, don't realize how successful animation can be for teaching math.

DISKETTE DEMO: Shuffling Triangles

From the DOS prompt, type:

>PLAY TRIANGLE

This animation demonstrates one of the ways that movement played a role in a mathematical discovery. It was by shuffling triangular tiles that Pythagoras and his apostles discovered the famous Pythagorean Theorem:

$$C^2 = A^2 + B^2$$

where C is the long side (or hypotenuse) of the triangle and the other two sides are A and B (see Figure 2.10). There are actually several ways of proving this, but the one illustrated here is the most obvious. You start with four triangles in the corner of a square. By sliding the triangles around, you uncover different areas of the underlying square. In one configuration, there is one area: C^2 (see Figure 2.11). In the other, there are two areas: A^2 and B^2 (see Figure 2.12). Whereas the square doesn't change size, the sum of A^2 and B^2 must equal C^2.

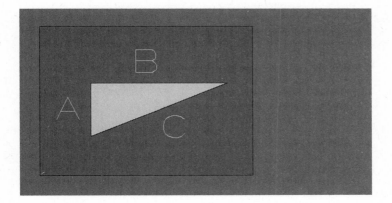

Figure 2.10.
The starting triangle with a hypotenuse C.

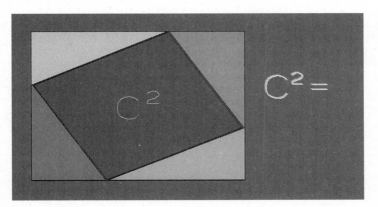

Figure 2.11.
With the triangles distributed so their hypotenuses are toward the center, the open area = C^2.

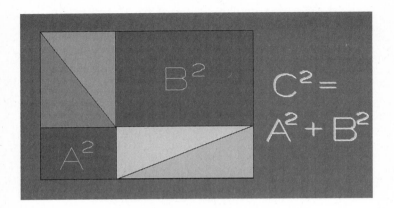

Figure 2.12.
Slide the triangles to expose two other areas, B^2 and A^2. This is a visual proof that $C^2 = A^2 + B^2$.

But enough of this labored description. Watch the movie!

DISKETTE DEMO: The Top-hat Fractal

From the DOS prompt, type:

>PLAY FRACTAL

The movie is composed of three key frames. They show a fractal being morphed, of all things. A fractal is a magnificent mathematical creature that looks the same no matter how you magnify it. That little trick is managed by making each basic part of the pattern repeat, on a smaller and smaller scale. For instance, this movie shows a "top hat" in frame one composed of five lines. I know it's not much of a top hat artistically, but play along with me.

You can stop a Fantavision movie at any time by pressing the space bar. You might find it handy in this and other movies when you want to study a frame. Do it now to stop the movie at the simple top hat.

Now imagine that you could replace each line on that top hat with another top hat. Press the space bar again twice—once to continue animating and again to stop at the next key frame. For every straight line in the original, there have now sprouted new top hats. Press the space bar twice again to skip to the next key frame. One more time, each straight line is replaced by a top hat. Things are getting pretty baroque. If I had more time and patience, I might have drawn the next step. But you get the idea.

Press the space bar again to continue the movie. What does this show? Although this is strictly a mathematical progression, it is oddly reminiscent of crystal formation. Other fractals—such as a bowler hat—might look like clouds. In other words, fractals make natural-looking pictures. This might say something about the nature being depicted. Namely: nature might be fractal.

Fractals are on the "bleeding" edge of mathematics. They may unlock the secrets of turbulence, feedback, and other chaotic behavior. They could provide the transition between quantum and classical physics. They may help us understand the convoluted chemical cascades of developmental biology—life itself.

On the other hand, there are a few scientists who think the whole fractal affair is an overblown exercise in public relations with pretty pictures.

Time will tell, but only if a new generation of scientists can be exposed to the issues. Their young minds will reflect a fresh light on this exciting new field.

Moving Words

Words come alive when they are animated on a computer screen. Words can be self-demonstrating, such as the word *roll* rolling across the screen. The interested educator can make the word *dive* take a plunge, or the word *shrink* vanish into a dot. These simple exercises are facilitated by an animation program that does tweening. On the disk, you will find some movie shorts that illustrate these concepts.

It isn't hard to imagine a whole animated dictionary. Kids would look through it just to enjoy the show. Along the way, they can't help but learn a few words. An obvious enhancement is sound. When IBMs regularly come equipped with good sound (there are some great products already available), you will see more multimedia products like this.

It isn't news that animation can help teach English and numbers. Sesame Street has been proving that for years. What *is* new is that educators have access to the tools they need to create their *own* customized course-work.

DISKETTE DEMO: Look Before You Leap

From the DOS prompt, type:

```
>PLAY LOOKLEAP
```

This will play a Fantavision movie that briefly illustrates the concept behind "moving words" (see Figure 2.13).

Figure 2.13.
Words can become actors in Fantavision.

Animated Motion Studies

Animation has been used in sports for years to analyze the dynamics of motion with an eye to improving performance. A typical analysis starts with placing dots on the athlete's joints: wrist, elbow, shoulder, hips, knees, and ankles. Then they are filmed performing their sport or event. The dots are entered into a computer manually on a digitizing pad or (preferably) by automated software.

Then the computer plays back the animation, and the sports gurus analyze it for efficiency. They can suggest new techniques for bettering the athlete's performance.

DISKETTE DEMO: Taking a Dive

From the DOS prompt type:

```
>PLAY DIVE
```

This movie was created with a digitizing pad and a time-series exposure of a high-dive. Although it is only a stick figure, the essence of the dive is well-defined. A coach might advise this diver to straighten his legs a bit before entering the water.

To see the dive in slow motion, press the '4' key. It introduces twice as many key frames and slows down the motion. Press the '5' key to resume the normal animation speed.

The study of motion is applied to nature as well as sports. It was by studying bird flight, you might remember, that airplanes were designed. And from the viewpoint of an aspiring animator, a knowledge of body motion—animal as well as human—is highly desirable.

Sometimes animation is used to bring back the dead. Paleontologists gain an important insight into the day-to-day life of a dinosaur when they can visualize its gait or its attack or defense posture. This is animation at its best—you can't go out and film a bunch of dinosaurs (except, possibly, if you're Steven Spielberg). So animation is the only way to bring these extinct creatures to life.

Naturalists are interested in what kind of energy expenditures are involved with different modes of locomotion. The way to analyze this is to use motion studies. Combine animation with a little physics, and you can calculate the effort involved with each step or flap of a wing.

DISKETTE DEMO: Flap Happy

From the DOS prompt, type:

>PLAY GULL

This movie has four key frames that represent the upstroke and the downstroke of a seagull's wing-beat. Notice how the wings fold on the upstroke. The gull is getting lift on all parts of this beat because of the shape of the wing (see the **Tweening takes Wing** section earlier in the chapter). The flapping provides both lift and forward thrust. There are still questions about the physics of bird-flight, and each bird is different, but this gull is a good start on an exploration.

Morphing in the Laboratory

"The structure of the DNA molecule, as ferreted out by James Watson and Francis Crick, depended critically upon the ability to sketch the various ways in which molecules might be bound with one another. These experiments—sometimes constructed in the scientists' heads, sometimes on paper, and sometimes using an actual three-dimensional model—led in the end to the correct reconstruction of the double helix."

Howard Gardner, *Frames of Mind*, 1983,
Basic Books, Inc.: New York

Logic is the way to *prove* a good theory, but inspiration is the way to *invent* one. When creative people are polled on the subject, they often say that visualizing is key to their talent.

Einstein said that the words of the language didn't play much role in his thinking. Instead, visual images guided his creativity. He was famous for his *gedenken,* or thought experiments. He didn't set out to do idle physics. Instead, he asked simple, visually oriented questions. The theory of relativity resulted from this simple question: What happens if you go the speed of light and then look in a mirror? Would you see yourself or would you beat the light and just see nothing?

This is what motivates all great researchers. They are not looking to add another digit to some cosmological constant. They have deceptively and ingeniously simple questions to answer.

These days you are likely to see a workstation at the researcher's desk. At the start of a new project, the researcher uses the computer to verify some ideas or sketch out the problem. Often, a simple animation can clarify the interactions of different pieces of the puzzle.

For instance, a biochemist might quickly animate the chain of reactions that regulatory proteins use to accomplish their mission. Some new insights might pop out of this preliminary animation. Because the major actors here are perambulating proteins, this is a perfect job for tweening. The proteins act on other molecules by folding into new configurations. This can be depicted with a simple morphing animation.

An engineer might use one of the popular new computer programs that have the laws of physics built-in. These amazing programs take carefully described objects such as a car or a lawn chair and subject them to the laws of physics. If you drop the chair on the car, it will bounce and clatter to the ground. The incredible realism of these simulations is almost eerie. This is non-linear tweening, where the paths are usually parabolas, not straight lines.

There is great interest in this field. If you can crash a car on the computer instead of the test track, you can save a lot of cash per crash. Of course to be useful you must have a very good model in the computer. The oldest cliche in the computer business has been around long enough to earn its own acronym: GIGO—Garbage In, Garbage Out. For this reason, cars still will be crashed. But perhaps not as often.

Visualization has just started to make an impact in all areas of science. It is not without critics. Some scientists believe more in a raw equation than a picture of it. But even the hard-liners are coming around. There are too many compelling reasons to use animation in research. And animation just won't go away.

Morphing and Tweening Hit the Conference Trail

When a scientist is ready to wow crowds with her new discovery, she can show the standard slides and overhead projections. Or she can whip out her latest animation and really get their attention.

It works. Animation is compelling. But more importantly, it is appropriate for most subjects. Every science deals with change or motion of some kind, from the frenzy of atoms in physics to the stately march of time in archeology. Change is the essence, and animation is its medium.

Biology is charting new, mind-bending territory. Already, scientists are presenting the fruits of their research as choreography, where proteins dance around and DNA calls out the steps.

Recently, some of the important chemical pathways in human embryology were spotlighted with the research video called "Meiosis in Motion," parts of which are on the included disk (and discussed earlier in the chapter). The video was well-received at several conferences where it was shown. Attendees remarked that it was easy to get a "gut feeling" for the concepts with animation as a guide. For packaging dense information and then disseminating it, few media can compare to animation.

These ideas only scratch the surface of animation in education and research. Tweening and morphing are two of the more powerful tools that are leading to a wider audience for animation. With teachers and researchers using this software, we can expect to see a major shift in education and communication toward a more visual and kinetic future.

This chapter has tossed out some teasing examples of where educational animation might go, and how tweening and morphing are a part of it. They have been object-oriented, polygon animations. This is a good expository style that is easy to implement. And it's stingy with your disk space.

In the next chapter, you will see how these polygons apply to the prepress and printing industry.

Tweening and Morphing in Design

3

"Art is a lie that makes us realize truth, at least the truth that is given us to understand."

Pablo Picasso

Animal stills courtesy of the Indianapolis Zoo.

Thirty thousand years ago, in the caves of Altamira, Spain, an artist I'll call Trog painted a boar on his living-room wall. It wasn't an ordinary boar (Figure 3.1).

His friends were fond of pointing out—that's what friends are for—the boar he drew had eight legs, not the regulation four. But in the flickering firelight, as they sat upon the floor, even his meanest critic saw the trotting of that boar.

Besides bad doggerel, Trog had hit upon tweening. And in drawing the extra legs in-between the other legs, he created animation. We're pretty smug about today's high technology, but thirty thousand years ago people were sitting in Trog's living room watching animations. That's when popcorn was invented, too. So much for progress.

Figure 3.1.
A sketch of an eight-legged boar from the Altamira caves in Spain.

Since then, there have been many forays into the magical worlds of animation, tweening, and metamorphosing, from ancient Egyptian comic strips to computer-assisted Disney features.

Morphing and tweening are intriguing design motifs. In this chapter, you will discover the roots of morphing as well as today's proliferating branches of art and computer illustration. Computers have fertilized the arts, and they are blossoming wildly in response.

Let's travel through time and smell a few flowers:

A Brief Time of History

"History gets thicker as it approaches recent times."

A.J.P. Taylor, *English History*

African Wall Decorations

African cave-dwellers rate among the oldest storytellers who left evidence. Look at the hunting party in Figure 3.2. This scene is from a cave in the Sahara desert near Tassili-n-Ajjer, Algeria. These characters really come alive. Although in-betweening isn't employed, there is a definite sense of motion—and a harbinger of things to come.

Figure 3.2. A wild hunting party in Algeria, about thirty thousand years ago.

To document war, sports, or just a royal party, the pharaoh's historians created beautiful wall paintings. These stories are immediately recognizable by a modern teenager—they are like comic strips.

There is quite a lot of this art around. There are sequences of wrestling action—the Egyptian version of a slow-motion replay on ESPN. There are scenes of workers in the fields and the preparation of food—Egyptian PBS. And, of course, religious paeans to their gods—Egyptian PTL.

In a way, early writing (such as hieroglyphics or Chinese pictograms) can be thought of as a cartoon strip. The text is really a string of pictures, each standing for a word or phrase.

Over time, the pictures became stylized. In a magical transformation, they came to symbolize *sounds* that could be strung together to represent the spoken language. Today, the words are still scanned like panels in a comic strip, even if they have lost their old pictorial roots.

A strip is an effort to include another dimension into a drawing—time. With the addition of time, a picture becomes a story. It invites deeper scrutiny and sucks in the audience. The extra richness of the experience helps to explain the remarkable success of movies, television, and animation in our culture. They are the culmination of over thirty thousand years of illustrated storytelling.

William Hogarth 1750s

In the mid 1700s, William Hogarth was the reigning satirist of England. He also was an excellent engraver. He wrote a short treatise called "The Analysis of Beauty" in 1753. It had two engraved plates with it, shown in Figures 3.3 and 3.4.

These engraved plates have several numbered figures around them that he referred to in his text. His inspiration for the first scene is the messy yard of Clito, a friend of Socrates. One day while visiting his friend, Socrates fell to musing about beauty as he tripped over the junk in Clito's yard.

Hogarth included many silly things in his yard. He was serious about teaching art, but he wanted to keep it lively. Unfortunately, this caused most of the critics of his day to scoff at his entire enterprise. There are still people today who believe nothing is learned unless the lesson is dry.

Notice the many examples of morphing and warping that surround the central image in Figure 3.3. At the top you see a table leg being warped into a more sinuous form. At the bottom left is a series of images numbered one through seven showing a girdle undergoing some contortions. At the bottom right is a group of faces numbered 97 through 105 that make a great morphing sequence. It seems to show the degeneration of art to childish cartooning.

Figure 3.3.

"Analysis of Beauty," by William Hogarth, plate 1. This plate is Hogarth's whimsical statuary yard containing the objects of art he wants to talk about. Notice the morphing and warping sequences around the periphery of the picture.

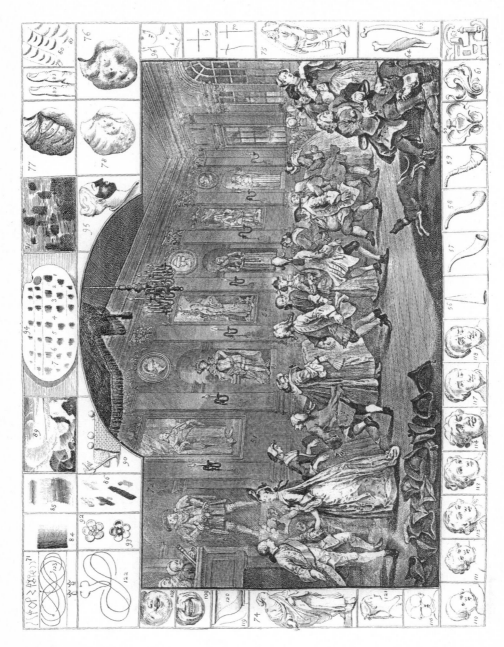

Figure 3.4.

"Analysis of Beauty," by William Hogarth, plate 2. This plate is a country-dance with more examples of art theory.

The printing press had been around for three hundred years, and it seemed to Hogarth that every idiot in Britain had taken up engraving. They were glutting the market with inferior and base illustrations. These plates were meant to teach those untutored oafs the secrets of the arts.

In Figure 3.4, surrounding the central image of a country dance, there are more warping and morphing sequences. At the bottom, a girl grows up, a cone turns and twists into a horn, and a pelvis becomes a decorative cornice.

Hogarth had a great imagination. He also was an amazing storyteller. Some of his etchings take hours to peruse, with details hiding in every corner. Many of his engravings were serialized, with some accompanying text. Although there were some Italian "comic books" that used pictures and text to tell religious stories, they were clumsy amateur productions. Hogarth was the first to create new contemporary stories with realistic illustrations and good printing techniques.

With his devotion to detail and his love of story, Hogarth would have been a natural animator. He was born two hundred years too early. Of course, twentieth-century critics probably would be no kinder to him. Like Steven Speilberg, he was too popular to earn critical respect.

Eadweard Muybridge 1880s

In the 1870s, Eadweard Muybridge figured out a great method of taking sequential shots of humans and animals in motion. It all started with horses. Leland Stanford, a railroad tycoon and founder of Stanford University, was a racehorse breeder. In a little wager with a friend, he bet $25,000 that all four hooves of a trotting horse left the ground at once.

I would faint if I heard that wager today. And in 1870, $25,000 was real money. But hey, if a millionaire can't have fun, what's the point of life?

Stanford enlisted Muybridge to prove his theory. At a cost considerably exceeding the $25,000 bet, Muybridge set up a series of twenty-four cameras along a racetrack on Stanford's estate. He set up a white background across from each camera to eliminate extraneous background. From each camera a thread ran across the track. As the horse ran past the camera, it would break the thread and trip the shutter. By taking pictures that were only fractions of a second apart, Muybridge was able dissect the motion. The pictures settled the argument forever. All four hooves do leave the ground at once. Flush with this success, Muybridge extended his studies to include other animals and humans.

This was finally the level of tweening that made motion understandable. In the early 1920s, a young man named Walter Elias Disney found Muybridge's photographic sequences in the public library. Together with his partner Ubbe Ert Iwwerks (I didn't make that up), Disney studied the photographs to learn about animal locomotion.

Animators, cartoonists, and artists in general owe a great debt to Muybridge for these studies of real motion. Disney owes a great debt to Ubbe, too—but that's another story. These photographs, which preceded movies, are still a treasured reference for animators.

Winsor McCay

Winsor McCay was an artistic prodigy who was, of course, scolded for his propensity to draw. Nevertheless, by the time he was nineteen, he was making a pleasant living at it. While pretending to attend classes at Cleary's Business College in Ypsilanti, Michigan, McCay was actually drawing portraits for patrons of a Detroit dime museum.

Dime museums were the brainchild of P. T. Barnum, who opened the first one in New York. They were sort of a primitive Disneyland—a cross between vaudeville and a funhouse. There McCay observed and drew acrobats, clowns, and "freaks." He also took notice of the hall of mirrors, with their distorted, warped reflections.

That wasn't the only place he encountered visual warping. In the portraits he did, he tried his best to improve on the original while still retaining enough "character" to keep the subject recognizable. McCay became a master of the medium, subtly warping here and there to please the customer.

Before long, McCay was drawing cartoons for *Life* magazine. Figure 3.5 shows a sample of his beautiful work, called *Saved*. The panels could have served as the key frames for an animation. There is an amazing cinematic quality to the sequence. All the more amazing because the cinema was only five years old.

The strip starts with four people being held hostage by the Indians. Notice the detail—the woman crying in frame one and fainting in frame two. Then the Indians notice another car, and race off after it. As they gallop across the desert, you can follow the individual paths of each horse and rider. Nothing is accidental—the motion is carefully choreographed. The drawing of the horses is flawless, indicating that McCay was familiar with Muybridge's motion studies.

While the Indians chase the car, McCay goes farther with the cinematic metaphor as the "camera" tracks back to follow the action. Notice the original foursome getting progressively smaller in frames three through five.

In frame five, the car unexpectedly explodes. McCay draws a wonderful explosion. If you look carefully, you can see all six horses, drawn with radial lines. In the last frame, the Indians manage to ride away, and the others are saved.

McCay was destined to animate, but the technology wasn't ripe yet. So he busied himself with cartoon strips that took warping and morphing to a new level. The cartoon strip was just being born, and McCay was the most talented midwife. He created strips such as *Mr. Goodenough* and *Little Sammy Sneeze* before he hit his stride with *Dream of the Rarebit Fiend*.

This new strip, being a nightmare sequence, gave McCay license to experiment. Figures 3.6 and 3.7 show the outrageous warping that McCay routinely employed to give physical weight to psychological tortures.

Figure 3.8 shows how much fun he could have, as he metamorphoses one animal into another to make silly chimeras.

These strips ran in the *Evening Telegram* and were more adult-oriented than *Sammy Sneeze*. To contrast the different styles of his creations, McCay was forced to use an alias. Somewhat defiantly, he chose Silas, the name of the *New York Herald* garbageman. But the work was undeniably Winsor McCay.

In 1905, McCay created another concurrent strip, *Little Nemo in Slumberland*. *Slumberland* gave him room to play with fantastic images. Preceding Freddy Kreuger by about 80 years, the strip describes another world that exists only in Little Nemo's dreams.

In Figure 3.9, Little Nemo's bathtub is metamorphosed first into a jungle swamp, then into an arctic sea, complete with icebergs and polar bears. In Figure 3.10, a banister takes on a life of its own in the beautifully warped frames of Little Nemo's dream. These frames always suggest key frames from an animated sequence.

In Chapter 6, I will come back to Winsor McCay. His mastery of the cartoon strip led him straight into a new method of animation that would one day be called tweening.

Figure 3.5.

"Saved," by Winsor McCay in Life Magazine, 1903. Notice the cinematic feel to this strip. McCay was drawing "key frames" before anyone knew what they were.

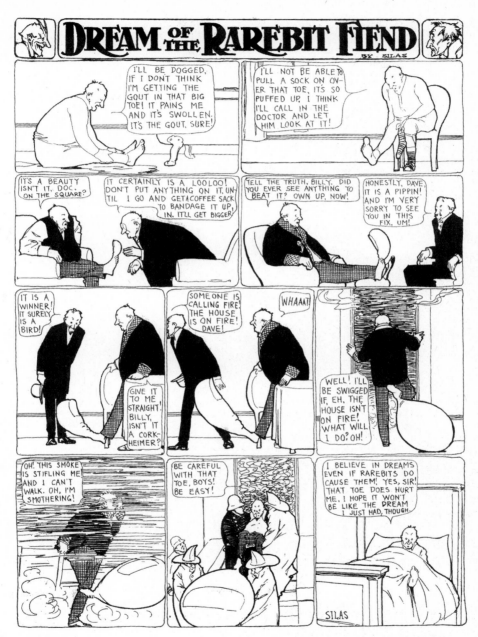

Figure 3.6.

"Dream of the Rarebit Fiend," by Winsor McCay, March 2, 1907. A man's gouty toe takes on a physical size to match the pain it's causing. A beautifully executed warp.

Figure 3.7.

"Dream of the Rarebit Fiend," October 14, 1908. A woman's mouth takes on amphitheater proportions in a dream brought on by a Welsh rarebit dinner. A typically smooth warp by Winsor McCay.

Figure 3.8.

"Dream of the Rarebit Fiend," by Winsor McCay, 1907. A man waits patiently for a deer to shoot, while a parade of strange metamorphosed animals passes by.

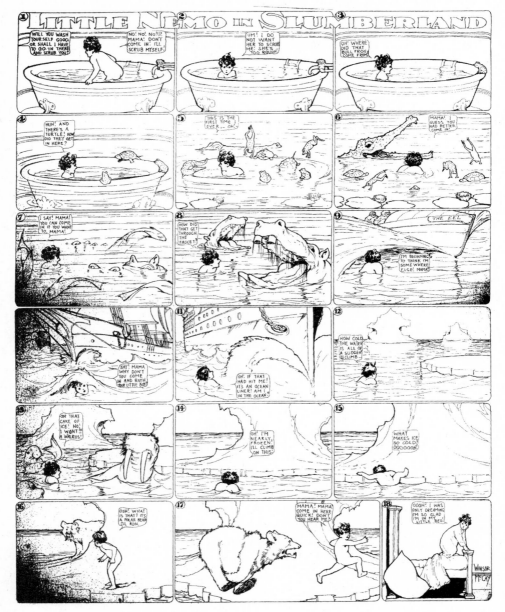

Figure 3.9.

"Little Nemo in Slumberland," by Winsor McCay. Little Nemo's bathtub morphs into an exotic swamp, then into a cold arctic sea in this 1908 strip.

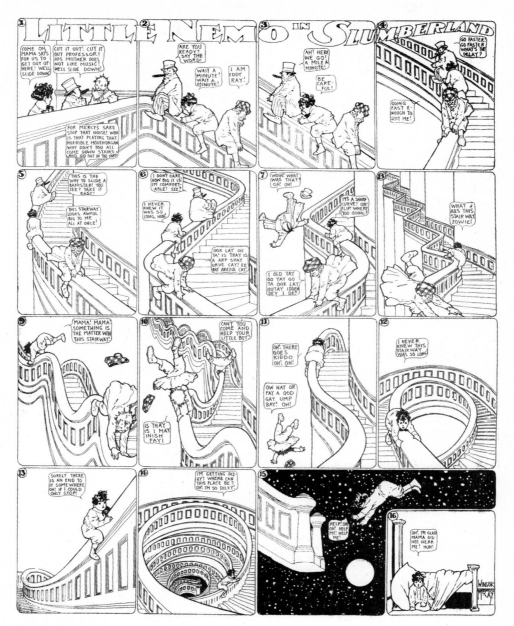

Figure 3.10.

"Little Nemo in Slumberland," by Winsor McCay, 1908. Nemo and some friends take on a
bucking, twisting banister in this wild warping sequence.

Marcel Duchamp 1912

"The movement of the form in a given time inevitably brings you into the realm of geometry and mathematics: it is like when you are constructing a machine."

Duchamp, discussing *Nude Descending A Staircase*

In 1912 a twenty-five-year-old artist, punster, and chess-player named Marcel Duchamp painted *Nude Descending a Staircase.* It was inspired by Eadweard Muybridge, Thomas Eakins, Etienne Jules Marey, and other photographers who were experimenting with multiple exposures of motion. There also was a resonance with cubism in its repeated, angular forms.

The painting is simply an abstract representation of a nude who is—yes—descending a staircase. The work does a great job of communicating motion with overlaid tweening.

It was a big break from Duchamp's previous work. In fact, it was a big break from anyone's work. It was inspirational to his fellow artists in Paris. They were inspired to organize a protest against it. They were furious with Duchamp. He had broken all the rules. And—they weren't positive—he seemed to be making fun of them.

They were successful in banning the painting, thus catapulting it into instant international fame. Its future was assured. By the time it was shown a year later in New York, it was already a controversial sensation.

But his artist friends had abandoned him, and he was a loner in his hometown. Finally, he came to the United States in 1915. He made a movie with Man Ray, the surrealist. He made a few sculptures and machines. His output was remarkably small, especially as measured against its impact.

One of his unfinished works, a mixed media called *Large Glass*, took him eight years to not finish. It is displayed nevertheless, and academics still battle over its interpretation. When he was asked about the intellectual genesis of the project, Duchamp said it was mostly the technical things that occupied him. He ended up learning about metallurgy, glass work, mirrors, dyes, etching, and a dozen other techniques.

That idea—that art can be driven by, or related to, new technologies—will ensure the lasting vigor of the arts, for better or worse. From perspective to morphing, technology has informed and guided art throughout history.

Let us hope we continue to find creative, unshackled minds to expose and interpret technology for the rest of us. How we use technology is a matter of survival, and we can use all the insight we can get.

M.C. Escher 1930-1968

"A brush or a tuft of animal hair or of plant fibers is in his hand, and with it he brushes over the rough surface of the stone. Look! The head of a bull appears on the rock wall, an image so alive that it looks as if it moves. It looks as if the damp nostrils tremble."

M.C. Escher, describing the Lascoux cave paintings in France,
August 1, 1950

Escher was simultaneously thrilled and chastened by the thirty-thousand-year-old cave drawings. Their beauty and color surprised him. But he was quick to see that artistic technique had developed very little in the ensuing millennia.

"Primitive" man with his hair brush was already a brilliant copycat. And, as Escher noticed, there was a vibrancy to the pictures that made them come alive. Escher wasn't sure how far the arts had really come.

In school, Escher was a fair student. But he had a hard time with arithmetic and algebra. He was quite resistant to the abstraction of numbers. He did somewhat better with geometry, but all in all, math was not his game. Later in his life, this would be ironic—mathematicians would compose the largest part of his audience.

Although he was a master woodcutter and illustrator, Escher was little-known outside of a small circle of admirers. For thirty years, he and his family enjoyed the fruit of artistic labor—chronic unemployment.

Actually, his parents and in-laws were well-to-do, so Escher never actually hungered for food. Only critical acclaim. To cheer him up, his father would say "You produce wallpaper." That must have encouraged him greatly.

In his early Dutch studies, Escher started to toy with tiling. *Tiling* is just what it sounds like—placing tiles on a surface, or as in his father's taunt, repeating patterns on wallpaper. For a normal, square tiling, there is no mystery. But if the shapes are irregular, all sorts of things pop out.

His studies lay dormant, however, until a trip to the Alhambra, in Spain. There Escher found a primal resonance with the Moorish mosaics on the walls and floors. It had a transforming effect on him. He copied all the designs he could find. These were to serve as fodder for future musings.

In 1924, he produced his first tiled piece and included it in a showing. No one was even remotely interested in it. Having at least a little business sense, he abandoned the whole line of inquiry for a dozen years. Then he went to Alhambra again and re-infected himself with the tiling madness. This time, there was no turning back.

Escher tiled his prints with opposites. One character forms the background for its antithesis. In Escher's vision, neither one predominates. Each is the background for the other. As he was fond of pointing out, every line serves double duty, defining a form both inside and outside of itself.

That made the design of the tiles a long, painstaking procedure. Test after test was tried and discarded, before something that worked started to form on the paper. Escher felt a great catharsis when two shapes finally snapped together.

To jog his imagination for this strange task, he used a trick described by Leonardo da Vinci. He would stare at a rough, stained wall or a gravel bed and let images coalesce out of the chaos. In the sixties, of course, a lot of people were staring at walls and seeing things. They also were staring at day-glo versions of Escher's prints. In fact, the hallucinogenic sixties paved the way for cinematic morphing, but that's a topic for Chapter 6.

Duality is an undeniable headache for the artist, but it also poses a problem for the eye. Try as you might, you can't see the foreground and background shapes at the same time. When you look at one of the background shapes, it becomes the foreground, and the other shapes fade back. The picture becomes dynamic as your eye fastens on one, then the other, of the tiled images.

In this delicate see-saw balance, Escher approaches animation. Even though the shapes are simple, they are imbued with a motive force that sweeps them across the page. The repetition of the tile pattern reinforces the motion, like a Muybridge sequence.

Often the conflicting concepts are basic, like light versus dark. In many of his prints, black birds fly in one direction against a backdrop of white birds flying the other way. In *Day and Night,* the black birds fly from a nighttime scene, while the white birds are leaving a daytime scene.

In *Symmetry Work 45* and *Circle Limit IV,* he contrasted black devils with white angels. In *Symmetry Work 63,* the antagonists are pessimism in black and optimism in white.

These stark opposites are the stuff of most metamorphic art. Like the tales of Dr. Jekyll and Mr. Hyde or Beauty and the Beast, the contrast is played to the maximum. From that juxtaposition comes high drama.

Sometimes the two players in an Escher woodcut are not opposites so much as complements, such as birds and fish representing air and water. But Escher wanted to put the third element—earth—into that picture. He didn't know it yet, but he needed a new axis.

Escher knew that with squares as tiles, there were only two axes and two colors needed. With two colors he could alternate tiles both horizontally and vertically. He created a basic checkerboard design, a simple foreground-background duality. From the printing perspective, this was ideal—black ink on white paper.

But to get a third player onto the page, Escher needed another color, and a place in space to put it. That's where the third axis comes in.

If you start with triangles instead of squares, you get a three-fold symmetry. To alternate the triangles across the plane, you need three colors. Thus, to put all three elements on the page, Escher started with triangular shapes and took off from there.

Escher's favorite trio was a fish, a bird, and a frog, but there are many variations on the theme, such as a fish, a devil, and a lizard. Sometimes the three characters were the same, but with different colors.

These trios endlessly pepper the print, alternating as they repeat to infinity—or the edge of the paper, which usually comes first.

Escher's first tilings, however, were just a prelude to the next step: metamorphosing. He realized that an extra dimension of storytelling could be achieved if the pattern changed as it repeated. To Escher, the concept was obvious and natural. The rest of us mortals might need a little more explanation.

Without ever knowing the math behind it, Escher invented tweened morphing. Instead of a relentless multiplication of the same image, Escher slowly mutated both the "foreground" and "background" characters.

One of his first methods was to gradually increase the detail of the tiled icons as they march across the page. At the same time the anti-tiles lose detail. The detailed characters are at the extremes of the page. In the middle just their silhouettes sift through each other. The raw outline is emphasized with this technique, so the outline must be simple and easily recognized.

This is like the cinematic or computer morph, where one image is cross-dissolved with another. The first image slowly fades away while the second picks up strength and finally dominates the first. The movie morph unfolds through time whereas the Escher morph spreads through space, but the concept is the same.

Another metamorphosing method Escher invented was to mutate the forms back to their embryonic geometry. That meant turning the binary tiles back into squares and the three-fold tiles into triangles. This is a wonderful way to illustrate the math underlying the art of tiling.

In *Verbum* (from the *Bible* "In principium erat Verbum"—in the beginning was the word), Escher plays with these primal shapes in his fantastic version of the genesis. The woodcut shows the separation of light and dark and the evolution of earth, air, and water, as represented by some archetypal denizens: frogs, birds, and fish. These shapes slowly metamorphose as they hop, fly, and swim out from the central triangles.

Escher's morphs were often like this—a mix of both twofold (light-dark) and threefold (earth-air-water) symmetries. That isn't easy. Try it if you don't believe me. An additional metamorphosis around the perimeter shows each animal changing into the other. A magnificent work, morphing on morphing on morphing.

As you might imagine, Escher wanted to know what lay beyond three-fold symmetries. This was the turf of crystallographers, so Escher did some research. He dug up some relevant journals. The math made him gag, but he devoured the pictures. He found out about quaternary and sesternary axes. He discovered that, mathematically, there are only a few ways to tile the plane. He mastered them all.

Besides mathematics and crystallography, there was another great influence on his work: music.

Escher often played music or sang while he worked. For his family's sake, I hope he had a good voice. As he played his iron across the wood, his hand would dance with the music, carving with the rhythm. Personally, I would ruin everything with that method, but it worked for Escher.

He described his pictures in terms of changing rhythms as one symmetry-type metamorphosed into another. Using an approach more intuitive than scientific, he related the second, third, fourth, and sixth quarter measures to the binary, ternary, quaternary, and sesternary axes—all ways of dividing the plane.

His favorite composer was Bach. Escher was enchanted with the way Bach squeezed, stretched, and overlaid his musical themes. Bach used reversals and reflections and played them simultaneously, one voice threaded through another, just as Escher intertwined his tiles. He called Bach a tonic for his creativity.

In the late 1930s, Escher created a thirteen-foot-long woodcut called *Metamorphosis*. The main design continuously and subtly changes through the entire thirteen feet. Several different tilings of the space are represented in this masterful mega-scroll.

It starts with the word *metamorphose*. The word is rotated ninety degrees and crossed with itself. The words intersect on the *O*, which stays the same when rotated, and the *M*, which becomes an *E* upon rotation. This crossword puzzle fades into a checkerboard, which then starts to mutate into interlocking lizard forms. As Escher said when describing this print, so far the rhythm is in two-quarter measure.

But then that rhythm changes. So far the print has used only black and white because only two forms have been contrasted. Now a third character is interposed. It divides the plane with three axes instead of two. And it requires a third color. In Escher's musical analogy, the rhythm has changed to three-quarter time.

The building blocks of the image continue to change. From lizards, they turn into hexagons, which suggest a honeycomb. Bees swarm around the comb, as eggs metamorphose into larva. As they hatch, they fly into the next phase of the picture. Their shapes change as they become the background for a school of fish swimming in the other direction. With only two opposed forms, Escher is back to two-quarter time.

But then the fish change into bird shapes, the background changes into bird shapes also, and a third bird shape starts out in miniature. As it grows, the rhythm moves back to three-quarter time, and the three flocks of birds intertwine.

The three shapes shift again, and become rhomboid. They coalesce to form cubes, which in turn become houses adorning a Mediterranean shoreline. A Saracen tower juts into the sea, joined to the land by a bridge. That tower becomes a rook on a chessboard, which is reminiscent of the squares at the beginning of the print. Accordingly, Escher ends his story here, with the word *Metamorphose* reappearing from the cracks between the chess squares.

In *Another World*, Escher uses metamorphosis to disorient the viewer. In the picture, walls become floors and ceilings become walls. Escher was influenced by Einstein's theory of relativity, which talks about the subjectivity of the observer. Escher's interpretation is more poetic than literal, of course. Artist's prerogative.

Escher's little morphing stories continued. In *Cycle*, there is a man running down a stairway. As he descends (represented by multiple images), he slowly changes into a flat shape, then by measures, into a simple rhombus. Three interlocking rhombuses (or rhombi to you Latin fiends), each providing the background for the others, start to suggest a cube. The cube becomes the house, and from the house comes our original little man. The story seems to say "A man is his castle."

In *Encounter*, Escher demonstrates the meshing of opposites again. This time the confrontation is between optimism and pessimism. A black figure symbolizing pessimism and a white one symbolizing optimism both appear from a foggy, gray background. As they gain contrast, they also gain dimensionality, finally seeming to pop out of the page. The two figures circle around each other, ultimately meeting at the bottom in a handshake, reconciling their opposite points of view.

Escher found philosophical meaning in image warping as well. In prints such as *Hand with Reflecting Sphere*, Escher demonstrates that spherical distortion compresses the entire environment into a small circle. As you peer into the sphere, you find yourself at the center of this universe—the focus of the world.

Escher played with distortion and reflection in many of his prints. In *Dewdrop*, he displays the warping due to both the reflecting and refracting aspects of water. In *Rippled Surface*, he shows his mastery of this type of optical deformation. In this minimalist print, the water surface is indicated only by the elliptical warping of the reflected tree branches.

As he explored warping, Escher discovered that the medieval theory of perspective was flawed. The eye does not really see straight lines going to a vanishing point. Rather, as we look around, we see curves connecting various points of view.

Straddle a railroad track, for instance. (Don't try this if a train is coming—take my word for it.) It is true that as the railroad track reaches toward the horizon it squeezes to a thin line. But if you look straight down, the tracks will seem parallel. As your head moves back up, the tracks go from parallel to convergent. There is no apparent discontinuity, so the lines must actually curve.

Indeed, that is what you see in a fish-eye lens. This lens (which is like a door's peep-hole), makes lines converge both above and below the horizon, curving to vanishing points at the circular edge of the picture. Thus the real theory of perspective should take this warping into account.

In a wonderful woodcut called *Print Gallery*, Escher warps the world into amazing contortions. He shows a visitor to the gallery looking at a painting. The painting being viewed arcs up and metamorphoses into a village that contains the gallery. This fantastic illusion puts the viewer into the picture. Here, Escher is using metamorphosis to involve the spectator in a unique way—as part of the painting.

In another print, *Reptiles*, a dragon-like lizard claws its way out of a flat drawing, and takes on a three-dimensional appearance. It crawls across objects on Escher's desktop. Then, after blowing out some smoke, the dragon crawls back into the flat drawing.

Some of Escher's customers thought the lithograph was a beautiful summation of reincarnation, another favorite metamorphosing theme. Escher denied any religious symbolism, but he seemed to enjoy adding symbolic layers to his work. He didn't protest too much.

Escher also used warping and morphing to represent infinity. In some of his woodcuts, such as *Circle Limit*, he tiles a circular space. Each tile becomes smaller as it leaves the center. In the limit, at the periphery of the circle, the tiles have become minute. The image has the feel of a spherical deformation. When Escher invented this reduction warping, he created a whole new slew of technical problems.

In describing a similar work with lizards shrinking toward the center, he said "By the time my small image surface had been reduced to a square centimeter, I needed a set of three magnifying glasses placed on top of one another in order to see clearly enough what I was doing. The smallest figure still recognizable as a complete animal shape, with head, tail, and four legs, had a total length of about two millimeters."

In 1951, out of the blue, an American journal published a favorable review of his work. That was followed by several other positive reviews. Suddenly Escher was famous. At the age of fifty, with thirty years of hard, lonely work behind him, Escher was an "overnight" success.

He deserved it. It reflected positively back into his work. At last he got feedback. The mathematicians had discovered M.C. Escher, and they let him know it. They bombarded him with ideas, many of which ended up on his woodblock.

One of the most famous of these is *Ascending and Descending*, an ever-ascending (or descending) stairway inspired by Professor L.S. Penrose. Your eye goes crazy trying to follow the monks as they patiently, infinitely, tread the stairs.

Professor Penrose's son, Roger, contributed another illusion, now called the Penrose triangle. Escher based many drawings on this visual trick. One of them, *Waterfall*, brilliantly transforms the illusion into a perpetual river with a waterfall that feeds itself.

These visual oddities manage to metamorphose in front of your eyes. It is as if things are changing just out of your view, barely glimpsed from the corner of your eye as you round each bend—only to end up back where you started.

These drawings, with their endless cycles, led Escher to deeper explorations of infinity and how to represent it on the page.

He discovered non-Euclidean math in an article by mathematician H.S.M. Coxeter. Albert Einstein had to learn non-Euclidean math to develop General Relativity, so the subject was becoming more popular at the time, if not less complicated.

Euclidean math, as developed by Euclid in 300 B.C., is your garden-variety geometry on a nice, flat piece of paper. Non-Euclidean math is like geometry on a curved surface, like a horse-saddle or a sphere. It's kind of a mess by comparison, but it gives you great pictures.

Escher used non-Euclidean principles in his *Circle Limit* series of woodcuts to suggest visual infinity. They do an admirable job.

As you can imagine, Escher spent a lot of time on each print. His dedication would have suited him well to animation. He surely proved that he could do repetitive work. It is strange and sad that he did not produce any films (that I know of). But his love was printed paper, and he was loyal to it.

By tiling the space, Escher tells a story that unfolds as your eye follows it. You are the narrator and you set the pace for the story.

In cinema, of course, the story is told on a screen, and your eye stares ahead. In that sense, viewing a film is more passive than looking at a painting. In fact, to follow a film, you must look at what the director wants you to look at, so movies are like visual bondage. You are not in control of the experience.

After twenty years of exploring and expanding the art of tiling, Escher noticed that no one else was interested in his passion. In his later years he would complain that he was walking around his geometrically-tiled garden all by himself. I don't think it ever occurred to him that no one else had the patience or genius to share his garden.

Escher died in 1972. A year later, Roger Penrose took Escher's tiling mania and harnessed it for further studies of "forced non-periodicity" (don't ask). Today those theories are central to the study of irregular crystals—a hot topic in physics, math, and crystallography.

Escher would have been pleased. He believed that underneath it all, the world was orderly.

His drawings inspired mathematicians and spurred them to deeper analysis. This humble, mathematically disinclined artist managed to enlighten some of the best mathematicians of our century.

This adds support to my thesis in Chapter 2, that imagery is of utmost importance in understanding. Sometimes, imagery is understanding.

Morphing in the Computer Age

How did the modern form of morphing arise? Was it just artistic experimentation? That would make a nice story, but the truth is somewhat more prosaic. It turns out that morphing and warping were important to scientists before the artists got hold of it.

One of the first uses was by NASA scientists in the 1960s. As they started to compile satellite pictures of the earth, they ran into a problem. The pictures didn't overlap properly, so it was hard to assemble a large mosaic. The camera lenses introduced some distortion, the angles of each shot were different, and some of the pictures were taken at widely different times. It was your basic mess.

By finding some common crossroads and other landmarks, they were able to warp the image to correct the distortions. After that, it was a simple matter to stitch the images together.

NASA found another use for warping when it got back pictures of other planets. Some of the spacecraft had unusual optics to perform extraordinary tasks in tight spots. They took strange pictures that had to be warped back to normalcy. The warping function used was the opposite of the warp introduced by the lens, so it was really *unwarping* the images. Most of the pictures of Mars, for instance, were unwarped before you ever saw them.

Another remarkable use of warping is in the medical field. A technique known as digital subtraction angiography (a typical medical mouthful) uses two X-rays of a patient. One X-ray is taken before and one after the injection of a dye. The dye is opaque to X-rays, so it shows up black on the pictures. To eliminate extraneous clutter, such as bones and organs, the first picture is subtracted from the second. That gets rid of everything except the dyed arteries.

It is a great technique, but it works only when the patient is completely motionless. Hopefully, the patient is still breathing. Unfortunately, that messes things up—unless, of course, you can warp the images into registration. Then you get some spectacular pictures of the patient's arteries.

So warping and morphing started out as serious scientific tools. And then an artist saw it.

In the early 1980s, Tom Brigham started to experiment with morphing as an art tool. He was at the New York Institute of the arts when he started to apply these scientific algorithms to an art project. For his first film trick, Tom turned a woman into a lynx.

The film premiered at the 1982 SIGGRAPH (Special Interest Group on Computer Graphics of the Association for Computing Machinery) convention. It has been described as a hallucination come to life.

Brigham also produced collages of pictures in the process of morphing. In one sequence, a kissing couple morphs into a monkey on a horse, then a man on a horse, then a frog on a horse. It continues as the horse turns into another frog, then the two embracing frogs morph into a man and a woman dancing.

Fame didn't rush up to meet Brigham. It took five years before Doug Smythe at Industrial Light and Magic (ILM) took another look at Brigham's concept. ILM is a division of LucasArts, set up by George Lucas to do the special effects for the movie industry.

Smythe needed a way to metamorphose several characters for Ron Howard's movie *Willow.* His clever solution is discussed in Chapter 6. But for now it is worth noting that Smythe is the person who coined the term "morphing." The rest is movie history.

Morphing in Computer Draw Programs

Prepress draw programs are a completely new tool for the artist. Unlike *paint* programs that strive to emulate a real-world painting environment, *draw* programs provide tools to create artwork for professional printing. They are not for the timid.

You might recall from Chapter 1 that when you enlarge an image that was painted on the computer screen, you also end up enlarging the pixels (see Figures 1.1 and 1.2). What looks like a diagonal line on the screen looks like a jagged staircase when you blow it up. That's really too bad, because the cure is to use a draw program and kiss your paintbrush good-bye.

The bad part about draw programs is that you are limited to line-drawing tools. No more airbrushing to get those graded colors. Yet they do manage to get color blends, so what's going on here? The answer is that they use tweening.

But what does tweening have to do with draw programs? Isn't tweening an animation technique?

Well, in a program such as Adobe Illustrator or Aldus Freehand, the tweening takes place on a single screen, one tweened shape overlapping the next. As the shapes tween, so do the colors.

For example, look at the two circles in Figure 3.11. If you include a single in-between you get Figure 3.12. Not only is the shape intermediate between the two circles, but the color is, too. If you add 60 circles in-between the two originals, you get Figure 3.13. That's pretty smooth shading, and it makes a circle look like a sphere.

Figure 3.11.
Two circles waiting to be tweened.

Figure 3.12.
A single tweened circle has a shape and a color in-between the other two.

Figure 3.13.
Sixty interpolations between each shape provide a smooth color blend.

Now you see how color blending is related to tweening and morphing.

Using methods similar to this, I drew the orchid in Figure 3.14.

In order to understand color tweening, which is also key to the next chapters, you must review a little color theory. I promise it won't be too hard.

Basic Color Concepts

"I mix them with my brains, sir."

John Opie (1761-1807) British painter, when asked what he mixed his colors with

The eye perceives color with specialized cells in the retina called cone cells. There are three types of cone cells and they are each receptive to a different color. It turns out that the three colors are close to red, green, and blue. When light strikes the cones, they compile their different inputs to produce the sensation of color.

Figure 3.14.
An orchid formed by color-blending petals.

As strange as it seems, a combination of red and green light looks yellow. Yellow light has its own frequency, as do red and green. But there are no yellow frequencies in a mix of red and green. Nevertheless, the eye can be fooled by this trick because of our tricolored cones.

When it came time to add color to television, the engineers wisely chose those three colors as fundamental. By combining different amounts of the three main colors, you can make almost any color of the rainbow—at least those that the human eye can see. This is called the red-green-blue or RGB color system.

Although this discussion is primarily concerned with computer displays, it is worth a little side trip to look at printing technology, too. After all, the book you are holding is an example of the latest printing art.

There is a big difference between a computer screen and a printed page. It might not seem so, but it is an enormous problem (maybe unsolvable) to match a computer screen to a printout. The first problem is that the physics are entirely different.

A TV monitor produces colors by *emitting* light from its tricolored phosphors. It is like a panel of little colored red, green, and blue light bulbs. Each member of a triplet glows at a specific frequency of light. If you light up all three colors at once, you get white. That's not obvious, but it is absolutely true.

A printed page produces colors by *absorbing* light from the environment. Each of the three primary printing colors absorbs light at a specific frequency. The colors are the *complement* of the TV colors. The complement of a color is like the opposite of the color. Instead of red-green-blue, you have cyan-magenta-yellow (CMY) colors. If you print all three colors at once, you get black.

Actually, you get mud brown, so black is usually added as a fourth color. It's called K because blue already took B. So the printing system is known as CMYK. Pretty poetic, eh?

This complement thing is interesting. Cyan is a blue-green color. The cyan pigment that is printed on a white page actually *absorbs* red. After the red is subtracted out of the white, you have a blue-green color left. That's what bounces back your eye as cyan.

So RGB and CMY are simply related: one is the color-complement of the other. In theory, you can translate easily from one to the other. That's what draw and prepress programs do more or less successfully. And that's what allows you to compose for print on the computer, even though the color systems are different.

To blend two colors, you need to blend their color components. This is just like the interpolation schemes mentioned in Chapter 1.

For the curious, here's a peek at the math behind computer colors:

THE MATH CORNER:

Color as a Vector

Because there are three components to an RGB color, you can plot it on a graph like any other three-dimensional variable, as in Figure 3.15. Each color can be represented by a vector whose tail is at the origin and whose head is the RGB coordinate in "color space."

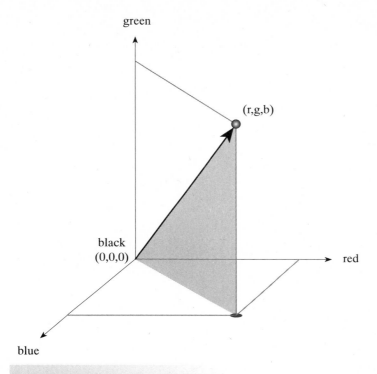

Figure 3.15.
A color as a vector in an RGB coordinate system.

All three components in a computer color system have the same number of shades, so the resulting space is a cube. Say you have four shades each of red, green, and blue. You then have a color cube with sides of four (see Figure 3.16). Of course, you are only seeing the front corner of the cube. There is a back corner and a middle as well.

The range for each color component is zero through three. Each cube can be referred to by its three-dimensional coordinate: (r,g,b). For instance, pure red is (3,0,0). It uses the maximum red and no other colors. It is the cube at the lower right of Figure 3.16.

We said all three colors together makes white and, sure enough, the front corner of the cube, (3,3,3) is white.

You can see that maximum green and maximum blue make cyan (0,3,3). Similarly, red and green make yellow (3,3,0), while red and blue make magenta (3,0,3).

Now you can visualize the *complement* of a color as "across the cube." Red is diagonally opposite cyan, its complement. Similarly, yellow is opposite blue and magenta is opposite green.

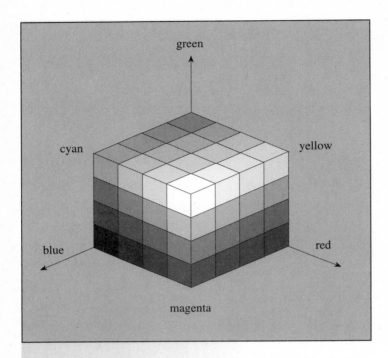

Figure 3.16.
A color cube with sides of four.

Does the eye have a color cube? Well, sort of. And this is a reasonable approximation of it. But everyone has slightly different light-sensing proteins, so two people don't necessarily see the same red.

And there are some colors in the rainbow that can't be displayed on your monitor. Most people don't seem to miss them. Do you?

Does this cube fit the CMY cube? Of course not! There are colors you can get in print that you can't get on the computer and vice-versa. When you consider how messy everything is, it's amazing what designers and printers are able to do.

The color space is *orthogonal* (every axis is perpendicular to the other two), so you can treat the components separately. That makes this a nice, well-behaved coordinate system.

That means you can use the trusty Pythagorean theorem to calculate the distance between two colors, (r_1, g_1, b_1) and (r_2, g_2, b_2).

RGB Color interpolation

The average of two colors, (r_1, g_1, b_1) and (r_2, g_2, b_2), lies in between them. It is the midpoint (r_m, g_m, b_m) of the line connecting the two, as seen in Figure 3.17. Notice that the average also represents the mid-point of each *component*. This can be seen in the projections of the vectors on the red-blue plane where the middle red, r_m, is halfway between r_1 and r_2, and the same goes for blue.

So the mid-point average is just:

```
r  = (r  + r )/2
 m     1    2
g  = (g  + g )/2
 m     1    2
b  = (b  + b )/2
 m     1    2
```

The same goes for a weighted average. The weighting function is applied to each component separately:

```
r  = f(w *r  + w *r ,w  + w )
 m      1  1    2  2   1    2
g  = f(w *g  + w *g ,w  + w )
 m      1  1    2  2   1    2
b  = f(w *b  + w *b ,w  + w )
 m      1  1    2  2   1    2
```

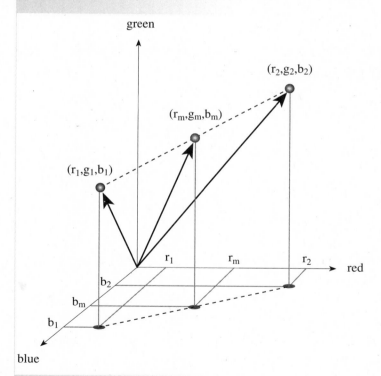

Figure 3.17.
The average of two colors lies at the mid-point of a line connecting them.

As you would hope, if the weights are both equal to one, these equations boil down to the mid-point average above. That's obvious but reassuring.

DISKETTE DEMO

To see some examples of tweening and morphing applied to color blending, get to the DOS prompt and type:

>BLEND

This program generates two different polygons and then tweens one into the other, without erasing. The colors are tweened as well, resulting in a fairly smooth blend of colors. The effect has a distinct 3D flavor, like strange extruded cones, or an aerial view of mountains.

To stop and examine a picture, press the space bar. Every time you press the space bar, another picture is displayed and the computer will wait for you to press a key again. To continue the automated show, press the Enter key instead of the space bar.

You might notice that some of the blending examples are not as smooth as others—they have a noticeable banding. The bands are caused when there are not enough colors to fit between the starting and ending colors. This happens whenever the two colors are too close to each other. The smoothest blends occur when the color range is the largest—darker darks and lighter lights.

Banding is usually about as welcome as the black plague; but as you can see, the technique can be exploited to produce swell-looking agates. The effect can be emulated even on a 24-bit color system by clipping the color resolution—should you be so perversely inclined.

Some of the polygons are rotated with respect to each other. This gives the blending a little twist. I did that to show you how important it is to correlate the points properly. Correlation—how the source polygon relates to the target—is one of the difficulties of this method.

Another problem with polygon blending is that, in most draw programs, the number of points in each polygon must match. So, in practice, one polygon is cloned from the other, then the points are moved to their new location. That guarantees that the number of points are the same, and that they are already correlated.

You might notice some funny horizontal lines on the screen. This is due to a bug in the Microsoft compiler. When the lowest edge of a polygon is horizontal, the compiler freaks out and extends the line too far. There is a worse bug that crashes the computer into a wall.

If a polygon is flat, the program totally chokes (I protect against that, so you don't need to worry). Hopefully, these bugs will be squashed in the next version of the compiler.

If you use a different compiler, this glitch should go away. Of course, another one might just show up.

This program is like an electronic Rorschach test. There are images that look like a tablecloth draped over a table, a shining gemstone, or an explosion. There are black holes, loony-tunes backdrops, spiderwebs, and tunnels. I know it sounds like I'm getting carried away, but these shapes are there because the color blending suggests them.

Now you know how color blending is accomplished in a draw program. And, in viewing the examples, you should see *why* people want to color blend. When you have had enough of this silly program, press the Esc key to quit.

FOR PROGRAMMERS ONLY: The Blend Program

BLEND.C

The blend program combines elements of the previous tweening programs with the image-morphing programs in the next chapters. It is self-contained, and shows how to create random colors and a blended color spread, and how to set the resulting palette.

```
BLEND.C
```

After the usual includes, some constants are defined, including the screen dimensions: XMIN, YMIN to XMAX, YMAX. It assumes the 320 x 200 VGA resolution with 256 colors. Notice that the mid-point of the screen is also defined: XMID, YMID. This is used to center the polygons to be tweened and morphed.

The number of colors is set to 256, and the starting color for this program is thirty-two. I could have started anywhere, but the first sixteen colors are traditionally set to mimic the sixteen colors of the EGA mode, and the second sixteen colors are a nice gray spread. I left them intact. In fact I use one of them, gray (color eight), as the background color.

FACTOR and **SHIFT_BITS** are defined for some of the fixed-point arithmetic used to tween the polygons and the colors. As you remember, by shifting bits you can make an integer simulate a fractional number without resorting to glacial-speed floating point.

The maximum number of points and tweens is defined here. If you want to vary the theme, play with these numbers.

It won't do you much good to increase **NTWEENS** very much. There are only thirty-two hues of each color component and you can't divide the color increments any finer than that. But it is interesting to see this for yourself. Raise the number to sixty-four and you will see the same banding as before. Thirty-two is the point of diminished returns.

Then come the structure definitions. First are the structures for the polygons and the fixed-point arrays that tween them. Then comes color, defined in terms of its red, green, and blue components.

The polygon arrays and the tweening arrays are declared globally. This makes the program more readable, but less modular. Ah, tradeoffs.

The main routine is ridiculously tiny, but that's because there is virtually no user interface for this program. It initializes the random number generator to the time, to guarantee that the sequences are always different, sets the graphics mode and then calls the subroutine blendPoly. It calls it over and over again until the user hits the Esc key. Then it resets the text mode and quits.

blendPoly is the central routine. It clears the graphics screen to gray, then it generates a color spread and two random polygons. Then it calls calcTweens to calculate the delta array that will be added to the polygon in order to tween it.

blendPoly calls tweenObject, which adds the deltas to the polygon and draws the resulting in-betweens. Then blendPoly waits for about three seconds, while reading the keyboard. If no keys are pressed, blendPoly returns 1 to the main program, telling it to continue. If the Esc key is pressed, blendPoly returns a 0, and the main loop is terminated.

The next two routines, `calcTweens` and `tweenObject`, are similar to the tweening routines introduced in earlier chapters. `calcTweens` creates two arrays, the `delta` array and the `tween` array. The tween array, `Tween[]`, is a fixed-point representation of the source array. The delta array, `Delta[]`, is a fixed-point increment to be added to `Tween[]`.

As the deltas are added in `tweenObject`, the tween array metamorphoses. After the desired number of tweens have been generated, the tween array is equal to the target array. It would be like magic if it wasn't so much like math.

`tweenObject` calls `drawObject` after adding the deltas. The main purpose of `drawObject` is to ensure that the Microsoft polygon routine doesn't get something it can't chew on. Otherwise, I would have called the polygon routine directly.

If you're interested in trying to avoid the polygons that fluster the Microsoft compiler, this is the routine to do it in. Hint: you need to search the polygon by Y, and make sure there is only one maximum. If there are two or more, the bottom is flat, and the compiler will burp.

`getPoly` is next, and it is the routine that creates the polygons to be tweened. It makes a polygon by sweeping a changing radius through as many angles as are needed to create the correct number of sides. For instance, a six-sided polygon divides the circle up into six parts of sixty degrees each. If all the radii are the same, you get a regular hexagon. If the radius is randomized, you get an irregular, six-sided polygon.

The variable named `jagFactor` is responsible for the regularity of the polygons. If the `jagFactor` is one, the radii are equal and a regular polygon is produced. A `jagFactor` of two means that the radius can fluctuate to half of the maximum. A `jagFactor` of three: one-third of the maximum. The larger the `jagFactor`, the greater the jaggedness of the polygon. Feel free to play with this number.

The `phase` variable controls the "twist" in the blending. It rotates one polygon with respect to the other. Right now the maximum phase is one-sixth of a circle, or sixty degrees. To experiment, alter the line:

```
phase = twoPi / random (6, 20);
```

This `random` function returns a random number between six and twenty, inclusively. *Decrease* the first number to *increase* the phase shifting (since it's in the denominator).

Next, `setSpread` creates a source and target color, then creates a spread, or blend of colors between them. It calls `setRandColor` to create a unique color with random red, green, and blue components.

The routine selects a random color between the desired min and max color. These parameters allow a generic "light" and "dark" color to be selected. At the toss of a random die, the spread is chosen to go from light to dark or vice-versa.

Then, using fixed-point arithmetic for speed, it calculates each color in the spread. It notifies the hardware of the palette change by calling `setPalColor`.

That covers the basic routines. There are several variables to play with, so rock out. Don't expect to improve the color blending much—32 shades of each primary are just not going to cut it. But you may enjoy playing with polygons and unusual visual effects.

You might enjoy trying to make the `setRandColor` routine return a more "pure" color, where one or two components predominate. Hint: pick a random component, and divide it (or the other two components) by some factor. Be bold, but don't forget to back up your work!

BLEND.C The Listing

```
/***************************************************************
 * FILE: blend.c
 * DESC: This program demonstrates how a color blend can be
 *       created by tweened morphing.
 *
 * HISTORY:   6/ 6/1993
 * LAST CHANGED:
 *
 *    Copyright (c) 1993 by Scott Anderson
 *
 ***************************************************************/

/* ----------INCLUDES------------- */

#include <conio.h>
#include <stdio.h>
#include <math.h>
#include <graph.h>
```

```
/* -----------DEFINES-------------- */

#define YES          1
#define NO           0

#define GRAY         8

#define XMIN         0
#define XMAX         319
#define XMID         ((XMAX + XMIN) / 2)
#define YMIN         0
#define YMAX         199
#define YMID         ((YMAX + YMIN) / 2)

#define COLORS       256
#define COLOR1       32

#define FACTOR       16   /* Bit rotate factor for fixed point */
#define SHIFT_BITS   8    /* Rotate factor for color blend */

#define MAX_POINTS   32
#define NTWEENS      32

#define ESC_KEY      27

#define PI           3.1415926535;

#define QUIT         (-1)
#define SKIP         1

/* -----------TYPEDEFS/STRUCTS---------- */

typedef struct {    /* for the screen coordinates */
    int x, y;
}
POINT;

/* Delta is the difference array that gets added to Tween */
typedef struct {
    long x, y;
}
DELTA;

typedef struct {    /* The high & low words in a long word */
    int lo, hi;
```

continues

BLEND.C continued

```
}
LO_HI;

/* A Fixed-point union:
 * a long word broken up into low & high words */
typedef union {
    long lword;                 /* The long word portion */
    LO_HI word; /* The high and low parts of this long word */
}
FIXED;

typedef struct {     /* A fixed-point coordinate pair */
    FIXED x, y;
}
TWEEN;

typedef struct {
    /* red, green, and blue color components */
    unsigned char r, g, b;
}
COLOR;

/* ----------PROTOTYPES------------ */

void    setGraphicsMode();
void    setTextMode();
int     blendPoly();
void    calcTweens(int npoints, int ntweens);
void    tweenObject(int npoints, int ntweens);
void    getXY(POINT *point);
void    getPoly(POINT array[], int npoints, int maxRad);
void    drawObject(int npoints, int color);
void    setSpread();
void    setRandColor (int min, int max, COLOR *color);
void    setPalColor(int index, int red, int green, int blue);
int     quitCheck();
int     keyCode(int key);

/* ----------GLOBAL DATA------------ */

POINT   Source[MAX_POINTS];
POINT   Target[MAX_POINTS];
DELTA   Delta [MAX_POINTS];
TWEEN   Tween [MAX_POINTS];
```

```
/*******************************************************************
 * FUNC: main (int argc, char *argv[])
 *
 * DESC: Kickstart the random number generator, set the graphics
 *       mode and run blendPoly until Esc is pressed.
 *******************************************************************/

main (int argc, char *argv[])
{
    srand((unsigned int) time());
    setGraphicsMode();
    while (blendPoly());
    setTextMode();
}

/*******************************************************************
 * FUNC: int blendPoly()
 *
 * DESC: blend a random polygon into another one.
 *******************************************************************/

int
blendPoly()
{
    int keyCode;
    long start;
    int npoints = random (3, MAX_POINTS);

    clearScreen(GRAY);
    setSpread();
    getPoly (Source, npoints, XMID);
    getPoly (Target, npoints, XMID/4);

    calcTweens(npoints, NTWEENS);
    tweenObject(npoints, NTWEENS);

    /* Wait a few seconds for a keystroke.
     * Return 0 if ESC is pressed */
    start = (long) time();
    while ((long) time() - start < 3) {
        keyCode = quitCheck();
        if (keyCode == QUIT)
            return 0;
        else if (keyCode == SKIP)
            return 1;
```

continues

BLEND.C continued

```
    }
    return 1;
}

/******************************************************************
* FUNC: void     calcTweens(int npoints, int ntweens)
*
* DESC: Calculate the Delta array from the Source and Target
*******************************************************************/

void
calcTweens(int npoints, int ntweens)
{
    int pt;
    for (pt = 0; pt < npoints; pt++)
    {   /* use fixed point long words to store the deltas */
        Delta[pt].x = ((long)(Target[pt].x - Source[pt].x)
                        << FACTOR) / ntweens;
        Delta[pt].y = ((long)(Target[pt].y - Source[pt].y)
                        << FACTOR) / ntweens;
        Tween[pt].x.word.hi = Source[pt].x; /* set high word */
        Tween[pt].y.word.hi = Source[pt].y;
        Tween[pt].x.word.lo = 0;            /* clear low word */
        Tween[pt].y.word.lo = 0;
    }
}

/******************************************************************
* FUNC: void     tweenObject(int npoints, int ntweens)
*
* DESC: Metamophose the Source polygon into the Target polygon
*       by adding the Delta array.
*******************************************************************/

void
tweenObject(int npoints, int ntweens)
{   /* Tween one object into another */
    int tween, point;
    int color = COLOR1;

    for (tween = 0; tween < ntweens; tween++)
    {   /* Add deltas to tween array & draw new polygon */
        for (point = 0; point < npoints; point++)
        {   /* Add delta to tween the line */
            Tween[point].x.lword += Delta[point].x;
```

```
                Tween[point].y.lword += Delta[point].y;
            }
            drawObject(npoints, color++);
        }
    }


    /*****************************************************************
     * FUNC: void     drawObject(int npoints, int color)
     *
     * DESC: Copy the points into an xycoord struct & draw the poly.
     *****************************************************************/

    void
    drawObject(int npoints, int color)
    {
        struct _xycoord poly[MAX_POINTS];
        int point;

        int fillOK = NO;
        int oldY = Tween[0].y.word.hi;

        for (point = 0; point < npoints; point++)
        {   /* get the coords from the hi word of the Tween array */
            poly[point].xcoord = Tween[point].x.word.hi;
            poly[point].ycoord = Tween[point].y.word.hi;

            /* The following code is to fix a fatal bug in the
             * Microsoft polygon fill routine that occurs when all
             * of the Y-values are the same (a horizontal line).
             * There is also a bug when the bottom line of the poly
             * is horizontal, but at least that bug doesn't crash
             * the machine...
             */
            if (poly[point].ycoord != oldY)
                fillOK = YES;   /* y is different, so fill poly */
        }
        _setcolor(color);
        if (fillOK)                    /* don't crash the system! */
            _polygon(_GFILLINTERIOR, poly, npoints);
    }


    /*****************************************************************
     * FUNC: void     getPoly(POINT array[], int npoints, int maxRad)
     *
     * DESC: Create a random polygon and put it in array
     *****************************************************************/
```

continues

BLEND.C continued

```c
void
getPoly(POINT array[], int npoints, int maxRad)
{   /* Generate a random set of points */
    int point;
    int rad, phase, jagFactor;
    float theta;
    float twoPi = 2 * PI;

    jagFactor = random(1, 4);
    phase = twoPi / random(6, 20);
    for (point = 0, theta = 0; point < npoints;
            point++, theta += twoPi / npoints) {
        rad = random(maxRad / jagFactor, maxRad);
        array[point].x = XMID + rad * cos(theta + phase);
        array[point].y = YMID + rad * sin(theta + phase);
    }
}

/****************************************************************
* FUNC: void     setSpread()
*
* DESC: Create a random color spread
****************************************************************/

void
setSpread()
{
    int index;
    int rotRed, rotGreen, rotBlue;
    int dRed,   dGreen,   dBlue;
    COLOR colorA, colorB;

    if (rand() & 1) {
        setRandColor ( 0, 16, &colorA);
        setRandColor (22, 32, &colorB);
    }
    else {
        setRandColor (22, 32, &colorA);
        setRandColor ( 0, 16, &colorB);
    }

    rotRed   = (int) colorA.r << SHIFT_BITS;
    rotGreen = (int) colorA.g << SHIFT_BITS;
    rotBlue  = (int) colorA.b << SHIFT_BITS;
```

```
        dRed    =  ((int)(colorB.r - colorA.r) << SHIFT_BITS)
                         / NTWEENS;
        dGreen  =  ((int)(colorB.g - colorA.g) << SHIFT_BITS)
                         / NTWEENS;
        dBlue   =  ((int)(colorB.b - colorA.b) << SHIFT_BITS)
                         / NTWEENS;

        for (index = 0; index < NTWEENS; index++) {
            setPalColor(index + COLOR1,
                        rotRed   >> SHIFT_BITS,
                        rotGreen >> SHIFT_BITS,
                        rotBlue  >> SHIFT_BITS);

            rotRed      += dRed;
            rotGreen    += dGreen;
            rotBlue     += dBlue;
        }
}

/****************************************************************
* FUNC: void setRandColor  (int min, int max, COLOR *color)
*
* DESC: Create a pointer to a random color with RGB components
*          between the min and max component value.
****************************************************************/

void
setRandColor (int min, int max, COLOR *color)
{
    color->r = min + random(0, max - min);
    color->g = min + random(0, max - min);
    color->b = min + random(0, max - min);
}

/****************************************************************
* FUNC: int random(int low, int high)
*
* DESC: Return a random number between the low and high values
****************************************************************/

int
random (int low, int high)
{   /* get a random number between low and high, inclusively */
    if (high < low) return (low);   /* don't divide by zero */
    return (low + (rand() % (high - low + 1)));
}
```

continues

BLEND.C continued

```
/**************************************************************
* FUNC: int quitCheck()
*
* DESC: Check keyboard. If there is no key waiting, return 0,
*       for OK. If a number from 1-9 is typed, change the wait
*       between frames. Otherwise, the user wants to quit,
*       so return 1.
**************************************************************/

int
quitCheck()
{
    int key;
    static int spaceWait = NO;

    if (spaceWait) {
        key = getch();
        if (key != ' ')
            spaceWait = NO;
        return keyCode(key);
    }
    else if (_kbhit()) {
        key = _getch();
        if (key == ' ') {
            /* turn on space bar stepping */
            spaceWait = YES;
            /* pause for space key */
            key = _getch();
        }
        return keyCode(key);
    }
    return 0;
}

/**************************************************************
* FUNC: int keyCode(int key)
*
* DESC: Parse the key and return a quit or skip code.
**************************************************************/

int
keyCode(int key)
{
    if (key == ESC_KEY || key == 'q' || key == 'Q')
        return QUIT;       /* a quit key */
```

```
        else return SKIP;    /* otherwise, skip */
}

/*****************************************************************
* FUNC: void    setGraphicsMode()
*
* DESC: Set up the graphics screen
*****************************************************************/

void
setGraphicsMode()
{
    _setvideomode(_MRES256COLOR);
}

/*****************************************************************
* FUNC: void    setTextMode()
*
* DESC: Set the screen to the startup text mode
*****************************************************************/

void
setTextMode()
{
    _setvideomode(_DEFAULTMODE);
}

/*****************************************************************
* FUNC: int clearScreen(int color)
*
* DESC: Clear screen to the given color
*****************************************************************/

int
clearScreen(int color)
{
    _setcolor(color);
    _rectangle(_GFILLINTERIOR, XMIN, YMIN, XMAX, YMAX);
}

/*****************************************************************
* FUNC: void setPalColor(int index, int red, int green, int blue)
*
* DESC:set the palette register to the color components
*****************************************************************/
```

continues

BLEND.C continued

```
void
setPalColor(int index, int red, int green, int blue)
{
    _outp (0x3c7, index-1);
    _outp (0x3c9, red);
    _outp (0x3c9, green);
    _outp (0x3c9, blue);
}
```

Now you know how useful warping, tweening, and morphing can be as design motifs. Artists are moved by the magic of a metamorphosis—and it's not just aesthetics. Literature abounds with references to metamorphosing. It is an irresistible metaphor for growth and renewal.

You also learned how morphing—as a technique—is used to blend colors in computerized draw programs. It is hard to imagine how this nasty problem could have been solved any other way.

In the next chapter, you will see how to apply these principles to photographic-quality images. The results can be startling.

Photographic Morphing and Warping

4

"The camera cannot lie. But it can be an accessory to untruth."

Harold Evans, *Pictures on a Page*

By now you can understand morphing polygons and colors, but how about those magnificent morphing scenes in *Terminator 2* or the Michael Jackson video "Black or White?" Surely those morphs aren't as easy. Well, they *are* different, but the territory is familiar. In fact, you need to know about morphing polygons and colors first.

In this chapter, you will learn about bitmapped images. Then you will proceed to warp and morph them to your heart's content. There is a lot of math in this chapter, just in case you are interested. But you don't need the math to understand what this kind of morphing can do and how you might use it.

Pictures on the PC

"The Greeks Had a Word for It."

Zoè Akins, Play title

There are many names for a picture on a PC screen. In the days when black and white was the standard, the pictures were called bitmaps. The idea was that the image was a raster map, and the values were black or white—zero or one. A single bit could stand for a pixel. That's not the case with color computers, yet once again, an old name has stuck to a concept that has evolved beyond its roots. For a fresh start, I propose pixel-map as the new nomenclature.

There are many graphics modes available on the average PC. Most of them are pretty hideous from an artistic point of view. CGA was the first graphics offering from IBM and it boasted 4 very strange, unpalatable colors.

Then came EGA (I am skipping some of the history to keep a boring story short). It offered sixteen colors, which didn't exactly ignite creative fires for the typical artist.

Then came VGA and it had 256 colors, the bare minimum for realistic-looking pictures. Suddenly, photography started showing up on computers.

The programs in this book work in 256-color mode. To conserve memory I stick to 320-by-200 resolution. This is very low resolution, but it works fine for our purposes, and the code is easy to scale up to higher resolution, should you need it.

The images on the disk are stored as PCX files. This is a popular graphics standard on the IBM, so there should be no problem incorporating any of these images into your own project. To get 256 colors, I use version five of the PCX "standard."

This is a good time to take a look at some of the images on the disk.

DISKETTE DEMO: LOAD

From the DOS prompt, type:

>LOAD BOB

The picture named BOB will be loaded and displayed. Notice that you don't have to type the ".PCX" entension because the program adds it for you. When you want to return to DOS, press the Esc key.

To list all of the PCX files that you can load, type:

>DIR *.PCX

You will be loading a lot of pictures in the pages to come. There are some more tricks that LOAD can do, but you'll get to that later.

Image Warping

There are two parts to the morphing algorithm: the warp and the dissolve. The dissolve is (theoretically) simple, but there are a thousand ways to morph. In this section I show you a user-friendly method for warping.

The first step in morphing—the warp—distorts the main outlines of the two images. The idea is to stretch and squeeze parts of one picture (such as the eyebrows) so that they match up with the equivalent parts of the target picture. This is the function of the warp algorithm.

Imagine that you have a map of the world printed on a sheet of rubber. What would happen if you grabbed some part of the picture, say New York, and pulled it south? Computers can address this question in a simple way.

The screen is a map of colored pixels, and they can be manipulated like any other mathematical coordinates. For instance, to slide the picture to the right, you could simply add one to the x-coordinate of all the pixels, and then replot them.

To rotate, squash, or skew the pixels, some standard equations will do the trick.

In short, a whole host of mathematical incantations can be brought to bear on the poor pixel, to shove it anywhere you want on or off the screen.

This process is fortuitously called "mapping" by the mathematicians. If the image stays connected through the transformation (no rips), it is called warping. In most warping routines, the warping is local, so if you pull New York south, Newark moves with it, but Chicago barely budges.

The simplest method is to indicate points on the screen, and then drag them where desired. Although relatively simple to program, this method poses difficulties for the user. The morphing artist must provide hundreds of points for effective warping and keep track of all of them. If even one point is misplaced, the warp will be wrong.

A better method is to use lines. With just two end-points, a line automatically specifies a string of points in between. Another benefit of this implementation is not as obvious: with lines, you can specify global changes. With one line, you can rotate or scale the entire image. This technique is much more powerful than local warping.

When there is more than one line, they each compete for influence, and the effect becomes more local.

Even though pixel-mapped images look different from polygons, they still can be treated as a collection of coordinates—and all the same rules apply. One difference is the number of points. In a typical Fantavision frame, there are a few hundred points. For a pixel-mapped image, there are thousands. The mode I use here, 320 by 200, has 64,000 pixels. And that is *very* low resolution. A Hollywood system would flaunt 1,000 by 1,000 pixels (in true, twenty-four bit color, no less). That's *one million* pixels.

So there will be a lot of calculating going on when you warp a pixel-map. That can take time. In this case, the low resolution is your friend. A workstation has ten times as many pixels to push as the average PC. Of course a workstation is a hundred times faster, so it still crosses the finish line first. And even a workstation can't always warp in real-time, so don't expect miracles from your PC.

Depending on the speed of your computer, a simple image warp can take seconds to minutes. Not great—somewhere between golf (really slow) and baseball (kind of slow) in terms of actual events per hour—but you can learn to live with it.

Warping has a long and varied history. A house of mirrors is a good metaphor for mathematical warping. In fact, any curvature at all in a mirror causes warping. A convex mirror creates a fish-eye effect, where close objects are normal size, but far objects appear smaller. Painters since the eighteenth century have been fascinated by these deviations from strict perspective.

In the 1970's, TV engineers figured out several ways to warp images. Using analog equipment, they were able to warp an image to fit on a rotating sphere or a 3-D cube. An analog device can do any calculation you design it for, at close to the speed of light. These wonderful contraptions can warp thirty frames per second easily for real-time motion.

This effect is now commonplace, yet comparable digital effects have lagged. Computers powerful enough to handle that many computed pixels per second are only now becoming available.

So why don't we all have analog video devices? The reason is that every special effect requires another analog circuit. If you want a new effect, you need to build the hardware. With digital effects, you just need to write some code. The digital effect will never run as fast as the analog effect, but it is much easier to produce, debug, and modify software than hardware.

To write that software, you need to know what a rubber sheet looks like to a mathematician.

THE MATH CORNER:

Warping

As mentioned earlier, this warping method uses lines instead of points to twist and stretch the image. The idea is to draw a line on the starting (source) image, and then move that line to a new position. Every point is affected by that line, and the rules are pretty simple:

1. Find the distance between a pixel and the source line by dropping the perpendicular, d (see Figure 4.1).

2. Find the fractional distance f along the source line to the perpendicular. The fraction goes from zero to one.

3. Move the point to a spot that is the same distance from, and fraction of, the *target* line.

Figure 4.1 shows what you want to calculate. Given point P in the source image, you want to deduce point P' in the target image. By inspecting the diagram, you see that the distance d is the projection of vector **AP** (I'm using boldface for vectors) on the perpendicular, which yields AP cos α

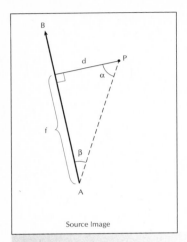

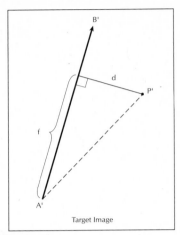

Figure 4.1.
A given point P has a relationship to the line AB that gets translated to the warping line A'B'.

You might remember from vector arithmetic that the dot product of vector **AP** with the perpendicular to **AB** (denoted ⊥**AB**) is defined as:

AP . ⊥AB = ¦¦AP¦¦ * ¦¦⊥AB¦¦ cos α = (AP$_x$ * ⊥AB$_x$ + AP$_y$ * ⊥AB$_y$)

where ||AP|| and ||AB|| are the magnitudes of the vectors. You can see that the solution in terms of components, (APx * ⊥ABx + APy * ⊥ABy), doesn't involve any trig. Now solve for d:

$$d = AP \cos \alpha$$
$$= \frac{AP \cdot \perp AB}{\|AB\|}$$

Equation 1.

Notice that the magnitude of the line itself, ||AB|| is used instead of the magnitude of the perpendicular, ||⊥AB||. This is for two good reasons: one is that they are equal and the other is that you can use this number again, as you're about to see.

Also note that the vector dot product allows you to calculate the desired values without computing any angles or using any trig. That makes it both simple and fast.

Again by inspection of Figure 4.1, you see the distance represented by f is the projection of AP on AB itself—AP cos β—which is the quantity:

$$\frac{AP \cdot AB}{\|AB\|}$$

To get just the fraction of line AB, from zero to one, you divide by the length of AB again:

$$f = \frac{AP \cdot AB}{\|AB\|^2}$$

Equation 2.

Equations 1 and 2 represent a translation into a new, scaled, orthogonal coordinate system based on d and f instead of x and y. The d and f "axes" are perpendicular, just like the x and y axes they are converted from. Now you are ready to transfer these two important relationships over to the new line, A'B'.

The fractional part—the "f-axis"—is easy. It is the same fraction, but of the new line:

$$f * A'B'$$

You also will want to apply the distance to the new "d-axis." This axis is perpendicular to the new line. The unit d-vector is:

$$\frac{\perp A'B'}{\|A'B'\|}$$

So, with the new origin at A', the source pixel P is transformed into the destination pixel P':

$$P' = A' + f * A'B' + d * \frac{\perp A'B'}{\|A'B'\|}$$

Equation 3.

That's what a rubber sheet looks like in math-talk. It uses the relationship a point has with the original line, and applies it to the new line. That's how it makes surrounding points move along with the line.

It's like gluing a stick onto the rubber sheet and then pulling and twisting it around.

To be of any use, however, you need more lines. They all have to compete for pixels. A useful metaphor is gravity. If each line represented mass, its effect (weight) would be proportional to one over the distance squared:

$$\text{weight} \propto \frac{1}{d^2}$$

That is what this program uses, but you also could experiment with weightings that are proportional to some power of the line length, so longer lines have more "pull:"

$$\text{weight} \propto \frac{\text{length}^n}{d^2}$$

Here n would typically range from zero to two.

Here's how the calculation goes for two control lines: From each line, the distance to the point is computed, and a new pixel is calculated as before. But this time there are two pixels instead of one, so some further work is needed. As shown in Figure 4.2, from the original point P to the new points P_1' and P_2' there are two displacements, D_1 and D_2:

$$D_1 = P_1' - P$$
$$D_2 = P_2' - P$$

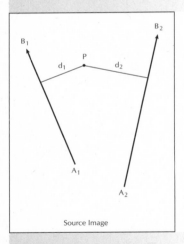 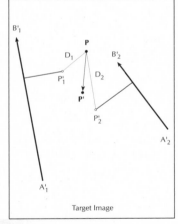

Source Image

Target Image

Figure 4.2.
Where two lines contribute influence, the warped point is the weighted average of the displacements D1 and D2.

As mentioned previously, there is a weighting factor based on how far the original point is from each line. Using this factor, the routine calculates the weighted average of the two displacements to arrive at the final position, P':

$$P' = P + \frac{D_1 W_1 + D_2 W_2}{W_1 + W_2}$$

As you might expect, the new point is on a line between P1' and P2'. If there are three lines, there are three displacements to average, and so on. For n lines:

$$P' = P + \frac{\sum\limits_{i=1}^{n} D_i W_i}{\sum\limits_{i=1}^{n} W_i}$$

If the warping is severe, this can look more like a taffy sheet than a rubber sheet. When you twist lines around relative to others, you get wild results. The routine does its best to resolve the conflicts, but be ready for eight-eyed people if you flip a nose upside-down!

DISKETTE DEMO: Warp

The warping routine on the included disk uses the line method. It is adapted from Thaddeus Beier and Shawn Neely's algorithm, the one used in Michael Jackson's rock video "Black or White."

To explore the warping routines, get to the DOS prompt and type:

>WARP BABY

where BABY.PCX is the name of a PCX image with 320-by-200 resolution and 256 colors. You don't need to type the ".PCX" extension—the program adds it automatically.

If there are any pre-defined control lines for this image, the program asks you if you want to use them. Type N for no. A new prompt appears to inform you that you are about to create new control lines. Press Enter.

The image will appear on the screen, and then a mouse cursor will appear on top of it. The idea is to draw a series of lines on the screen, then to move them and stretch them. The warping routines will then move and stretch the *image* to follow the *lines*. This is a lot easier than trying to move the image itself a pixel at a time, which is definitely not recommended.

Draw a line by pressing the mouse button to indicate the starting point. With the mouse button *still down*, drag out a line from the starting point. As a useful first exercise with a single control line, start at the top and draw a vertical line down the screen (see Figure 4.3). Then press the Enter key. This tells the computer that you are finished entering lines.

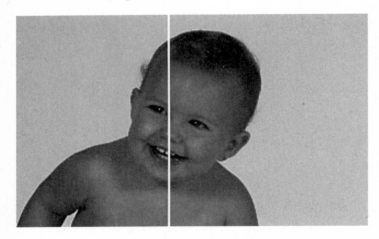

Figure 4.3.
The control line is a vertical line down the screen.

The program then reminds you that you are about to edit the control lines. Press Enter, and the image is redisplayed with the control line on top of the picture.

Grab this line and drag it. Put the mouse close to the top point and hold down the mouse button. Still pressing the mouse button, drag the point halfway down the screen and over to the right (see Figure 4.4). If nothing happens, you were probably not close enough to an end-point. Try again, putting the tip of the mouse arrow right on the point. Next, grab the bottom point of the line and drag it over to the left of the screen—also halfway down—to make the line horizontal.

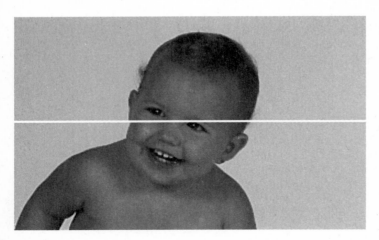

Figure 4.4.
The control line has been rotated 90°.

Press the Enter key to tell the computer that you are through dragging the lines around. It will commence calculating. Starting at the top of the screen, you should see a new image scanning down. It is a rotated version of your first image (see Figure 4.5). The top of the screen is now on the right and the bottom is now on the left, just as your control line dictated. Before you get a pain in the neck, press Esc to quit.

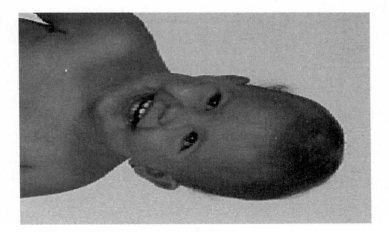

Figure 4.5.
The image is rotated by the control line.

A single line can be used to *move* the image as well. Just drag the lone control line and the image will move with it. In addition, a single line can be used to squash or stretch the image by elongating or shortening the control line. A global manipulation like this can work only with a single line. Any extra lines will compete for influence, and the results will not be so simple.

Now let's wave the flag. Start the program again, with the command:

```
>WARP FLAG
```

This time, when the picture is loaded in, draw five or six vertical lines spaced regularly across the screen (see Figure 4.6). Press Enter to get to the edit screen. Grab the end-points of each line and move the first line up, the next line down, the next line up, etc., for each vertical line (see Figure 4.7). When you are done, press Enter. The image should warp into a rippling flag (Figure 4.8).

Figure 4.6.
The flat flag with some vertical control lines.

Figure 4.7.
The flag with the displaced control lines.

Figure 4.8.
The warped flag.

Experiment with other images. Although you can warp things in really spectacular ways, the best effects usually occur with only a slight movement of the control lines.

You can use lines to keep things anchored down as well. To prevent the edges from warping, for instance, you could draw four lines around the perimeter of the screen. Simply leave these lines untouched to keep the border intact.

Finally you have the tool you need to turn a few heads, raise some eyebrows, twist an arm or pull a leg. Experiment and have some fun!

FOR PROGRAMMERS ONLY: The Warp programs

DEFINE.H

This is the header file for all of the image warping and morphing programs. It includes the defined constants, macros, and structures that I use to deal with the images and control lines.

The constants are for dimensioning the screen and certain arrays and limits.

The macros include `PIXEL(p,x,y)`. It returns the color of the `x,y` coordinate in the pixmap array of `p`.

The structures include `point`, `line`, `color`, and `picture` types, as well as some structures that are discussed in the next chapter:

DEFINE.H—the listing

```
/*****************************************************************
 * FILE: define.h
 * DESC: These are the main defines for dissolve, warp,
 *       morph, load and fix.
 *
 * HISTORY:  Created  1/11/1993
 * LAST CHANGED:  5/ 6/1993
 *
 *    Copyright (c) 1993 by Scott Anderson
 *
```

continues

DEFINE.H—continued

```
**********************************************************************/

/*--------------------DEFINES----------------------------*/

#define ON              1
#define OFF             0


#define MAX_TWEENS      99      /* Maximum tweens (2 digits) */
   /* minus 2 digit tween# appended to end */
#define MAX_NAME_SIZE (8-2)
#define HEADER_LEN      128     /* PCX header length */
     /* Number of colors in the palette */
#define COLORS 256
/* bytes in palette (COLORS*3) */
#define PALETTE_SIZE    (3*COLORS)


/* Maximum number of morphing lines */

#define MAX_LINES       32
/* max number of pixels wide we handle */
#define MAX_WIDE        320
/* max number of pixels tall we handle */
#define MAX_TALL        200
/* Size of screen buffer */
#define MAX_BYTES       (MAX_WIDE*(long) MAX_TALL)
/* Number of components per color (RGB)   */
#define COMPS           3
/* largest color component value */
#define MAX_COMP        32
/* the midpoint of the colors - for gray  */
#define MID_COMP        (MAX_COMP/2)
/* enough to handle about 10 different palettes  */
#define MAX_FREQ        1023
#define MAX_FILES       10
/* length of a file name including directory */
#define MAX_PATHLEN 80
#define ENTER           13      /* Keyboard values */
#define ESC             27


#define HTAB            18      /* Position for text messages */
#define VTAB            8

/* The mouse button & keyboard constants */
#define NO_BUTTON 0
```

```
#define LEFT_BUTTON      1
#define RIGHT_BUTTON     2
#define KEYPRESS         4

/* the square of min dist for grabbing pt */

#define GRAB_DISTANCE 25

        /* Some of the graphics colors */
#define BLACK 0
#define WHITE 255

#define EXT_PCX          ".PCX"  /* pcx file extension */
   /* primary line file holder extension */
#define EXT_LINE1        ".LN1"
#define EXT_LINE2        ".LN2"  /* aux file for warp lines */

#define ERROR            -1      /* General-purpose error code */

typedef enum {
    NO_ERROR,           /* first entry means everything is ok */
    MEMORY_ERR,         /* Not enough memory */
    READ_OPEN_ERR,      /* Couldn't open file for reading */
    READ_ERR,           /* Trouble reading the file */
    WRITE_OPEN_ERR,     /* Couldn't open the file for writing */
    WRITE_ERR,          /* Couldn't write the file */
    MOUSE_ERR,          /* No mouse driver found */
    WRONG_PCX_FILE,     /* PCX file format not supported yet */
    READ_CONTENTS_ERR   /* error in .LN file */
}
ERR;

/*---------------------MACROS----------------------------*/

#define MIN(a,b)        (((a)<(b)) ? (a) : (b))
#define PIXEL(p,x,y)    (p->pixmap[y * (long) p->wide + x])
#define SQUARE(x)       (((long) x)*(x))

/* ---------------------TYPEDEFS----------------------------*/

typedef struct {
    int x,y;                    /* the screen coordinates of the point */
}
POINT;
```

continues

DEFINE.H—continued

```c
typedef struct {
    POINT p[2];
}
LINE_SEGMENT;

typedef struct {
    int number;        /* number of segments to follow */
    LINE_SEGMENT line[MAX_LINES];
    char *filename; /* name of file holding the line list */
}
LINE_LIST;


typedef struct {
    POINT p[2];             /* the endpoints */
    int delta_x, delta_y;   /* x & y displacement */
    float length;           /* the precalculated length of the line */
    long length_square;     /* the length squared */
}
LINE;

typedef struct {
/* red, green, and blue color components */
    unsigned char r, g, b;
}
COLOR;

typedef struct {
    COLOR c[COLORS];        /* a 256 entry palette */
}
PALETTE;

typedef struct {
    int xmin, ymin;         /* the upper left corner */
    int xmax, ymax;         /* the lower right corner */
    int wide, tall;         /* the width and height */
    int pal_id;             /* an ID number for each palette */
    PALETTE pal;            /* the actual palette is here */
    unsigned char far *pixmap;  /* a pointer to the pixel map */
}
PICTURE;

typedef struct linko {
    struct linko *next;
```

```
    char        *str;
}
LINKED_LIST;

/* --------------------PROTOTYPES------------------------ */

/**** file handling routines ****/
extern PICTURE *loadPicture(char *filename);
extern int loadPalette(FILE *fp, PALETTE *palette);
extern int getBlock (unsigned char *byte, int *count,
FILE *fp);
extern int mustRead(FILE *fp, char *buf, int n);
extern int saveScreen(PALETTE *pal);
extern int putBlock(unsigned char num, unsigned char color,
FILE *fp);
extern int writeByte(unsigned char *byte, FILE *fp);

/**** screen and color routines ****/
extern int defaultPalette(PALETTE *palette);
extern int setPalette(PALETTE *palette);
extern int displayPicture(PICTURE *picture);
extern int displayNoPal(PICTURE *picture);
extern int freePicture(PICTURE *pic);

/**** mouse routines ****/
extern int initMouse();
extern int hideMouse();
extern int showMouse();
extern int mousePos(int *x, int *y);

/**** general purpose routines ****/
extern int clip(int num, int min, int max);
extern int quitCheck();
extern void quit(int err, char *name);
extern int wait(int count);
extern int waitForKey();
extern char lineAsk(char *name);

/* --------------------GLOBAL DATA------------------------ */

extern int     TargFlag;
extern int     Key;
```

WARP.C

The main program in WARP.C gets the command-line arguments and makes sure they are within bounds. This program is set up to do multiple, tweened warping, but don't concern yourselves with that until the next chapter.

Then the program loads in the desired picture. It checks to see whether there are any pre-defined control lines attached to this image. If there are, the program asks you whether you want to use these lines or create new ones. After the desired control lines are defined and placed into SrcLine and DstLine, the program calls tweenWarp to do the hard part.

Before ending, the current before-and-after control lines for this image are saved.

tweenWarp is the next routine and it displays the source image while it ponders how to warp. It goes through a tween loop, adjusting the control lines (warpLine[]) to move from the source location to the target (also called the destination) location.

Inside that loop is the actual warping loop. Rather than picking a pixel from the source and warping it, the program does the opposite. It selects a pixel from the *warped* image and finds out what *source* pixel would give rise to it, by using the inverse transformation. That way every pixel in the warped image gets a value. If the algorithm went from the source to the warped image, it might miss certain target pixels.

It goes through every pixel in the warped picture and finds the color to plot by calling sumLines. This routine is in the file LINECALC.C, listed later in the chapter. It contains the actual warping calculations.

After the picture is composed, the computer beeps in triumph and waits for the user to hit a key. Let's look at the code:

WARP.C—the listing

```
/*****************************************************************
* FILE: warp.c
* DESC: This program lets you specify a file to warp, then
*       prompts you for control lines. It uses the lines to
*       warp the underlying image, going a step at a time,
*       tweening to the target and optionally saving the
*       sequence as numbered PCX files.
*
```

```
* HISTORY:  Created  1/13/1993
* LAST CHANGED: 5/ 6/1993
*
*    Copyright (c) 1993 by Scott Anderson
*
********************************************************************/

/* ---------------------INCLUDES---------------------------*/

#include <conio.h>
#include <stdio.h>
#include <io.h>
#include <dos.h>                 /* for the mouse */
#include <math.h>
#include <graph.h>
#include <memory.h>
#include <string.h>

#include "define.h"

/* ---------------------DEFINES---------------------------*/

#define WARP_TWEENS      2


/* ---------------------PROTOTYPES---------------------------*/

int     tweenWarp(PICTURE *src);

/* ---------------------EXTERNALS---------------------------*/

/**** line routines ****/
extern void      editLines(PICTURE *pic, LINE_LIST *lineList);
extern void      createLines(PICTURE *pic, LINE_LIST *lineList);

/**** warping and morphing routines ****/
extern int       sumLines(PICTURE *picture, COLOR *color,
                 LINE *origline, POINT *warp, LINE *warpline);
extern int       setLength(LINE *line);

/**** i/o routines ****/
extern LINE_LIST    *loadLines(char *filename, char *extension);
extern void         saveLines(char *filename,
                    LINE_LIST *lineList, char *extension);
```

continues

WARP.C—continued

```
/**** external variables ****/
extern char     *OutFilename;
/* set from last picture loaded */
extern int      Xmin, Ymin, Xmax, Ymax;

/* --------------------GLOBAL DATA------------------------*/

PICTURE *Src;              /* source picture pointer */

LINE SrcLine[MAX_LINES];
LINE DstLine[MAX_LINES];

int     Tweens;
int     StartLine;
int     NumLines;

/****************************************************************
* FUNC: main (int argc, char *argv[])
*
* DESC: Read in a filename to warp
****************************************************************/


main (int argc, char *argv[])
{
    int     segment;
    LINE_LIST *lineSrcList;
    LINE_LIST *lineDstList;
    char    answer;

    /* load the pcx file if one is given */
    if ((2 > argc) || (argc > 4)) {
        printf("Usage: warp <[source] file> [<steps> [<output>]]\n\n");
        printf("Where: <[source] file> is the source PCX filename\n");
        printf("        <steps>    is the optional sequence size \n");
        printf("                       (the max is %d, the default is \
                            %d)\n", MAX_TWEENS, WARP_TWEENS);
        printf("        [[]<output>[]]    is the optional output [\]
               filename\n");
        printf("                       (defaults to no output)\n\n");
        printf("Note:  The output filename can be at most %d \
               characters long.\n",
                                MAX_NAME_SIZE);
```

```
        printf("         The PCX extension is added automatically, \
            so don't\n");
        printf("         include it in the filename.\n");
        printf("         Morph only accepts PCX files with %d X %d \
            resolution\n",
                                  MAX_WIDE, MAX_TALL);
        printf("         and %d colors.\n", COLORS);
        exit(0);
    }
    if (argc > 2) {
        Tweens = clip (atoi(argv[2]), 1, MAX_TWEENS);
        if (argc > 3)
            OutFilename = argv[3];
    }
    else
        Tweens = WARP_TWEENS;

    printf("Loading the file %s\n", argv[1]);
    Src = loadPicture(argv[1]);
    if (Src == NULL)
        quit(MEMORY_ERR, "");

    lineSrcList = loadLines(argv[1], EXT_LINE1);
    lineDstList = loadLines(argv[1], EXT_LINE2);
if (lineSrcList->number != 0) {
        if (lineAsk(argv[1]) == 'N') {
            createLines(Src, lineSrcList);
            lineDstList->number = 0;
        }
        else
            editLines(Src, lineSrcList);
    }
    else [{]
        createLines(Src, lineSrcList);
        [lineDstList->number = 0;
    }]

    TargFlag = 1;    /* For the screen intro message */
    NumLines = lineSrcList->number;
    if (NumLines ) {[) {]
        /* Make sure the number of lines match */
        if (lineDstList->number !=  NumLines)    {
            /* didn't match, so copy the source lines */
            lineDstList->number = NumLines;
            for (segment = 0; segment < NumLines; segment++)
```

continues

WARP.C—continued

```
                    lineDstList->line[segment]
                    = [lineSrcList->line[segment];
    }

        editLines(Src, lineDstList);
    saveLines(argv[1], lineSrcList, EXT_LINE1);
    saveLines(argv[1], lineDstList, EXT_LINE2);
    beep();
    for (segment = 0; segment < NumLines; segment++) {
        DstLine[segment].p[0] = lineDstList->line[segment].p[0];
        DstLine[segment].p[1] = lineDstList->line[segment].p[1];
        setLength(&DstLine[segment]);
        SrcLine[segment].p[0] = lineSrcList->line[segment].p[0];
        SrcLine[segment].p[1] = lineSrcList->line[segment].p[1];
        setLength(&SrcLine[segment]);
    }
    tweenWarp(Src);
    }

    setTextMode();

}

/****************************************************************
 * FUNC: int tweenWarp(PICTURE *src)
 *
 * DESC: In-between the warping lines to the final warped image.
 *        Display the warped image as you go.
 ****************************************************************/

int
tweenWarp(PICTURE *src)
{
    POINT warp;
    COLOR scolor;
    LINE warpLine[MAX_LINES];
    int tween, line, p;

    setGraphicsMode();
    displayPicture(src);
    if (Tweens > 1) {
        saveScreen(&src->pal);
    Tweens--;
    }
```

```
/* src is already on screen, now tween to the target */
    for (tween = 1; tween <= Tweens; tween++) {
        /* Tween the control lines used to warp the images */
        for (line = 0; line < NumLines; line++) {
            /* tween each point of each line */
            for (p = 0; p < 2; p++) {
                warpLine[line].p[p].x = SrcLine[line].p[p].x +
                    ((DstLine[line].p[p].x
                        -SrcLine[line].p[p].x) * tween) /Tweens;
                warpLine[line].p[p].y = SrcLine[line].p[p].y +
                    ((DstLine[line].p[p].y
                        -SrcLine[line].p[p].y) * tween) /Tweens;
            }
            setLength(&warpLine[line]);
        }
        /* Go through the screen [positions] and get warped [
           ]source pixels */
        for (warp.y = Ymin; warp.y <= Ymax; warp.y++)    {
            for (warp.x = Xmin; warp.x <= Xmax; warp.x++)    {
                _setcolor (sumLines(src, &scolor, SrcLine,
                    &warp, warpLine));
                _setpixel (warp.x, warp.y);
            }
        }
        if (!OutFilename) { /* no output file name */
            beep();
            waitForKey();          /* so pause to enjoy the pictures */
        }
        else
            saveScreen(&src->pal);
    }
}
```

LINECALC.C

LINECALC.C does the real math behind the warping. The two important routines
are sumLines and getSourceLoc. If you had only one control line, you would need
getSourceLoc only. To include the contributions of the other control lines, you
need sumLines.

For every single pixel in the warped image, sumLines must go through all the control lines and sum up the contribution of each one. The weighting is determined by the distance of the point from each line.

I use an inverse distance-squared formula, but you might play around with this particular equation for different results. The line to alter is:

```
weight = 1/(.001 + distance * distance);
```

The addition of .001 in the denominator is to avoid a division-by-zero error when the point is on the line and the distance is zero. Notice that the calculations use floating-point arithmetic, which accounts for the leisurely pace of these computations.

The distance is calculated in getSourceLoc, which is the next routine in the file. It carries out the math described previously, returning the warped coordinate as well as its distance from the line.

The rest of LINECALC.C is mainly involved with drawing and editing the control lines. Let's take a look:

LINECALC.C—the listing

```
/*****************************************************************
* FILE: linecalc.c
* DESC: These routines include the warping calculations and
*       the line-handling functions.
*
* HISTORY: Created   3/11/1993
* LAST CHANGED: 5/ 6/1993
*
*    Copyright (c) 1993 by Scott Anderson
*
*****************************************************************/

/* --------------------INCLUDES-------------------------- */

#include <conio.h>
#include <stdio.h>
#include <io.h>
#include <math.h>
#include <graph.h>
```

```
#include <malloc.h>
#include <memory.h>
#include <string.h>

#include "define.h"



/* --------------------MACROS---------------------------- */

#define PIXEL(p,x,y)     (p->pixmap[y * (long) p->wide + x])
#define SQUARE(x)        (((long) x)*(x))



/* --------------------PROTOTYPES------------------------*/

/**** line routines ****/
int     xorLine(int x1, int y1, int x2, int y2);
int     getLine(int *argx1, int *argy1, int *argx2, int *argy2);
int     findPoint(LINE_LIST *lineList, int * line, int * point,
                  int x, int y);
int     movePoint();

/**** warping and morphing routines ****/
int     sumLines(PICTURE *picture, COLOR *color, LINE *origline,
                 POINT *warp, LINE *warpline);
float   getSourceLoc(POINT *orig, LINE *origline, POINT *warp,
                     LINE *warpline);
int     setLength(LINE *line);

void    setupScreen(PICTURE *pic, int editFlag);

/* --------------------EXTERNALS--------------------------*/

/* set from last picture loaded */
extern int      Xmin, Ymin, Xmax, Ymax;

extern int      NumLines;

extern LINE     SrcLine[MAX_LINES];
extern LINE     DstLine[MAX_LINES];

/* --------------------GLOBAL DATA------------------------*/
```

continues

129

LINECALC.C—continued

```
int     TargFlag=0;

/********    These are the basic warping calculations    **********/

/****************************************************************
* FUNC: int sumLines(PICTURE *picture, COLOR *color,
*         LINE *origline, POINT *warp, LINE *warpline)
*
* DESC: Sum and weight the contribution of each warping line
****************************************************************/

int
sumLines(PICTURE *picture, COLOR *color, LINE *origline,
         POINT *warp, LINE *warpline)
{
    int     x, y;
    float   weight, weightSum;
    float   distance;
    int     line;
    POINT   orig;
    int     paletteIndex;
    float   deltaSumX = 0.0;
    float   deltaSumY = 0.0;

/* if no control lines, get an unwarped pixel */
    if (NumLines == 0)
        orig = *warp;
    else {
        weightSum = 0.0;
        for (line = 0; line < NumLines; line++,
                origline++, warpline++) {
            distance=get SourceLoc(&orig,origline,warp,
                                   warpline);
            weight = 1/(.001+distance*distance);
            deltaSumX += (orig.x - warp->x) * weight;
            deltaSumY += (orig.y - warp->y) * weight;
            weightSum += weight;
        }
        orig.x = warp->x + deltaSumX / weightSum+ .5;
        orig.y = warp->y + deltaSumY / weightSum+ .5;
    }

    /* clip it to the nearest border pixel */
    x = clip(orig.x, Xmin, Xmax);
```

```
    y = clip(orig.y, Ymin, Ymax);
    paletteIndex = PIXEL (picture, x, y);
    color->r = picture->pal.c[paletteIndex].r;
    color->g = picture->pal.c[paletteIndex].g;
    color->b = picture->pal.c[paletteIndex].b;
    return (paletteIndex);
}

/************************************************************
* FUNC: float getSourceLoc(POINT *orig, LINE *origline,
*                          *POINT *warp, LINE *warpline)
*
* DESC: For a given line, locate the corresponding warped pixel
************************************************************/

float
getSourceLoc(POINT *orig, LINE *origline, POINT *warp,
             LINE *warpline)
{
    float fraction, fdist;
    int dx, dy;
    float distance;

    dx = warp->x - warpline->p[0].x;
    dy = warp->y - warpline->p[0].y;
    fraction = (dx * (long) warpline->delta_x + dy
               * (long) warpline->delta_y)
               / (float) (warpline->length_square);
    fdist = (dx * (long) -warpline->delta_y + dy
            * (long) warpline->delta_x)
               / (float) warpline->length;
    if (fraction <= 0 )
        distance = sqrt(dx*(long) dx + dy * (long) dy);
    else if (fraction >= 1) {
        dx = warp->x - warpline->p[1].x;
        dy = warp->y - warpline->p[1].y;
        distance = sqrt(dx*(long) dx + dy * (long) dy);
    }
    else if (fdist >= 0)
        distance = fdist;
    else
        distance= -fdist;
    orig->x = origline->p[0].x + fraction * origline->delta_x -
              fdist * origline->delta_y
```

continues

LINECALC.C—continued

```
                         / (float) origline->length+ .5;
     orig->y = origline->p[0].y + fraction * origline->delta_y +
                  fdist * origline->delta_x
                         / (float) origline->length+ .5;
     return distance;
}

/*****************************************************************
 * FUNC: int setLength(LINE *line)
 *
 * DESC: Set the deltas, the length and the length squared
 *       for a given line.
 *****************************************************************/

int
setLength (LINE *line)
{
    line->delta_x = line->p[1].x - line->p[0].x [+ 1];
    line->delta_y = line->p[1].y - line->p[0].y [+ 1];
    line->length_square = SQUARE(line->delta_x)
                          + SQUARE(line->delta_y);
    line->length = sqrt(line->length_square);
}

/******************** The line routines  ********************/

/*****************************************************************
 * FUNC: int xorLine(int x1, int y1, int x2, int y2)
 *
 * DESC: Draw a line on the screen using the XOR of the
 * screen index.
 *****************************************************************/

int
xorLine(int x1, int y1, int x2, int y2)
{
    int oldcolor = _getcolor();

    _setcolor(WHITE);            /* Use white as the xor color */
    _setwritemode(_GXOR);
    _moveto (x1,y1);
    _lineto (x2,y2);
    _setcolor(oldcolor);     /* restore the old color */
}
```

```
/****************************************************************
* FUNC: int getLine(int *argx1, int *argy1, int *argx2, int *argy2)
*
* DESC: Input a line on the screen with the mouse.
****************************************************************/

int
getLine (int *argx1, int *argy1, int *argx2, int *argy2)
{
    int     x1,y1, x2,y2;
    int     oldx, oldy;
    int     input;

/* save the current mode */
    short   old_mode = _getwritemode();
/* get input until we have a real line, not just a point */
    do {
        /* wait for button or key press */
        while (!(input = mousePos (&x1, &y1)));
        if (input & KEYPRESS) {
            _setwritemode(old_mode);
            return 1;
        }
        oldx=x1, oldy=y1;
        hideMouse();
        /* prime the pump with this dot */
        xorLine (x1, y1, oldx, oldy);
        showMouse();
        while (input = mousePos (&x2, &y2)) {
            /* rubber band a line while the mouse is dragged */
            if (x2 != oldx ¦¦ y2 != oldy)
            {
                hideMouse();
                xorLine (x1, y1, oldx, oldy);
                xorLine (x1, y1, x2, y2);
                showMouse();
                oldx=x2, oldy=y2;
            }
        }
    } while (x1 == x2 && y1 == y2);

    *argx1 = x1, *argy1 = y1;
    *argx2 = x2, *argy2 = y2;
```

continues

LINECALC.C—continued

```
    _setwritemode(old_mode);              /* get out of XOR mode */
    return (0);
}

/*****************************************************************
 * FUNC: int findPoint(LINE_LIST *lineList, int * line,
 *                     *int * point, int x, int y)
 *
 * DESC: loop thru dstline and find point within GRAB_DISTANCE,
 *       return 1 if found, 0 otherwise.
 *****************************************************************/

int
findPoint (LINE_LIST *lineList, int * line, int * point,
           int x, int y)
{
    int l, p;
    int minl, minp;
    long length;
    long minlength = SQUARE(640) + SQUARE(480);

    for (l = 0; l < lineList->number; l++) {
        for (p = 0; p <= 1; p++) {
            length = SQUARE(lineList->line[l].p[p].x - x)
                    + SQUARE(lineList->line[l].p[p].y - y);
            if (length < minlength) {
                minlength = length;
                minl = l;
                minp = p;
            }
        }
    }
    if (minlength > GRAB_DISTANCE)
        return 0;
    *line = minl;
    *point = minp;
    return 1;
}

/*****************************************************************
 * FUNC: int movePoint(LINE_LIST *lineList)
 *
 * DESC: Grab a point and move it. Return 1 when key is pressed,
 *       else return 0.
 *****************************************************************/
```

```
int
movePoint(LINE_LIST *lineList)
{
    int     stuckx, stucky, movex,movey;
    int     oldx, oldy;
    int     input;
    int     line, point;

/* save the current mode */
    short   old_mode = _getwritemode();

    do {
        /* keep getting input until we have a mouse button */
        while (!(input = mousePos (&movex, &movey)));
        if (input & KEYPRESS) {
            _setwritemode(old_mode);
            return 1;
        }
        if (!findPoint(lineList, &line, &point, movex, movey)) {
            _setwritemode(old_mode);
            return 0;
        }

        /* establish fixed end point */
        stuckx = lineList->line[line].p[1-point].x;
        stucky = lineList->line[line].p[1-point].y;

        oldx=movex, oldy=movey;
        hideMouse();
        /* erase the old line */
        xorLine (stuckx,
                 stucky,
                 lineList->line[line].p[point].x,
                 lineList->line[line].p[point].y);
        /* and prime the pump with the new line */
        xorLine (stuckx, stucky, oldx, oldy);
        showMouse();

        while (input = mousePos (&movex, &movey)) {
            /* rubber band a line while the mouse is dragged */
            if (movex != oldx || movey != oldy) {
                hideMouse();
                xorLine (stuckx, stucky, oldx, oldy);
                xorLine (stuckx, stucky, movex, movey);
```

continues

LINECALC.C—continued

```c
                    showMouse();
                    oldx=movex, oldy=movey;
                }
            }
        } while (stuckx == movex && stucky == movey);

        lineList->line[line].p[point].x = movex;
        lineList->line[line].p[point].y = movey;

        _setwritemode(old_mode);        /* get out of XOR mode */
        return (0);
}

/*****************************************************************
* FUNC: void    createLines(PICTURE *pic, LINE_LIST *lineList)
*
* DESC: create a list of line segments for a picture
*****************************************************************/

void
createLines(PICTURE *pic, LINE_LIST *lineList)
{
        setupScreen(pic, 0);     /* set for enter prompt */

        initMouse();
        showMouse();
        for (lineList->number = 0;lineList->number < MAX_LINES;
             lineList->number++) {
            if (getLine(&lineList->line[lineList->number].p[0].x,
                        &lineList->line[lineList->number].p[0].y,
                        &lineList->line[lineList->number].p[1].x,
                        &lineList->line[lineList->number].p[1].y))
                break;
        }
        hideMouse();
}

/*****************************************************************
* FUNC: void    editLines(PICTURE *pic, LINE_LIST *lineList)
*
* DESC: move around some existing lines
*****************************************************************/
```

```
void
editLines(PICTURE *pic, LINE_LIST *lineList)
{
    int segment;

    setupScreen(pic, 1);    /* set for edit prompt */

    initMouse();
    for (segment = 0; segment < lineList->number; segment++) {
        xorLine(lineList->line[segment].p[0].x,
                lineList->line[segment].p[0].y,
                lineList->line[segment].p[1].x,
                lineList->line[segment].p[1].y);
    }
    showMouse();
    /* move the endpoints around */
    while(!movePoint(lineList));
    hideMouse();
}

/****************************************************************
 * FUNC: void    setupScreen(PICTURE *pic, int editFlag)
 *
 * DESC: Print a message introducing the screen, wait for input,
 *       then set the graphics mode and display the screen.
 ****************************************************************/

void
setupScreen(PICTURE *pic, int editFlag)
{
    static char *editMess[2] = {"enter", "edit"};
    static char *targMess[2] = {"source", "target"};
    setTextMode();

    _settextposition(VTAB, HTAB);
    printf("When you are ready to %s the control lines",
            editMess[editFlag]);
    _settextposition(VTAB+2, HTAB);
    printf("for the %s image, press any key.",
            targMess[TargFlag]);
    waitForKey();

    setGraphicsMode();
    displayPicture(pic);
}
```

Image Dissolving

"Cross-dissolving is simple."

Thaddeus Beier and Shawn Neely, "Feature-Based Image Metamorphosis,"
Computer Graphics, Vol 26, Number 2, July 1992

I'm not talking about Salvadore Dali here. This section is about dissolving, not melting. You need to mix two images together by blending their colors. And contrary to what Thad and Shawn say, cross-dissolving isn't so simple—at least, not on a PC.

In the previous chapter you learned about RGB colors, the Red-Green-Blue color system. There I talked about how nice 24-bit color is. But most of us have regulation-vanilla VGA cards, so we must settle for less.

On the PC, you can mix thirty-two shades of each of these primary colors to produce a little more than thirty-two thousand different colors (32,768 to be exact). That sounds like a lot (the amount definitely surpasses a crayon box), but an ordinary human eye can distinguish almost *half a million* colors! A computer that can display all those (and more) is called a true-color system. A true-color system has 256 shades of each primary color, and is the ultimate in color graphics.

On these workstations, cross-dissolving is as simple as averaging color values. But not on a PC. On most PCs, you can display only 256 colors at a time. When you combine two colors on a PC, the resulting color might not be in the group of 256 that you have available.

Given these formidable limitations, it's a wonder you can do any kind of graphics at all on a PC. But there are tricks you can use to beat the system.

The trick used here is to pretend you have more colors than you actually have. I know it sounds crazy, but this is not a Zen trick, and it works. When you blend two colors together, you calculate the exact RGB value and enter it into a big color table with all 32,768 possible entries (32 reds times 32 greens times 32 blues).

After you have blended every pixel on the screen, you look through the color table for the 256 most popular colors. That's your new color table. Then you force all the leftover colors to shift to the closest.

It's not elegant—in fact it seems klunky—but the algorithm usually picks a pretty good palette.

THE MATH CORNER:

Cross-dissolves

To blend two colors together, you need to compute the weighted average of their component primaries:

$$r = \frac{w_1 * r_1 + w_2 * r_2}{(w_1 + w_2)}$$

$$g = \frac{w_1 * g_1 + w_2 * g_2}{(w_1 + w_2)}$$

$$b = \frac{w_1 * b_1 + w_2 * b_2}{(w_1 + w_2)}$$

where $r_1 g_1 b_1$ and $r_2 g_2 b_2$ are the primary colors for the first and second pixels and w_1 and w_2 are the weighting factors for each pixel. For example, with a color 20 percent of the way between two others, w_1 is 20, w_2 is 80 and their sum is 100.

If the weighting for the first pixel is zero, the color takes the value of the second pixel, as you would expect. Similarly, if the second weight factor is zero, the first pixel is selected.

To find a close color, you need to look through the 256 colors and check for the nearest rgb color in the batch. The color "distance" is calculated just like any other distance in a three-dimensional space:

$$\text{distance} = \sqrt{(r - r_i)^2 + (g - g_i)^2 + (b - b_i)^2}$$

where $r_i g_i b_i$ is the ith entry into the color table. In the program, I use the distance squared. I only need it for comparison purposes, and the square gives the same result—but without the square-root calculation.

DISKETTE DEMO: Dissolve

The fifty-fifty cross-dissolve is just a double exposure. Given two images, you want to combine the colors equally from both. To play with the computerized version of this, type:

>DISSOLVE BABY GRANDMA

Here BABY and GRANDMA are the two images you want to blend.

The program displays the starting picture, while it calculates the double-exposure. It beeps when it is done and waits for you to inspect the resulting image. When you have had enough, hit Esc.

FOR PROGRAMMERS ONLY: The DISSOLVE program

DISSOLVE.C

The `main` routine of DISSOLVE.C collects the command-line inputs and loads the source and target frames. Then it calls `tweenDissolve` to do the simultaneous fade-in/fade-out of the cross dissolve.

You might notice that `tweenDissolve` (like `tweenWarp`) is designed to accommodate more than one in-between frame. The next chapter covers this interesting feature in greater detail.

`tweenDissolve` goes through each pixel on the two screens and computes a third value somewhere between them, using the weighted averaging method just discussed.

It accumulates colors in the `Freq[r][g][b]` array, named for the frequency (which is the measure of popularity) of each rgb triplet. Each pixel of a given rgb color is logged into this 32K table. The most frequently occuring colors have the largest entries in the table. This table is a histogram of the color table.

Then `tweenDissolve` saves the full rgb color map in three separate arrays, to avoid memory-model overloads. Most PCs are still trying to figure out how to address more than 64K of memory at a whack. Really! One day, all computers will have at least 32-bit addressing and we can get beyond *this* kludge and on to the *next* kludge.

tweenDissolve calls `collapseColors` in COLOR.C. Its function is to strip the most popular 256 colors off the top of the `Freq` array. Notice that there are some non-kosher code optimizations in this fun routine. It has a dreaded `GOTO` statement, but it's for a good reason—and it's fast.

The first algorithm you might come up with to collapse the colors would be to go through the array and pick out the most popular color. Then go through it again, looking for the second most popular color. This works fine, but it sends you cycling through a large array 256 times.

It would be great to know what the popularity cutoff is. That way you could go through the array just once, picking all the colors above the cutoff. There is a way to do that, but you need a new array, called `freqCount`. Here's how it works:

First, the routine scans through `Freq`, the big color table. It counts the frequency of the frequencies (this sort of thing happens in all tricky routines), and stores it in the `freqCount` array.

For example, if a color is used by 200 pixels, `freqCount[200]` is incremented to one. If another color is used by 200 pixels, `freqCount[200]` is bumped to 2. Now you know that two pixels have a popularity of 200.

After filling this array, the routine starts at the top of the `freqCount` array, and scans down to see how many colors are most popular.

Currently the maximum frequency, `MAX_FREQ`, is set to 1023. If five thousand pixels have the same rgb color, it peaks out and just enters 1023 into `Freq[r][g][b]`. This means the `freqCount` array must be dimensioned to 1024 because it needs an entry for every frequency. To include higher frequencies, you must be prepared to increase the size of `freqCount`.

`FreqCount[1023]` contains the number of different colors that have 1023 pixel references (or more). These colors are the most popular, so they are definitely going to make the grade into the small palette. Let's say there are 100 of them, and the rest of the array looks like:

```
freqCount[1023] = 100          100
freqCount[1022] = 50           150
freqCount[1021] = 40           190
freqCount[1020] = 10           200
freqCount[1019] = 20           220
freqCount[1018] = 10           230
freqCount[1017] = 40           270
```

The column on the right records a running total of the counts. If you look at the big color table, you will see 100 colors that had the highest count, 50 that have the next highest count and so on. The number of colors that are the most popular are in the running sum column. There are 190 colors that are used by 1021 pixels or more, 200 that are used by 1020 pixels or more, and so on.

From this you see that for colors used by 1017 pixels or more, you need 270 colors—and that's too many. So the cutoff frequency is 1018. Any color that popular or better will gain automatic entry into the exclusive club of the 256-color palette. And there is room for only 26 of the next less popular group of colors.

You are almost done. Now the program goes through the `Freq` array and quickly selects the desired small palette. While doing so, it modifies the `Freq` table to reflect the selection. For an rgb color that doesn't make the grade, a zero is placed in `Freq[r][g][b]`. If it does survive the cut, the value in the `Freq` table is replaced by the index into the small palette (0 through 255).

Then `tweenDissolve` goes through the rgb color map and finds the closest fit of each pixel to the 256-color table by calling `closestColor`. This routine uses the modified `Freq` table to speed things up. For a given rgb color, the value of `Freq[r][g][b]` is either zero or the desired index. If it is zero, the closest color from the small palette is substituted. That index then replaces the zero in `Freq[r][g][b]`. The next pixel of this color finds this index and doesn't need to recalculate it.

It's really too bad that so much rigmarole is involved with just averaging colors. The underlying math is so simple, but the hardware throws a monkey-wrench into the whole thing.

My friends remind me that if the hardware was easy to use, I would be out of a job. Perhaps I complain too much.

Here's the listing of DISSOLVE.C:

DISSOLVE.C—the listing

```
/*****************************************************************
* FILE: dissolve.c
* DESC: This file accepts two PCX files and does a dissolve
*       between them.
*
* HISTORY:  Created  1/13/1993
```

Morphing MAGIC

Learning can be fun and easy when the tutorial is visual and animated. Play with the Fantavision player and sample movies included on the disk and covered in Chapter 2. This example makes the theory of continental drift come alive. On the next two pages, jazz music becomes a bright and colorful montage.

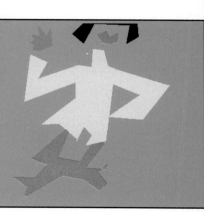

As you will see over the next four pages, morphing has made a big splash in Hollywood. Here are two scenes from the 1992 blockbuster *Terminator 2*. The Terminator is hidden as part of a linoleum floor, but now he's reforming to kill an unsuspecting police officer. (Courtesy of Carolco © 1991)

A scene from the Ron Howard film *Willow™*, one of the first films to use morphing. Here a turtle morphs into a tiger, and then the tiger morphs into a woman. See Chapter 6 for more information about this effect. (Courtesy of Lucasfilm Ltd.)

Indiana Jones and the Last Crusade™— Indiana and the Nazis are racing each other to find the Holy Grail. Confronted with a choice of goblets, the Nazi agent grabs what he thinks is the Grail. Drinking from the Grail is supposed to confer immortality, so he chugs down the contents of the goblet. Whoops, wrong goblet. The villain quickly ages, then dries up for good measure. (Courtesy of Lucasfilm Ltd.)

("Last Crusade"™ & ©Lucasfilm Ltd. (LFL) 1989. All rights reserved.)

This is not the type of mom you want mad at you. From the 1992 film *Sleepwalkers*, actress Alice Kreig mutates into the mother from Hell. (Sleepwalkers © 1992 Columbia Pictures Inc.—All rights reserved.)

Morphing has made a big splash on Madison Avenue. There's nothing like a visual image to get TV viewers to open their wallets. In this powerful use of the effect, a speeding car morphs into a speeding tiger. (Courtesy of Exxon Co. USA)

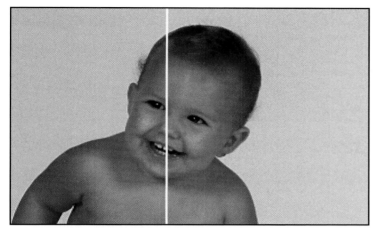

Now you don't have to leave morphing to the professionals—you can do it yourself! However, you want to take things slowly, just a few baby steps at first. These three figures, discussed in Chapter 3, demonstrate a simple figure rotation you can perform with WARP.

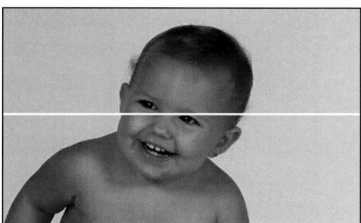

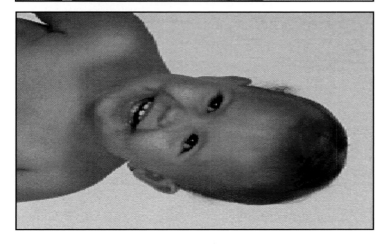

If you're feeling a little more patriotic, try this flag-waving exercise, also described in Chapter 4. (For the best effect, you should have the National Anthem playing in the background, preferably as loud as you can.)

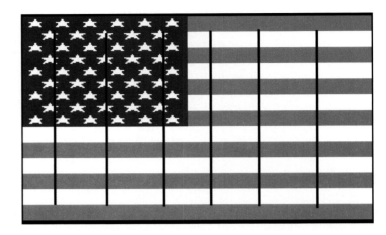

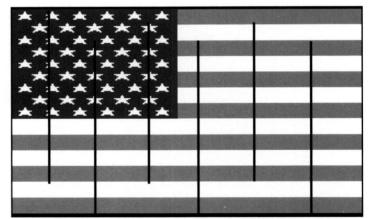

You can save a series of warped images and then load them to create an animation.

In this example, you've taken a single image and created an animation from it. A single frame of a belly dancer has become an actual dance!

Here's a color version of the morphing tutorial covered in Chapter 5. With the morphing software included in this book, you easily can change a boy to a woman. The next two pages contain animal morphs performed with the

software on the book. (All these images are included on the disk, so you can try these morphs yourself.)

Animal photos courtesy of
the Indianapolis Zoo.

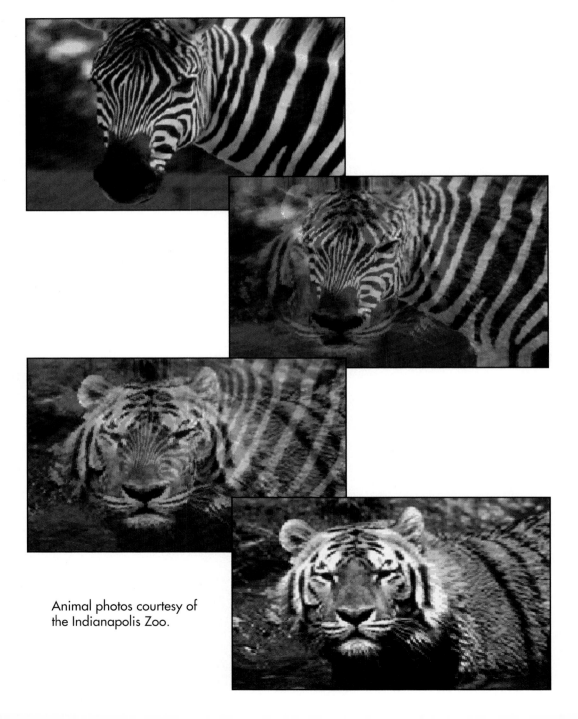

Animal photos courtesy of
the Indianapolis Zoo.

You've seen people morph into people and animals morph into other animals, but how about a person morphing into an animal? There are plenty of other figures provided on the disk: try a myraid of combinations! (Photos courtesy of Mike Morrison)

```
* LAST CHANGED: 3/10/1993
*
*    Copyright (c) 1993 by Scott Anderson
*
*****************************************************************/

/* --------------------INCLUDES-------------------------- */

#include <conio.h>
#include <stdio.h>
#include <io.h>
#include <math.h>
#include <graph.h>
#include <malloc.h>
#include <memory.h>
#include <string.h>

#include "define.h"

/* --------------------DEFINES-------------------------- */

#define DISSOLVE_TWEENS 1


/* --------------------PROTOTYPES----------------------- */
int getColor(PICTURE *pic, int x, int y, COLOR *color);

int     tweenDissolve(PICTURE *src, PICTURE *dst);

/* --------------------EXTERNALS------------------------ */

/**** color routines ****/
extern int      closestColor(int r, int g, int b, PALETTE *palPtr);
extern void     collapseColors(PALETTE *palPtr);

/**** other variables ****/
/* ID of palette currently being displayed */
extern int      CurrentPal;
extern char     *OutFilename;

/* set from last picture loaded */
extern int      Xmin, Ymin, Xmax, Ymax;

/***** variables used to compute intermediate images ****/
/* number of colors in tweened image before reduction*/
```

continues

DISSOLVE.C—continued

```
extern int       Ncolors;

/* r, g, b frequency counter array */
extern unsigned int far Freq[MAX_COMP][MAX_COMP][MAX_COMP];

/* tweened images red, grn, and blu components*/
extern unsigned char far Red[MAX_WIDE][MAX_TALL];
extern unsigned char far Grn[MAX_WIDE][MAX_TALL];
extern unsigned char far Blu[MAX_WIDE][MAX_TALL];

extern PALETTE TweenPal;                /* resulting palette */


/* --------------------GLOBAL DATA------------------------ */

PICTURE *Src;                /* source & destination picture pointers */
PICTURE *Dst;

int     Tweens;

/****************************************************************
* FUNC: main (int argc, char *argv[])
*
* DESC: Read in a filename to load
****************************************************************/

main (int argc, char *argv[])
{
    int      segment;

    /* load the pcx file if one is given */
    if ((3 > argc) || (argc > 5)) {
        printf("Usage: dissolve <source> <dest> [<steps>
[<output>]]\n\n");
        printf("Where: <source>      is the source PCX
filename\n");
        printf("       <dest> is the destination filename\n");
        printf("       <steps>      is the optional sequence size
\n");
        printf("                        (the max is %d, the default is
%d)\n",
                        MAX_TWEENS,
DISSOLVE_TWEENS+2);
        printf("       <output>     is the optional output
```

```
filename\n");
        printf("                              (defaults to no output)\n");
        printf("Note:  The output filename can be at most %d \
                characters long.\n", MAX_NAME_SIZE);
        printf("        The PCX extension is added automatically, \
                so don't\n");
        printf("        include it in the filename.\n");
        printf("        Morph only accepts PCX files with %d X %d \
                resolution\n", MAX_WIDE, MAX_TALL);
        printf("        and %d colors.\n", COLORS);
        exit(0);
    }
    if (argc > 3) {
        /* subtract two from the sequence count (for the source
           and target) to get the tween count */
        Tweens = clip (atoi(argv[3]) - 2, 1, MAX_TWEENS);
        if (argc > 4)
            OutFilename = argv[4];
    }
    else
        Tweens = DISSOLVE_TWEENS;
    printf("Loading the file %s\n", argv[1]);
    Src = loadPicture(argv[1]);
    if (Src == NULL)
        quit(MEMORY_ERR, "");
    printf("Loading the file %s\n", argv[2]);
    Dst = loadPicture(argv[2]);
    if (Dst == NULL)
        quit(MEMORY_ERR, "");

    setGraphicsMode();
    tweenDissolve(Src, Dst);
    setTextMode();
}

/*****************************************************************
* FUNC: int tweenDissolve(PICTURE *src, PICTURE *dst)
*
* DESC: calculate a pixel to plot, from the warping function
*****************************************************************/

#define TOTAL_WEIGHT        (100)    /* Good for up to 99 tweens */

tweenDissolve(PICTURE *src, PICTURE *dst)
{
```

continues

DISSOLVE.C—continued

```c
int color;
int x,y;
COLOR scolor, dcolor;
int t, i, p;
int r, g, b;
unsigned int srcweight, srcpaletteindex;
unsigned int dstweight, dstpaletteindex;

displayPicture(src);
saveScreen(&src->pal);

/* src is on screen, now tween to the target */
for (t = 1; t <= Tweens; t++) {
    dstweight = t * TOTAL_WEIGHT / (Tweens+1);
    srcweight = TOTAL_WEIGHT - dstweight;

    /* Zero out the buffers */
    initFreq();
    _fmemset(Red, 0, sizeof Red);
    _fmemset(Grn, 0, sizeof Grn);
    _fmemset(Blu, 0, sizeof Blu);

    /* Go through the screen positions */
    for (y = Ymin; y <= Ymax; y++)  {
        if (quitCheck())
            quit(0, "");
        for (x = Xmin; x <= Xmax; x++)  {
            getColor(src, x, y, &scolor);
            getColor(dst, x, y, &dcolor);
            r = (scolor.r * srcweight + dcolor.r * dstweight)
                / TOTAL_WEIGHT;
            g = (scolor.g * srcweight + dcolor.g * dstweight)
                / TOTAL_WEIGHT;
            b = (scolor.b * srcweight + dcolor.b * dstweight)
                / TOTAL_WEIGHT;
            if (Freq[r][g][b] == 0)      /* A new color */
                Ncolors++;
             /* Keep it to one byte */
            if (Freq[r][g][b] < MAX_FREQ)
                Freq[r][g][b]++;
            /* put the RGB components of each pixel into a
                temporary screen buffer */
            Red[x][y] = r;
            Grn[x][y] = g;
```

```
                    Blu[x][y] = b;
                }
            }
        collapseColors(&TweenPal);
        setPalette(&TweenPal);

        for (y = Ymin; y <= Ymax; y++)  {
            if (quitCheck())
                quit(0, "");
            for (x = Xmin; x <= Xmax; x++)  {
                color = closestColor(Red[x][y],
                                     Grn[x][y],
                                     Blu[x][y],
                                     &TweenPal);

                _setcolor (color);
                _setpixel (x, y);
            }
        }
        if (!OutFilename) { /* no output file name was given */
            beep();
            beep();
            waitForKey();        /* so pause to enjoy the pictures*/
        }
        else
            saveScreen(&TweenPal);
    }
    CurrentPal = 0;           /* force a new palette */
    displayPicture(dst);
    saveScreen(&dst->pal);
}

/*****************************************************************
* FUNC: int getColor(PICTURE *pic, int x, int y, COLOR *color)
*
* DESC: Return the index         and the RGB color at the given
*       x,y coordinate.
*****************************************************************/

int
getColor(PICTURE *picture, int x, int y, COLOR *color)
{
    int      paletteIndex;

    paletteIndex = PIXEL (picture, x, y);
    color->r = picture->pal.c[paletteIndex].r;
```

continues

DISSOLVE.C—continued

```
    color->g = picture->pal.c[paletteIndex].g;
    color->b = picture->pal.c[paletteIndex].b;
    return (paletteIndex);
}
```

COLOR.C

As well as `collapsePalette` and `closestColor`, COLOR.C has a few other utility routines. The only one of interest to you now is `initFreq`, at the end. It clears out the `Freq` array and initializes it to include black, gray, and white. You will want to refer back here when you get to the next chapter and read about multiple images.

Here are the color routines:

COLOR.C—the listing

```
/****************************************************************
* FILE: color.c
* DESC: This file contains the color routines used by morph,
*       dissolve and fix.
*
* HISTORY:  Created  3/18/1993
* LAST CHANGED: 5/ 6/1993
*
*    Copyright (c) 1992 by Scott Anderson
*
****************************************************************/

#include <stdio.h>
#include <memory.h>

#include "define.h"

/* --------------------DEFINES------------------------- */

/* --------------------TYPEDEFS/STRUCTS------------------ */

/* --------------------PROTOTYPES----------------------- */

int    closestColor(int r, int g, int b, PALETTE *palPtr);
```

```
void      collapseColors(PALETTE *palPtr);
int       mergePalette(PICTURE *pic);
int       remapPicture(PICTURE *picPtr, PALETTE *palPtr);
int       initFreq();

/* --------------------EXTERNALS-------------------------- */

/* set from last picture loaded */
extern int        Xmin, Ymin, Xmax, Ymax;

/* --------------------GLOBAL DATA------------------------ */

/* number of colors in tweened image before reduction*/
int Ncolors;

/* r, g, b frequency counter array */
unsigned int far Freq[MAX_COMP][MAX_COMP][MAX_COMP];

/* tweened images red, grn, and blu components*/
unsigned char far Red[MAX_WIDE][MAX_TALL];
unsigned char far Grn[MAX_WIDE][MAX_TALL];
unsigned char far Blu[MAX_WIDE][MAX_TALL];

PALETTE TweenPal;               /* resulting palette */

/*****************************************************************
* FUNC: void      collapseColors(PALETTE *palPtr)
*
* DESC: Collapse the colors in the Freq table until
* Ncolors < COLORS, then put it in the given color palette.
*****************************************************************/

void
collapseColors(PALETTE *palPtr)
{
    int freqCutoff;
    int r, g, b;
    int index;
    int ncolors;

    static int freqCount[MAX_FREQ+1];

    memset(freqCount, 0, sizeof freqCount);
    for (r = 0; r < MAX_COMP; r++)
        for (g = 0; g < MAX_COMP; g++)
```

continues

COLOR.C—continued

```
                for (b = 0; b < MAX_COMP; b++)
                    freqCount[Freq[r][g][b]]++;

    ncolors = 0;
    for (freqCutoff = COLORS-1; freqCutoff > 1; freqCutoff--) {
        ncolors += freqCount[freqCutoff];
        if (ncolors > COLORS) break;
    }

    /* Collapse color space to 256 colors */
    r = g = b = 0;
    while (Ncolors >= COLORS) {
        for (; r < MAX_COMP; r++, g=0) {
            for (; g < MAX_COMP; g++, b=0) {
                for (; b < MAX_COMP; b++) {
                    if (Freq[r][g][b] && Freq[r][g][b]
                        <= freqCutoff)
                        goto castOut;   /* the ultimate no no */
                }
            }
        }
        r = g = b = 0;
        freqCutoff++;
        continue;
castOut:
        Freq[r][g][b] = 0;  /* just remove this low freq color */
        Ncolors--;
    }

    /* build a palette out of all the remaining non zero freq's */
    index = 0;
    for (r = 0; r < MAX_COMP; r++)
        for (g = 0; g < MAX_COMP; g++)
            for (b = 0; b < MAX_COMP; b++)
                /* we have a color we need to map */
                if (Freq[r][g][b]) {
                    palPtr->c[index].r = r;
                    palPtr->c[index].g = g;
                    palPtr->c[index].b = b;
                    /* remember index in palette */
                    Freq[r][g][b] = index;
                    index++;
                }

}
```

```
/***************************************************************
* FUNC: int closestColor(int r, int g, int b, PALETTE *palPtr)
*
* DESC: return the palette index of the color closest to rgb.
***************************************************************/

int
closestColor(int r, int g, int b, PALETTE *palPtr)
{
    int index;
    int distance;
    int min_distance = 3200;     /* a big number */
    int min_index;

    /* The value in Freq is now the index into the color table */
    if (Freq[r][g][b]) return Freq[r][g][b];

    /* If zero, search for the closest color */
    for (index = 1; index < Ncolors; index++) {
        /* this is really the distance squared, but it works */
        distance =  SQUARE (r - palPtr->c[index].r) +
                    SQUARE (g - palPtr->c[index].g) +
                    SQUARE (b - palPtr->c[index].b);
        if (distance < min_distance) {
            min_distance = distance;
            min_index = index;
            if (distance <= 2) break;    /* close enough! */
        }
    }

/* New index - for future reference */
    Freq[r][g][b] = min_index;
    return min_index;
}

/***************************************************************
* FUNC: int mergePalette(PICTURE *picPtr)
*
* DESC: Merge a palette into Freq count table.
***************************************************************/

int
mergePalette(PICTURE *picPtr)
{
```

continues

COLOR.C—continued

```c
    int     r, g, b;
    unsigned int    pos;
    unsigned char   index;
    PALETTE *palPtr = &picPtr->pal;
    unsigned char far *bufPtr = picPtr->pixmap;

    for (pos = 0; pos < MAX_BYTES; pos++) {
        index = *bufPtr++;
        r = palPtr->c[index].r;
        g = palPtr->c[index].g;
        b = palPtr->c[index].b;
        if (Freq[r][g][b] == 0)        /* A new color */
            Ncolors++;
        if (Freq[r][g][b] < MAX_FREQ)   /* Keep it managable */
            Freq[r][g][b]++;
    }
}

/*****************************************************************
* FUNC: int remapPicture(PICTURE *picPtr, PALETTE *palPtr)
*
* DESC: Remap a picture with a different palette.
*****************************************************************/

int
remapPicture(PICTURE *picPtr, PALETTE *palPtr)
{
    int     x, y;
    int     index;
    int     r, g, b;
    unsigned int    pos;
    unsigned char   lookup[COLORS];
    unsigned char far *bufPtr;

    /* Create the cross-reference lookup table */
    for (index = 0; index < COLORS; index++) {
        r = picPtr->pal.c[index].r;
        g = picPtr->pal.c[index].g;
        b = picPtr->pal.c[index].b;
        lookup[index] = closestColor(r, g, b, palPtr);
    }

    /* Save the new palette in the picture's palette */
```

```
    for (index = 0; index < COLORS; index++) {
        picPtr->pal.c[index].r = palPtr->c[index].r;
        picPtr->pal.c[index].g = palPtr->c[index].g;
        picPtr->pal.c[index].b = palPtr->c[index].b;
    }

    /* Remap the individual pixels to point to the new colors */
    for (bufPtr = picPtr->pixmap, pos = 0; pos < MAX_BYTES;
            bufPtr++, pos++)
        *bufPtr = lookup[*bufPtr];
}
/****************************************************************
* FUNC: int initFreq()
*
* DESC: zero out the frequency color space table
****************************************************************/

int
initFreq()
{
    int bytes = (sizeof Freq) / 2;

    _fmemset(Freq, 0, bytes);
    /* divide because of element size */
    _fmemset(Freq+(bytes/sizeof *Freq), 0, bytes);

    /* Guarantee a black color */

    Freq[0][0][0] = MAX_FREQ;
    /* a grey color */
    Freq[MID_COMP-1][MID_COMP-1][MID_COMP-1] = MAX_FREQ;
    /* and a white color */
    Freq[(long)MAX_COMP-1][MAX_COMP-1][MAX_COMP-1] = MAX_FREQ;
        Ncolors = 3;
}
```

Morphing to a target image

"A very profitable algorithm."

Thaddeus Beier and Shawn Neely, "Feature-Based Image Metamorphosis,"
Computer Graphics, Vol 26, Number 2, July 1992

Surprisingly, the concept of digital-image warping, especially as used by artists and movie-makers, is only about ten years old. In the early 1980s, Tom Brigham did some of the first work at the New York Institute of Technology.

By the late eighties morphing was a staple at all the big effects studios.

In 1993, Brigham won an Oscar for his wonderful contribution to cinema. It was the first time the Academy awarded a prize to an algorithm. It probably won't be the last.

Morphing is a combination of warping and dissolving. Let's say you want to morph a panther into a person. While the panther is being warped to fill the outline of the person, the person is being warped *backward* to fill the outline of the panther. Both warp sequences are blended together, with the panther fading out and the person fading in—a cross dissolve.

DISKETTE DEMO: Morph

From the DOS prompt, type:

>MORPH BABY GRANDMA

BABY is the source image and GRANDMA is the target image. The program will load the two images. If there are any pre-defined control lines for this image, a message will be displayed asking if you want to use them. For this example, just say no by pressing the N key. If there are no lines associated with the picture, you won't be bothered by this question.

The program then displays a prompt, reminding you that you are about to create control lines for the source image. Press Enter.

The program displays the source image and waits for you to draw your control lines. For this example draw seven control lines:

1. From one eye to the other.

2. From one nostril to the other.

3. Across the upper lip.

4. Across the lower lip.

5. Under the chin.

6. Down the left side of the face.

7. Down the right side of the face.

When you are done, press Enter. The computer will display a prompt telling you that you are about to edit the control lines for the target image. Press Enter again. The target picture is displayed. The lines you drew will pop up on top. Now grab the lines (remembering which one goes where) and move them to the corresponding spot on this picture. For instance, move the old eye line to connect up the new eyes.

When you have moved all the lines, press Enter again. The program will display the source image while it is calculating the in-between morph. This can take some time. The more lines, the longer the wait. For these seven lines, it takes my 33MHz 486 about a minute and a half to do the computations.

When the computer is done, it will alert you with a beep. What you see on the screen is a morph of your two original pictures. The result should look a little like each one of them.

You might notice some "fringing" around the edges, where things don't line up properly. This is because there are just seven control lines. With a few more lines, you can make things overlap perfectly—give it a try.

It's kind of fun, isn't it? I'm hooked on it, but you shouldn't tell people you're addicted to morphing. The Drug Enforcement Agency has a lousy sense of humor.

FOR PROGRAMMERS ONLY:
The Morph program

MORPH.C

This program, like dissolve before it, is set up to do more than one morphed image. Multiple images, or sequences, are covered in the next chapter, so don't be alarmed by references to multiples. Just look the other way for now.

main takes the two given filenames and loads them. Then it looks on the disk for control lines that might be associated with the source or target image. If the user OKs the old control lines, these files are loaded in. Otherwise, the user creates a new set of control lines from scratch.

Then tweenMorph is called to do the real work. After that, the program saves the control lines used for these images and exits back to DOS. Program over.

tweenMorph is the next routine in the file. It displays the source screen while it calculates the morphed image. The warp lines are tweened, and the source and destination weights are apportioned.

The color tables are zeroed out and then the main loop starts. As in tweenWarp, the pixels are mapped in reverse. The warped pixel is inverse-mapped to its source pixel to avoid gaps.

There are two images getting warped here. The source and the target are both being warped. For each pixel in the morphed image, you need a contribution from both images.

For the single images produced so far, each picture is warped halfway toward the other and then combined. A new color is computed that is halfway between the two. That color is logged into the Freq array. The pixel is also recorded in the component arrays, Red[x][y], Grn[x][y], and Blu[x][y]. These are saved as three arrays to avoid running into the 64K data limit.

As in DISSOLVE.C, the Freq array is used to collapse the color set to 256 colors. The palette is set to the new collapsed palette, and the picture is displayed by finding the closest color for each pixel and plotting it.

That's really all there is to it. Except for the little bit of math and the hardware color problems, this is a fairly simple piece of code:

MORPH.C—the listing

```
/*****************************************************************
* FILE: morph.c
* DESC: Create a metamorphosing sequence between two given
*       images. This program lets you specify two files to
*       morph, then prompts you for control lines. It uses
*       the lines to warp the underlying images a step at
*       a time, combine them, and optionally save them as
*       numbered PCX files.
*
* HISTORY:  Created  1/13/1993
* LAST CHANGED:  5/ 6/1993
*
*    Copyright (c) 1993 by Scott Anderson
*
*****************************************************************/

/* --------------------INCLUDES------------- */

#include <conio.h>
#include <stdio.h>
#include <io.h>
#include <math.h>
#include <graph.h>
#include <malloc.h>
#include <memory.h>
#include <string.h>

#include "define.h"

/* --------------------DEFINES---------------------------- */

#define MORPH_TWEENS    1

/* --------------------PROTOTYPES------------------------- */

int     tweenMorph(PICTURE *src, PICTURE *dst);

/* --------------------EXTERNALS------------------------- */

/**** color routines ****/
extern int  closestColor(int r, int g, int b, PALETTE *palPtr);
extern void collapseColors(PALETTE *palPtr);
```

continues

MORPH.C—continued

```
/**** line routines ****/
extern int  setLength(LINE *line);
extern int  sumLines(PICTURE *picture, COLOR *color,
                    LINE *origline, POINT *warp, LINE *warpline);


/**** io routines ****/
extern LINE_LIST    *loadLines(char *filename, char *extension);
extern void          saveLines(char *filename,
                        LINE_LIST *lineList, char *extension);


/***** variables used to compute intermediate images ****/

/* number of colors in tweened image before reduction*/
extern int  Ncolors;

/* r, g, b frequency counter array */
extern unsigned int far Freq[MAX_COMP][MAX_COMP][MAX_COMP];

/* tweened images red, grn, and blu components*/
extern unsigned char far Red[MAX_WIDE][MAX_TALL];
extern unsigned char far Grn[MAX_WIDE][MAX_TALL];
extern unsigned char far Blu[MAX_WIDE][MAX_TALL];

extern PALETTE TweenPal;            /* resulting palette */


/**** other variables ****/
extern char     *OutFilename;
/* set from last picture loaded */
extern int      Xmin, Ymin, Xmax, Ymax;
/* ID of palette currently being displayed */
extern int      CurrentPal;

/* --------------------GLOBAL DATA------------------------ */

PICTURE *Src;        /* source & destination picture pointers */
PICTURE *Dst;

LINE    SrcLine[MAX_LINES];
LINE    DstLine[MAX_LINES];

int     Tweens;
int     NumLines;
```

```
/****************************************************************
* FUNC: main (int argc, char *argv[])
*
* DESC: Read in a filename to load
****************************************************************/

main (int argc, char *argv[])
{
    int      segment;
    LINE_LIST *lineSrcList;
    LINE_LIST *lineDstList;
    char     answer;

    /* load the pcx file if one is given */
    if ((3 > argc) || (argc > 5)) {
        printf("Usage: morph <source> <dest> [<steps>
[<output>]]\n\n");
        printf("Where: <source> is the source PCX filename\n");
        printf("       <dest>   is the destination filename\n");
        printf("       <steps>  is the optional sequence size\n");
        printf("              (the max is %d, the default is
%d)\n",
                            MAX_TWEENS, MORPH_TWEENS+2);
        printf("       <output> is the optional output
filename\n");
        printf("              (defaults to no output)\n\n");
        printf("Note:  The output filename can be at most %d\
                    characters long.\n",
                        MAX_NAME_SIZE);
        printf("        The PCX extension is added automatically,\
                so don't\n");
        printf("       include it in the filename.\n");
        printf("       Morph only accepts PCX files with %d X %d\
                resolution\n",
                        MAX_WIDE, MAX_TALL);
        printf("       and %d colors.\n", COLORS);
        exit(0);
    }
    if (argc > 3) {
        /* subtract two from the series count to get the tweens
         * since the starting and ending frame are included. */
        Tweens = clip (atoi(argv[3]) - 2, 1, MAX_TWEENS);
        if (argc > 4)
            OutFilename = argv[4];
    }
```

continues

MORPH.C—continued

```
else
    Tweens = MORPH_TWEENS;

printf("Loading the file %s\n", argv[1]);
Src = loadPicture(argv[1]);
if (Src == NULL)
    quit(MEMORY_ERR, "");

printf("Loading the file %s\n", argv[2]);
Dst = loadPicture(argv[2]);
if (Dst == NULL)
    quit(MEMORY_ERR, "");
lineSrcList = loadLines(argv[1], EXT_LINE1);
if (lineSrcList->number != 0) {
    if (lineAsk(argv[1]) == 'N')
        createLines(Src, lineSrcList);
    else
        editLines(Src, lineSrcList);
}
else
    createLines(Src, lineSrcList);

TargFlag = 1;    /* For the screen intro message */
NumLines = lineSrcList->number;
if (NumLines) {
    lineDstList = loadLines(argv[2], EXT_LINE1);
        /* inconsistent warp target*/
    if (lineDstList->number !=  NumLines)
        lineDstList->number = 0;
    if (lineDstList->number) {  /* ask what he wants to do */
        if (lineAsk(argv[2]) == 'N')
            lineDstList->number = 0;
    }
    if (lineDstList->number == 0) { /* create a warp target */
        /* copy the source lines */
        lineDstList->number = NumLines;
        for (segment = 0; segment < NumLines; segment++)
            lineDstList->line[segment]
                            = lineSrcList->line[segment];
    }

    editLines(Dst, lineDstList);
    saveLines(argv[1], lineSrcList, EXT_LINE1);
    saveLines(argv[2], lineDstList, EXT_LINE1);
```

```
            beep();
            for (segment = 0; segment < NumLines; segment++) {
                DstLine[segment].p[0]=lineDstList->line[segment].p[0];
                DstLine[segment].p[1]=lineDstList->line[segment].p[1];
                setLength(&DstLine[segment]);
                SrcLine[segment].p[0]=lineSrcList->line[segment].p[0];
                SrcLine[segment].p[1]=lineSrcList->line[segment].p[1];
                setLength(&SrcLine[segment]);
            }
        }

    tweenMorph(Src, Dst);
    setTextMode();
}


/*****************************************************************
* FUNC: int tweenMorph(PICTURE *src, PICTURE *dst)
*
* DESC: calculate a pixel to plot, from the warping function
*****************************************************************/

#define TOTAL_WEIGHT        (100)    /* Good for up to 99 tweens */

tweenMorph(PICTURE *src, PICTURE *dst)
{
    int color;
    POINT warp;
    int x,y;
    COLOR scolor, dcolor;
    LINE warpLine[MAX_LINES];
    int t, i, p;
    int r, g, b;
    unsigned int srcweight, srcpaletteindex;
    unsigned int dstweight, dstpaletteindex;

    displayPicture(src);
    saveScreen(&src->pal);

    /* src is on screen, now tween to the target */
    for (t = 1; t <= Tweens; t++) {
        /* Tween the lines used to warp the images */
        for (i = 0; i < NumLines; i++) {
            for (p = 0; p < 2; p++) {
                warpLine[i].p[p].x = SrcLine[i].p[p].x +
                    ((DstLine[i].p[p].x - SrcLine[i].p[p].x) * t)
```

continues

MORPH.C—continued

```
                    /(Tweens+1);
            warpLine[i].p[p].y = SrcLine[i].p[p].y +
                ((DstLine[i].p[p].y - SrcLine[i].p[p].y) * t)
                /(Tweens+1);
        }
        setLength(&warpLine[i]);
    }

    dstweight = t * TOTAL_WEIGHT / (Tweens+1);
    srcweight = TOTAL_WEIGHT - dstweight;

    /* Zero out the buffers */
    initFreq();
    /* set background to black */
    _fmemset(Red, 0, sizeof Red);
    _fmemset(Grn, 0, sizeof Grn);
    _fmemset(Blu, 0, sizeof Blu);

    /* Go through the screen and get warped source pixels */
    for (warp.y = Ymin; warp.y <= Ymax; warp.y++)    {
        if (quitCheck())
            quit(0, "");
        for (warp.x = Xmin; warp.x <= Xmax; warp.x++)    {
            sumLines(src, &scolor, SrcLine, &warp, warpLine);
            sumLines(dst, &dcolor, DstLine, &warp, warpLine);
            r = (scolor.r * srcweight + dcolor.r * dstweight)
                        / TOTAL_WEIGHT;
            g = (scolor.g * srcweight + dcolor.g * dstweight)
                        / TOTAL_WEIGHT;
            b = (scolor.b * srcweight + dcolor.b * dstweight)
                        / TOTAL_WEIGHT;
            if (Freq[r][g][b] == 0)       /* A new color */
                Ncolors++;
            /* Keep it to one byte */
            if (Freq[r][g][b] < MAX_FREQ)
                Freq[r][g][b]++;
            /* put RGB components into temporary buffer */
            Red[warp.x][warp.y] = r;
            Grn[warp.x][warp.y] = g;
            Blu[warp.x][warp.y] = b;
        }
    }
    collapseColors(&TweenPal);
    setPalette(&TweenPal);
```

```
        for (y = Ymin; y <= Ymax; y++)  {
            if (quitCheck())
                quit(0, "");
            for (x = Xmin; x <= Xmax; x++)  {
                color = closestColor(  Red[x][y],
                                       Grn[x][y],
                                       Blu[x][y],
                                       &TweenPal);
                _setcolor (color);
                _setpixel (x, y);
            }
        }
        /* no output file name on command line */
        if (!OutFilename) {
            beep();
            waitForKey();    /* so pause to enjoy the pictures */
        }
        else
            saveScreen(&TweenPal);
    }
    if (OutFilename) {  /* save the last pic in this series */
        CurrentPal = 0;          /* force a new palette */
        displayPicture(dst);
        saveScreen(&dst->pal);
    }
}
```

In the next chapter, you will use the insights you have gained about warping, color dissolves, and morphing to create miniature "movies." Instead of producing just one picture (fun as that is) the next chapter will introduce you to *tweening* with warping and morphing. You will create short sequences that you can play back at something approaching real-time speeds.

I don't know about you, but I can hardly wait!

Morphing
in Motion

5

"In motion-picture animation, a chief designer draws only inter-
mittent 'key-frames' to define the motion of the character. 'In-
betweeners' traditionally draw the frames representing the motion
connecting the key-frames. In recent years, computer programs
have been designed to partially automate this process by interpolat-
ing frames between key-frames with algorithms."

Richard Mark Friedhoff,
The Second Computer Revolution: Visualization

In the last chapter, you warped, dissolved, and morphed pictures to create a new image. This chapter brings everything to life—you're going to make the images move.

You will use the concept of tweening developed in Chapter 1, "Morphing Helps Animators," to accomplish this task. Did you think you had seen the last of tweening? Not by a long shot.

As I briefly mentioned in the last chapter, the four programs (DISSOLVE, WARP, MORPH and LOAD) are built to handle more than one image. Let's exploit that feature to create animated sequences.

Producing a sequence

"An Englishman, even if he is alone, forms an orderly queue of one."

George Mikes, *How to be an Alien*

So far, like the Englishman, you have created one-image "sequences" only. To produce those singlets, you used control lines that directed the warping process.

To make a real sequence, you need to *tween* the control lines. As the control lines tween, the warped pixels tween along with them. All you need to do is specify the number of frames in your sequence. Aren't computers fun?

The programs MORPH and WARP compute the tweened images, display them for you, and save them to the disk as part of a numbered sequence. Although DISSOLVE has no control lines, it still tweens the fade-in and fade-out. Have you ever seen so much tweening?

For each program, the commands to create the sequence are similar. In addition to specifying the PCX filenames, you include the number of tweens and the output filename for the numbered sequence.

Once you save the sequence to disk, you can play it back with the LOAD program. LOAD grabs as many pictures in the sequence as it can squeeze into memory and displays them consecutively. Now you're making movies!

If you have some fancy equipment, you can record a screen image onto videotape, one frame at a time. Or you can simply tape the sequence right off the screen with your video camera. Or you can have a standard animation program, such as Autodesk Animator or Quicktime, play back the files, although you might need to convert the images to another format first.

These are just the rudiments of animation, yet the power of the PC is being stretched to the limit. With faster machines and better memory management, this task will become easier.

Until that fateful day, you can still have fun playing with these short little sequences.

Warping a sequence

"Warp us out of here, Scotty!"

Captain Kirk

Each frame in the sequence is a numbered PCX file, so you should have copious disk space available before you start. You can have ninety-nine frames in a sequence, but in practice you can expect each frame to use about 60K—that means an eight-frame sequence easily can use a megabyte of storage. Aren't you sorry you didn't buy that bigger hard disk?

If you don't have the room, don't worry. Saving the resultant files is optional. You still can view the sequence one frame at a time, but you won't be able to animate the results.

The general form of the command is:

```
WARP <File> [<Steps> [<OutFile>]]
```

<File> is the name of a PCX image with 320-by-200 resolution and 256 colors.

<Steps> is the optional number of frames you want in the sequence. If you don't specify the number, you can't make a sequence and the program just produces a single image for preview only. That's what you did in the last chapter. But if that was a fish egg, this is caviar.

<OutFile> is the optional name for saving the frames. The program will use the output filename as the root sequence name and append a number from one to ninety-nine as the step number.

Because two digits are used for the step number and DOS filenames can only have eight characters, the sequence name (also called the root name) must be at most six characters long. A little cramped, I'm afraid—but hey, this is DOS.

If you don't define *<Steps>*, you can't specify an output file. The program does what it did in the last chapter: produces one picture and quits. That's what I'm trying to indicate with the square brackets: *<OutFile>* is an option only if *<Steps>* is defined.

The process might look a little intimidating, but the following example should clear things up:

DISKETTE DEMO: Warp

To morph an image called DANCER.PCX in 5 steps and save it in the files named DANCE1.PCX through DANCE5.PCX, get to the DOS prompt and enter:

>WARP DANCER 5 DANCE

As usual, you don't have to type the PCX extension—the program adds it for you automatically.

The program asks whether you want to use the pre-defined control lines for this image. In the last chapter, I told you to just say no and make your own. Now I will spare you. Say yes and take the easy way out.

The program displays the DANCER.PCX file and draws the control lines on top (see Figure 5.1). It is waiting for you to edit those lines. Press Enter to indicate your approval.

The warped control lines are displayed (Figure 5.2). If you feel the need, you can edit these lines. Otherwise, just press Enter. The original image is then saved as the first picture in the sequence, DANCE1.PCX.

Figure 5.1.
The starting image for the warp, with control lines indicating the features to warp.

Figure 5.2.
The warped control lines.

The warped image scans down the screen as the new pixels are computed. In the last chapter this produced the final warped image. Now, however, you want to take it a step at a time. A five-frame sequence starts with the original picture, then rounds off the set with four warped images. So the first warp goes only one-quarter of the way to the final warp.

If you hadn't specified an `<OutFile>`, the computer would beep and wait for you to examine the image. This gives you a chance to preview a sequence before committing it to the disk.

Of course, you did specify an `<OutFile>`, so the program saves this warped image as the second in the sequence, DANCE2.PCX (Figure 5.3).

Figure 5.3.
The first interpolation, or tween, of the warping lines.

After three more warps, you arrive at the final orientation (Figures 5.4–5.6). When you are through admiring your handiwork, press Enter.

Figure 5.4.
The second tween of the warping sequence.

Figure 5.5.
The third tween of the warping sequence.

Look at your disk. From the DOS prompt type:

```
>DIR DANCE*.PCX
```

The five numbered files you saved should be listed on the screen.

Congratulations, you have created your first sequence! That wasn't too painful, was it? Now you can see that warping is a powerful algorithm in its own right. It allows you to create multiple images from a single picture.

Figure 5.6.
The final tween
of the warping
sequence.

Loading a sequence

"Everything flows."

> Heraclitus, an ancient Greek philosopher who
> obviously never had an 8088 computer

Now that you have a warping sequence, what are you going to do with it?

Depending on the speed of your computer, you can view the sequence as a flowing animation, or for some old, slow computers, a slide show. (Sorry, Heraclitus.) To do it, use the LOAD program.

In the last chapter, you used LOAD to view the individual files on the disk. Now you will see how to load a sequence as well. The general command structure is:

```
LOAD <File>
```

<File> is the root name of the sequence—the same name the sequence was created with, happily enough. If you want to avoid some confusion, don't end your root names with a number. A number is going to be added to the root, so things could get confusing. Believe me.

LOAD finds the sequentially numbered files that have the given root name and attempts to bring them all into memory. As each file is read in, it is displayed on the screen. The files load in much faster from a hard disk than from a floppy, so if you get tired of killing time, move the pictures over to your hard disk.

When all the files are read in or when the memory gags (whichever comes first), LOAD displays them in a loop.

Snatching a picture out of memory is several times faster than off the disk, so you can come very close to actual animation.

But enough of this shop talk. Let's see some action!

DISKETTE DEMO: Load

Play back the sequence you just created. From the DOS prompt, type:

```
>LOAD DANCE
```

The program loads as many files as will fit in memory, then it flips through them as fast as it can. The playback speed depends on your computer. On a 33MHz 486, the program runs about 15 frames per second—just fast enough to qualify as animation.

The number of frames you can load at one time depends on your hardware and software configuration also. If you have any TSRs (Terminate and Stay Resident programs), you might want to unload them to free up memory. In a standard 640K machine, you should be able to load seven frames into memory at one time.

To change the playback rate, press a key from one to nine, with one being the slowest and nine the fastest. To linger a little longer at the end frames, press E. This key is a toggle, so it switches back off when you press E again.

To stop a frame, press the space bar. You can step through the pictures one frame at a time by tapping the bar. To continue normal playback, press Enter.

Now you know how to warp an image and play back the sequence. This is really quite an interesting achievement. You took a single frame and made an animation! As I mentioned in Chapter 1, animation is supposed to be a *lot* harder than that. And, depending on what you choose for your starting frame, it doesn't have to look *cartoonish*. This is a power tool for animators.

In just a couple more steps, you will be morphing—adding another great gadget to your animation tool kit.

FOR PROGRAMMERS ONLY: The LOAD program

LOAD.C

LOAD is a very short program that examines the command line and calls the appropriate routines in the IO.C file. That's why it's short. All the hard stuff is in IO.C, as you will soon find out.

First, the program looks on the disk for a sequence of files with the proper root name. It creates a linked list of files with a call to rootSequence. The linked list is a structure that contains the name of the file and a pointer, or link, to the structure of the next file. Given the "head" of the list, the rest can be found with these pointers.

The routine loads these files into memory until the memory is crammed, saving the address of each picture's starting point in the array Src[ ].

Then the routine goes though the pictures, displaying them as quickly as possible (which usually isn't fast enough). While it does, the program checks the keyboard with a call to quitCheck, in IO.C.

The program goes forward through the pictures to the end, then it switches direction and goes backward to the start. Until you hit a key it will continue to loop back and forth through the pictures. If you created a fairly subtle sequence, this should look nicely animated. When you press Esc, the program terminates.

LOAD.C—The Listing

```
/******************************************************************
* FILE: load.c
* DESC: This program loads a PCX file or a list of them.
*       It crams as many into memory as it can, then it flips
*       quickly through them.
*
* HISTORY:  Created  1/13/1993
* LAST CHANGED:  3/20/1993
*
*    Copyright (c) 1993 by Scott Anderson
*
******************************************************************/
```

continues

LOAD.C—continued

```c
/* --------------------INCLUDES------------------------- */

#include <conio.h>
#include <stdio.h>
#include <io.h>
#include <math.h>
#include <graph.h>
#include <string.h>

#include "define.h"

/* --------------------EXTERNALS----------------------- */

/* External functions */
extern int   quitCheck();
extern LINKED_LIST  *rootSequence(int argc, char *argv[]);

/* External variables */
extern int  Wait;
extern int  Key;
extern int  EndWait;

/* --------------------GLOBAL DATA--------------------- */

PICTURE *Src[MAX_FILES];                /* source picture pointer */

/*******************************************************************
* FUNC: main (int argc, char *argv[])
*
* DESC: Display the file or sequence passed on the command line.
*        Read in as many files as will fit in memory, then display
*        them in a loop, forward and backward.
*******************************************************************/

main (int argc, char *argv[])
{
    int file, fileNum;
    int direction;
    int i;
    LINKED_LIST *pcxList;
    LINKED_LIST *pcxListHead;

    if (argc == 1) {
        printf("Usage: load <name>\n\n");
```

```
        printf("Where: <name> is the root name of a sequence\n");
        exit(23);
    }
    setGraphicsMode();

    file = 1;
    pcxListHead =  rootSequence(argc, argv);
    for (pcxList = pcxListHead; pcxList; pcxList = pcxList->next) {
        Src[file] = loadPicture(pcxList->str);
        if (Src[file] == NULL)
            break;
        displayPicture(Src[file++]);
    }

    fileNum = file - 1;
    if (fileNum == 1)/* there's only one file */
        waitForKey();/* so wait for the user to quit */
    else if (fileNum > 1 ) {
        file = 1;
        direction = 1;
        while (!(quitCheck())) {
            if ((file += direction) >= fileNum)
                direction = -1;
            if (file <= 1)
                direction = 1;
            displayPicture(Src[file]);
            if (EndWait && (file == 1 ¦¦ file == fileNum))
                wait(Wait);
        }
    }
    /* Reset to original mode, then quit */
    setTextMode();
}
```

IO.C

This file contains all the input and output routines used by the other programs, such as LOAD, MORPH, and WARP. The DOS load and save routines, as well as the keyboard and mouse functions, are in this file.

After various constant definitions, there are a couple of structures defined here for handling the PCX files. Some global input and output variables for the keyboard and file handling then follow.

The first routine, saveScreen, saves the picture currently being displayed. You pass it the color palette to save with it. PutBlock and writeByte are two subroutines used by `saveScreen` to implement the run-length encoding scheme used in PCX files.

Run-length encoding (RLE) is a method of compacting a file that contains repetitive data. For instance, if there is a string (or run) of eighty zeros in a file, you could represent it with a count of eighty and a value of zero. That's two bytes versus eighty—a forty-fold compaction. Unfortunately, the PCX encoding algorithm is not quite that efficient in practice. With files that have very few runs, this compaction implementation sometimes doesn't help much at all.

Luckily for you, the pictures included on the disk have been specially prepared to take advantage of the PCX version of RLE, so they don't take up too much disk space.

The next routine is `loadPicture`. Given the name of the file, `loadPicture` allocates memory and then loads the PCX image into it. It unpacks the RLE file into a full 64K buffer. It uses the three subroutines, `getBlock`, `mustRead`, and `loadPalette`, to accomplish its tasks. Based on the image it loads, `loadPicture` sets the global clipping variables `Xmin`, `Ymin` and `Xmax`, `Ymax`.

`freePicture` is the next routine, and it frees up the memory that was allocated for a picture. This routine is used by DISSOLVE so that it can process more images than will fit in memory.

Each PCX file can have two attached line files. These are the control lines used by WARP and MORPH. The routines that manage these files are `loadLines` and `saveLines`. The first line file, with an extension of LN1, identifies the important features in the image for both WARP and MORPH. The second line file, with an extension of LN2, is the warped version of the first, and is used by the warp program only.

Next comes `rootSequence`, which implements the linked list used to load a sequence of files. It calls `appendName` to extend the linked list and `fixFilename` to examine and prepare the filename for sequencing.

This routine is followed by `setPalette` and `defaultPalette`. `setPalette` uses the output ports on the IBM to set the colors quickly. There is a C command to do this, but most implementations are ridiculously slow. `defaultPalette` is called only if there is no palette associated with the given file, which really should never happen.

Although the images are loaded into local memory, you need to move them into the video buffer if you want to see them. That is the purpose of `displayPicture`, which only needs a pointer to the image address to do its job. The actual moving is done in `displayNoPal`, which does a quick memory move command. As its name implies, it doesn't mess with the palette—that is done in `displayPicture`.

In order to make sure that the color palettes can be managed with some efficiency, `displayPicture` calls the routine named `paletteID`. If the desired palette is the same as the current palette, it doesn't have to change anything.

`paletteID` looks through the palettes already in memory to make sure that one like it doesn't currently exist. If it does, it returns the ID byte associated with that palette. Otherwise, it adds that palette to the list, assigns a new ID, and returns that value. It calls `samePal` to check through a pair of palettes, making sure that all the colors are identical.

`drawPalette` is a routine that is not called by anything, but I included it for the curious. It displays the current palette in the upper right corner of the screen. You can call it any time after the graphics mode has been set.

Next come the mouse routines. `initMouse` starts the whole thing up and is only called once. `hideMouse` and `showMouse` are the routines that deal with the mouse cursor on the screen. The cursor is the arrow that shows up after you load a file in the warp and morph programs. You need the cursor to know where your mouse is, but before you change anything on the screen (such as the control lines), you have to hide the cursor. Then you make your change and quickly show the cursor again. `mousePos` returns the X and Y coordinates of the mouse, as well as any mouse clicks or keystrokes.

Some miscellaneous input and output routines that deal with prompting, keyboard input, and timing follow. Among these routines is `wait`. This routine is called by the LOAD program in an attempt to synchronize with the raster scan of your monitor.

The idea is to redisplay the picture while the raster isn't looking. This can't really work on a PC because the video access is so slow, but it seems to make things a **little** better. If you want to explore the flashing problem discussed in the next section (dissolving), this is one of the routines to experiment with.

At the very end of IO.C is the `quit` routine. It resets the original text mode and prints out an error message if there is one.

This is a large chunk of code, but IO is always a large task on an IBM because very little is built in. If you were to rewrite this code for windows, much of it could go away.

IO.C—The Listing

```
/******************************************************************
* FILE: io.c
* DESC: These are the basic input/output routines. They include
*        disk-handling and keyboard I/O.
*
* HISTORY:  Created   3/11/1993
* LAST CHANGED: 5/ 6/1993
*
*    Copyright (c) 1993 by Scott Anderson
*
******************************************************************/

/* --------------------INCLUDES-------------------------- */

#include <conio.h>
#include <stdio.h>
#include <io.h>
#include <dos.h>                /* for the mouse */
#include <math.h>
#include <graph.h>
#include <malloc.h>
#include <memory.h>
#include <string.h>

#include "define.h"

/* --------------------DEFINES--------------------------- */

/* 0-99 (for tweens) appended to name */
#define MAX_NAME_SIZE    (8-2)

/**** PCX constants ****/
/* Set top 2 bits for the count bytes */
#define C0              (0xc0)
/* The inverse of C0: 0x3f = 63 */
#define MAX_RUN         (0x3f)
/* Signals a 256 color palette */
#define PAL_CODE        12


/* --------------------MACROS--------------------------- */

/* --------------------TYPEDEFS------------------------- */

typedef struct {
    char manufacturer;
```

```
        char version;
        char encoding;
        char bperpixelperplane;
        unsigned int xmin, ymin, xmax, ymax;
        unsigned int hres, vres;
        char rgbmap[3][16];
        char reserved;
        char nplanes;
        unsigned int bytesperline;
        unsigned int paletteinfo;
}
CORE_PCX_HEADER;

typedef struct {
        CORE_PCX_HEADER pcx;
        unsigned char filler[128-sizeof (CORE_PCX_HEADER)];
}
HEADER_PCX;

/* ---------------------PROTOTYPES--------------------------- */

char        lineAsk(char *name);
void        setTextMode();
void        setGraphicsMode();
int         fixFilename(char *userName, char *fixedName,
                        char *extension, int number);
LINE_LIST   *loadLines(char *filename, char *extension);
int         saveLines(char *filename, LINE_LIST *lineList,
                        char *extension);
LINKED_LIST *appendName(LINKED_LIST *head, char *name);
LINKED_LIST *rootSequence(int argc, char *argv[]);
int         waitForKey();

/* ---------------------GLOBAL DATA------------------------- */

int     CurrentPal = 0; /* ID of current palette */

int     Wait = 0;
int     Key;
int     EndWait = OFF;

/* from the last read file, used to save pic */
static HEADER_PCX    Header;

/* Global values set from last picture loaded */
int Xmin, Ymin, Xmax, Ymax;
```

continues

IO.C—continued

```c
/* no file output for NULL name */
char    *OutFilename = NULL;
long    TotalBytes;

int     Button;
int     Keystroke;

/**************   The file handling routines   ****************/

/*****************************************************************
* FUNC: int saveScreen(PALETTE *pal)
*
* DESC: Save the current screen with the given palette
*****************************************************************/

int
saveScreen(PALETTE *pal)
{
    static int      fileCount = 0;

    unsigned int    byteCount = 0;
    unsigned char   lastColor;
    unsigned char   color;
    /* The number of bytes in a run */
    unsigned char   num;

    int     index;
    int     x, y;
    /* big enough for number & '.PCX' */
    char    pcxName[MAX_PATHLEN];
    FILE    *fp;
    char    *p;

    if (!OutFilename)   /* no file name on command line */
        return 0;

    /* Create a numbered file name for output */
    fileCount++;
    fixFilename(OutFilename, pcxName, EXT_PCX, fileCount);

    /* Open the file and print the PCX file header */
    if ((fp = fopen (pcxName, "wb")) == NULL)
```

```
        quit (WRITE_OPEN_ERR, pcxName);
    byteCount = fwrite (&Header, 1, sizeof (Header), fp);
    if (byteCount != sizeof (Header))
        quit (WRITE_ERR, pcxName);

    /* pack the the screen lines before writing them */
    for (y = Ymin; y <= Ymax; y++) {
        num = 1;            /* prime algorithm with the 1st pixel */
        lastColor = _getpixel (Xmin, y);
        for (x = Xmin + 1; x <= Xmax; x++) {
            color = _getpixel (x, y);
            if (color == lastColor) {
                num++;        /* Accumulate same-colored pixels */
                if (num == MAX_RUN) {
                    byteCount += putBlock (num, lastColor, fp);
                    num = 0;
                }
            }
            else {  /* This is a pixel of a different color */
                if (num)
                    byteCount += putBlock (num, lastColor, fp);
                lastColor = color;
                num = 1;
            }
        }
        /* flush the last byte or batch of bytes on a line */
        if (num)
            byteCount += putBlock (num, lastColor, fp);
    }
    /* Finally, the color palette */
    num = PAL_CODE;        /* Write out the palette code byte */
    byteCount += writeByte (&num, fp);

    /* Write the color palette */
    for (index = 0; index < COLORS;  index++) {
        color = pal->c[index].r << 3;
        byteCount += writeByte (&color, fp);
        color = pal->c[index].g << 3;
        byteCount += writeByte (&color, fp);
        color = pal->c[index].b << 3;
        byteCount += writeByte (&color, fp);
    }
    fclose (fp);
    return byteCount;
}
```

continues

IO.C—continued

```c
/*****************************************************************
 * FUNC: int putBlock(unsigned char num, unsigned char color,
 *                                                  FILE *fp)
 *
 * DESC: Write out the 2 or 1 byte block for Run Length Encoding.
 *****************************************************************/

int
putBlock(unsigned char num, unsigned char color, FILE *fp)
{
    unsigned int byteCount = 0;

    /* Singlet colors with the top 2 bits set could be
        confused with a count, so first write the one-count. */
    if ((num > 1) || ((num == 1) && ((color & C0) == C0))) {
        num |= C0;
        byteCount += writeByte (&num, fp);
    }
    byteCount += writeByte (&color, fp);
    return byteCount;
}


/*****************************************************************
 * FUNC: int writeByte(unsigned char *byte, FILE *fp)
 *
 * DESC: Write one byte to the file and quit if there is an error.
 *****************************************************************/

int
writeByte(unsigned char *byte, FILE *fp)
{
    int count;

    count = fwrite (byte, sizeof (char), 1, fp);
    if (count != 1)
        quit (WRITE_ERR, "");
    return count;
}


/*****************************************************************
 * FUNC: loadPicture (char *filename)
 *
 * DESC: Read a PCX file from the disk into a buffer
 *****************************************************************/
```

```
PICTURE *loadPicture (char *filename)
{
    char        pcxName[MAX_PATHLEN];
    FILE        *fp;
    int         num, count;
    PICTURE     *picture;
    unsigned int        bytes_read;
    unsigned char       byte;
    unsigned char far   *bufptr;

    fixFilename(filename, pcxName, EXT_PCX, 0);

    fp = fopen(pcxName, "rb");
    if (fp == NULL)
        quit (READ_OPEN_ERR, pcxName);
    picture = malloc(sizeof (*picture));
    mustRead(fp, (char *) &Header, sizeof Header);

    Xmin = picture->xmin = Header.pcx.xmin;
    Ymin = picture->ymin = Header.pcx.ymin;
    Xmax = picture->xmax = Header.pcx.xmax;
    Ymax = picture->ymax = Header.pcx.ymax;
    picture->tall = Ymax - Ymin + 1;
    picture->wide = Xmax - Xmin + 1;
    picture->pal_id = 0;
    if (picture->tall != MAX_TALL
            || picture->wide != MAX_WIDE
            || Header.pcx.bperpixelperplane != 8
            || Header.pcx.nplanes != 1)
        quit (WRONG_PCX_FILE, pcxName);
    TotalBytes = picture->tall * (long) picture->wide;
    TotalBytes = MIN(TotalBytes, MAX_BYTES);

    picture->pixmap = (unsigned char far *)
                    _fmalloc((size_t) TotalBytes);
    if (picture->pixmap == NULL)
        return(NULL);
    bufptr = picture->pixmap;
    bytes_read = 0;

    while (getBlock(&byte, &count, fp) != EOF) {
        if ((bytes_read += count) > TotalBytes)
            break;
        for (num = 0; num < count; num++)
            *bufptr++ = byte;
```

continues

IO.C—continued

```
    }
    if (Header.pcx.version == 5)
        loadPalette(fp, &picture->pal);
    else
        defaultPalette(&picture->pal);

    fclose(fp);
    return picture;
}

/*****************************************************************
* FUNC: getBlock (unsigned char *byte, int *count, FILE *fp)
*
* DESC: get a Run Length Encoded block.  It's either a byte or a
*       string of bytes with a length given by count.
*****************************************************************/

int
getBlock (unsigned char *byte, int *count, FILE *fp)
{
    unsigned char input_byte;

    if (fread(&input_byte, sizeof(input_byte), 1, fp) != 1)
        return (EOF);
    *count = 1;      /* so far */
    if ((input_byte & C0) == C0) {
        /* Top 2 bits on, data stream to follow */
        /* mask out the byte count */
        *count = input_byte & MAX_RUN;
        mustRead(fp, &input_byte, 1);
    }
    *byte = input_byte; /* return the byte */
    return (0);      /* success */
}

/*****************************************************************
* FUNC: int mustRead(FILE *fp, char *buf, int n)
*
* DESC: Read bytes or quit.
*****************************************************************/

int
mustRead(FILE *fp, char *buf, int n)
{
    int nread;
```

```
        nread = fread(buf, sizeof(*buf), n, fp);
        if (nread != n)
            quit(READ_ERR, "");
    }

/****************************************************************
* FUNC: int loadPalette(FILE *fp, PALETTE *palette)
*
* DESC: Go to the end of the file and get the palette
****************************************************************/

loadPalette(FILE *fp, PALETTE *palette)
{
    unsigned char packed_pal[3*COLORS];
    int     color, component;
    int     red, green, blue;

    unsigned char input_byte;
    fseek(fp, -(PALETTE_SIZE+1L), SEEK_END);    /* -1 on error */

    mustRead(fp, &input_byte, 1);
    if (input_byte != PAL_CODE) {
        printf("The color palette is missing!\n");
        return (ERROR);
    }
    mustRead(fp, packed_pal, sizeof packed_pal);
    for (component = 0, color = 0;
            component < COMPS*COLORS; component += COMPS) {
        palette->c[color].r = packed_pal[component+0]>>3;
        palette->c[color].g = packed_pal[component+1]>>3;
        palette->c[color].b = packed_pal[component+2]>>3;
        color++;
    }
    palette->c[255].r = 0x1f;
    palette->c[255].g = 0x1f;
    palette->c[255].b = 0x1f;
    return (0);
}

/****************************************************************
* FUNC: int freePicture(PICTURE *pic)
*
* DESC: Free the memory allocated for this image.
****************************************************************/
```

continues

IO.C—continued

```c
int
freePicture(PICTURE *pic)
{
    _ffree(pic->pixmap);
    free(pic);
}

/****************************************************************
* FUNC: LINE_LIST    *loadLines(char *filename, char *extension);
*
* DESC: allocate and fill in LINE_LIST structure from file
****************************************************************/

LINE_LIST
*loadLines(char *filename, char *extension)
{
    char        lineName[MAX_PATHLEN];
    FILE        *fp;
    char        *p;
    LINE_LIST   *lineList;
    int         number;
    int         i;

    lineList = malloc(sizeof (*lineList));
    lineList->number = 0;

    /* condition the filename to be a line list file name */
    fixFilename(filename, lineName, extension, 0);
    lineList->filename = strdup(lineName);

    fp = fopen(lineName, "r");
    if (fp == NULL)
        return lineList;

    if (fscanf(fp, "%d\n", &number) != 1
                        || number < 1 || number > MAX_LINES) {
        fclose(fp);
        return lineList;
    }

    lineList->number = number;
    for(i=0;i<number;i++) {
        if (fscanf(fp, "%d %d %d %d\n",
                        &lineList->line[i].p[0].x,
                        &lineList->line[i].p[0].y,
```

```
                        &lineList->line[i].p[1].x,
                        &lineList->line[i].p[1].y) != 4)
            quit (READ_CONTENTS_ERR, lineName);
        lineList->line[i].p[0].x = clip(lineList->line[i].p[0].x,
                                   0, MAX_WIDE);
        lineList->line[i].p[0].y = clip(lineList->line[i].p[0].y,
                                   0, MAX_TALL);
        lineList->line[i].p[1].x = clip(lineList->line[i].p[1].x,
                                   0, MAX_WIDE);
        lineList->line[i].p[1].y = clip(lineList->line[i].p[1].y,
                                   0, MAX_TALL);

    }
    fclose(fp);
    return lineList;
}

/****************************************************************
* FUNC: saveLines(char *filename, LINE_LIST *lineList,
*                                         char *extension);
*
* DESC: save lineList to a file
****************************************************************/

saveLines(char *filename, LINE_LIST *lineList, char *extension)
{
    /* big enough for number & '.PCX' */
    char    lineName[MAX_PATHLEN];
    FILE    *fp;
    char    *p;
    int     i;

    /* condition the filename to be a line list file name */
    strcpy (lineName, filename);
    strupr (lineName);
    p= strstr(lineName, ".");
    if (p == NULL)
        p = lineName + strlen(lineName);
    strcat(p, extension);       /* add extension, it's needed */

    fp = fopen(lineName, "w");
    if (fp == NULL)
        quit (WRITE_ERR, lineName);

    fprintf(fp, "%d\n", lineList->number);
```

continues

IO.C—continued

```c
    for(i=0;i<lineList->number;i++) {
        fprintf(fp, "%d %d %d %d\n",
                        lineList->line[i].p[0].x,
                        lineList->line[i].p[0].y,
                        lineList->line[i].p[1].x,
                        lineList->line[i].p[1].y);
    }
    fclose(fp);
}

/****************************************************************
 * FUNC: LINKED_LIST *rootSequence(int argc, char *argv[])
 *
 * DESC: Process argument list and return a sequence of pcx files
 ****************************************************************/

LINKED_LIST
*rootSequence(int argc, char *argv[])
{
    LINKED_LIST *head = NULL;
    int arg, loaded, i;
    char filename[100];

    for (arg = 1; arg < argc; arg++) {
        if (fixFilename(argv[arg], filename, EXT_PCX, 0))
            head = appendName(head, filename);
        else {
            loaded = 0;
            for(i=1;i<MAX_TWEENS;i++) {
                fixFilename(argv[arg], filename, EXT_PCX, i);
                if(_access(filename, 4) == 0) {
                    head = appendName(head, filename);
                    loaded = 1;
                }
                else if (loaded == 1)
                    return head;  /* a break in the sequence */
            }
            /* didn't find a sequence, try using EXT_PCX */
            fixFilename(argv[arg], filename, EXT_PCX, 0);
            head = appendName(head, filename);
        }
    }
    return head;
}
```

```
/****************************************************************
* FUNC: LINKED_LIST *appendName(LINKED_LIST *head, char *name)
*
* DESC: add a data item to the end of the linked list
****************************************************************/

LINKED_LIST
*appendName(LINKED_LIST *head, char *name)
{
    LINKED_LIST *l;
    LINKED_LIST *end;

    l = (LINKED_LIST *) malloc(sizeof (LINKED_LIST));
    l->str = strdup(name);
    l->next = NULL;

    if (head == NULL)
        return l;

    /* find guy that points to end */
    for(end=head; end->next; end=end->next);
    end->next = l;
    return head;
}

/****************************************************************
* FUNC: int fixFilename(char *userName, char *fixedName,
*                               char *extension, int number)
*
* DESC: Create a valid filename with correct extension & number.
*       Returns true if the userName had an extension at end
****************************************************************/

int
fixFilename(char *userName, char *fixedName, char *extension,
                                            int number)
{
    char *p;
    char localbuf[100];
    int  extensionFound;

    strcpy (localbuf, userName);
    p = localbuf + strlen(localbuf) - 4;
    /* extension is there */
    extensionFound = strcmpi(p, extension) == 0;
```

continues

IO.C—continued

```c
        if (extensionFound)
            *p = '\0';
        if (number)
            sprintf(fixedName, "%s%d%s", localbuf, number, extension);
        else
            sprintf(fixedName, "%s%s", localbuf, extension);
        return extensionFound;
}

/***    These are the color and the screen handling routines    ***/

/*****************************************************************
* FUNC: int setPalette(PALETTE *palette)
*
* DESC: Set the 256 colors in the palette, using the output ports
*****************************************************************/

setPalette(PALETTE *palette)
{
    int     color;

    for (color = 0; color < COLORS; color++) {
        _outp (0x3c7, color-1);
        _outp (0x3c9, palette->c[color].r << 1);
        _outp (0x3c9, palette->c[color].g << 1);
        _outp (0x3c9, palette->c[color].b << 1);
    }
}

/*****************************************************************
* FUNC: int defaultPalette(PALETTE *palette)
*
* DESC: Create a gray-scale palette as a default
*****************************************************************/

defaultPalette(PALETTE *palette)
{
    int i;
    long j;
    long k;

    for (i=0;i<COLORS;i++) {
        j = i & 0x1f;
        palette->c[i].r = palette->c[i].g = palette->c[i].b = j;
    }
```

```
}
/*******************************************************************
* FUNC: int displayPicture(PICTURE *picture)
*
* DESC: set the video mode & palette, then draw from the buffer
*       to the screen.
*******************************************************************/

displayPicture(PICTURE *picture)
{
    int x, y, xb, yb;

    if (picture->pal_id == 0) { /* need to define palette */
        picture->pal_id = paletteID(&picture->pal);
    }
    if (CurrentPal != picture->pal_id) {
        setPalette(&picture->pal);
        CurrentPal = picture->pal_id;
    }
    displayNoPal(picture);
}


/*******************************************************************
* FUNC: int displayNoPal(PICTURE *picture)
*
* DESC: display a picture without messing with the palette
*******************************************************************/

int
displayNoPal(PICTURE *picture)
{
    /* This is the memory address of the VGA screen */
    unsigned char far *screen = (unsigned char far *) 0xa0000000;
    unsigned char far *bufptr = picture->pixmap;

    _fmemcpy (screen, bufptr, (unsigned int) MAX_BYTES);
    wait(Wait);
}

/*******************************************************************
* FUNC: int paletteID(PALETTE *pal)
*
* DESC: return a unique id for each unique palette
*******************************************************************/
```

continues

191

IO.C—continued

```
int
paletteID(PALETTE *pal)
{
    static PALETTE *definedPals[MAX_FILES];
    static int npals = 0;
    int i;

    for (i = 0; i < npals; i++) {
        if (samePal(definedPals[i], pal))
            return i+1;
    }
    definedPals[npals] = pal;
    npals++;
    return npals;
}

/****************************************************************
 * FUNC: int samePal(PALETTE *p1, PALETTE *p2)
 *
 * DESC: return 1 if same exact palettes, 0 otherwise
 ****************************************************************/

int
samePal(PALETTE *p1, PALETTE *p2)
{
    int index;

    for (index = 0; index < COLORS; index++) {
        if (p1->c[index].r != p2->c[index].r) return 0;
        if (p1->c[index].g != p2->c[index].g) return 0;
        if (p1->c[index].b != p2->c[index].b) return 0;
    }
    return 1;
}

/****************************************************************
 * FUNC: int drawPalette()
 *
 * DESC: Draw the 256 colors of the current palette in the top
 *       left of the screen.
 ****************************************************************/

int
drawPalette()
```

```
{
#define BT 4      /* block tall */
#define BW 6      /* block wide */

    int x, y, xb, yb;

    for (xb = 0; xb < 16; xb++) {
        for (yb = 0; yb < 16; yb++) {
            for (x = xb*BW; x < (xb*BW + BW); x++) {
                for (y = yb*BT; y < (yb*BT + BT); y++) {
                    _setcolor(yb * 16 + xb);
                    _setpixel (x, y);

                }
            }
        }
    }
}

/******************    The mouse routines    ******************/

/***************************************************************
 * FUNC: int initMouse()
 *
 * DESC: Initialize the mouse and quit if a driver isn't present.
 ***************************************************************/

#define MOUSE 0x33

int
initMouse()
{
    union _REGS regs;
    struct _SREGS sregs;
    regs.x.ax = 0x3533;
    _intdosx(&regs, &regs, &sregs);
    if((regs.x.bx | sregs.es ) == 0)
        quit(MOUSE_ERR, "");
    regs.x.ax = 0;
    _int86(MOUSE, &regs, &regs);
}

/***************************************************************
 * FUNC: int hideMouse()
 *
```

continues

IO.C—continued

```
* DESC: Hide the mouse cursor before we draw anything.
*        This uses the chunk of screen saved by showMouse.
*************************************************************/

int
hideMouse()
{
    union _REGS regs;

    regs.x.ax = 0x02;
    _int86(MOUSE, &regs, &regs);
}


/*************************************************************
* FUNC: int showMouse()
*
* DESC: Redisplay the mouse cursor after drawing something on the
*        screen. Save the chunk of screen under the cursor for
*        hideMouse.
*************************************************************/

int
showMouse()
{
    union _REGS regs;

    regs.x.ax = 0x01;
    _int86(MOUSE, &regs, &regs);
}


/*************************************************************
* FUNC: int mousePos(int *x, int *y)
*
* DESC: Return the x,y coordinates of the mouse and any
*        button or keystroke.
*************************************************************/

#define KEYHIT   0x0b    /* Check the keyboard */
#define STDIN    0x07    /* Read a char from standard input */

int
mousePos(int *x, int *y)
{
    union _REGS regs;
```

```
        char *buttons;
        int keystroke;

        regs.h.ah = KEYHIT;
        _intdos(&regs, &regs);
        keystroke = (regs.h.al == 0xff) ? KEYPRESS : 0;
        if (keystroke) {
            regs.h.ah = STDIN;
            _intdos(&regs, &regs);  /* STDIN */
            if (Key = regs.h.al == ESC)
                quit(0,"");              /* quit on Esc key */
        }
        regs.x.ax = 0x03;
        _int86(MOUSE, &regs, &regs);
        *x = regs.x.cx/2;              /* store the x & y coordinates */
        *y = regs.x.dx;
        /* return:  0 = none
                    1 = left
                    2 = right
                    4 = keypress */
        return (Button = (regs.x.bx & 0x03) | keystroke);
    }

/****************    A few utility routines    *****************/

/***************************************************************
 * FUNC: int waitForKey()
 *
 * DESC: Wait for a key to be pressed, then return the key.
 ***************************************************************/

int
waitForKey()
{
    int key;

    while (!_kbhit());
    key = _getch();
    if (key == ESC)
        quit(0,"");
    return (key); /* clear buffer and return keystroke */
}

/***************************************************************
 * FUNC: char     lineAsk(char *name)
 *
```

continues

IO.C—continued

```
* DESC: Ask the users if they want to use the pre-defined lines.
******************************************************************/

char
lineAsk(char *name)
{
    char c;

    setTextMode();

    _settextposition(VTAB, HTAB);
    printf ("The picture '%s' has some pre-defined", name);
    _settextposition(VTAB+2, HTAB);
    printf ("control lines. Would you like to use them?");
    _settextposition(VTAB+4, HTAB+8);
    printf ("(Y/N):");
    c = getche();
    if (c == ESC)
        quit(NO_ERROR, "");
    c = toupper(c);
    return c;
}

/*****************************************************************
* FUNC: int quitCheck()
*
* DESC: Check keyboard. If there is no key waiting, return 0,
*       for OK. If a number from 1-9 is typed, change the wait
*       between frames. Otherwise, the user wants to quit,
*       so return 1.
******************************************************************/

int
quitCheck()
{
    static int spaceWait = OFF;

    if (spaceWait) {
        Key = getch();
        if (Key != ' ')
            spaceWait = OFF;
    }
    else if (_kbhit()) {
        Key = _getch();
```

```
        if (Key == ' ') {
            /* turn on space bar stepping */
            spaceWait = ON;
            /* pause for space key */
            Key = _getch();
        }
        if (Key == ESC ¦¦ Key == 'q' ¦¦ Key == 'Q')
            return 1;                      /* a quit key */
        if (Key == 'E' ¦¦ Key == 'e')
            EndWait ^= ON;                 /* toggles on and off */
        else if (Key >= '1' && Key <= '9')
            Wait = '9' - Key;
    }
    return 0;
}

/*****************************************************************/

beep()
{
    printf("\a");
}

/******************************************************************
 * FUNC: int clip(int num, int min, int max)
 *
 * DESC: Clip the number to a value between min and max, inclusive.
 ******************************************************************/

int
clip(int num, int min, int max)
{
    if (num < min)
        num = min;
    else if (num > max)
        num = max;

    return num;
}

/******************************************************************
 * FUNC: int waitForTop() and waitForBottom()
 *
 * DESC: These routines wait for the TV scan line to get to the
 *       top and the bottom of the screen.
 ******************************************************************/
```

continues

IO.C—continued

```c
#define VID_PORT 0x3da
#define VID_RETRACE 0x8

waitForTop()
{
    /* wait till retrace ends */
    while(_inp(VID_PORT) & VID_RETRACE);
}
waitForBottom()
{
    /* wait till next retrace starts*/
    while(!(_inp(VID_PORT) & VID_RETRACE));
}

/****************************************************************
* FUNC: int wait(int count)
*
* DESC: Wait for a number of screen refreshes, based on count.
****************************************************************/

int
wait (int count)
{
    int i;

    if (!count)
        return 0;
    for (i = 1; i < 2 * count; i++) {
        waitForBottom();
        waitForTop();
    }
}

/****************************************************************
* FUNC: void     setGraphicsMode()
*
* DESC: Set up the graphics screen
****************************************************************/

void
setGraphicsMode()
{
    _setvideomode(_MRES256COLOR);
```

```
    CurrentPal = 0;                 /* Force a new palette */
}

/*****************************************************************
* FUNC: void      setTextMode()
*
* DESC: Set the screen to the startup text mode
*****************************************************************/

void
setTextMode()
{
    CurrentPal = 0;                 /* Force a new palette */
    _setvideomode(_DEFAULTMODE);
}

/*****************************************************************
* FUNC: void      quit(int err, char *name)
*
* DESC: Turn text back on, print the error message and quit.
*****************************************************************/

void
quit(ERR err, char *name)
{
    static char *ErrMess[] = {
        " ",
        "I can't get enough memory. Try turning off some TSR's.",
        "I can't find the file",
        "I can't read the file",
        "I can't open the file",
        "I can't write the file",
        "You must install a mouse driver to run this program.",
        "This is the wrong PCX type - I can't read the file",
    };

    setTextMode();
    if (err != NO_ERROR) {
        printf ("Error #%d:\n", err);
        printf ("%s %s\n", ErrMess[err], name);
        exit (err);
    }
    exit (0);
}
```

Cross-dissolving a sequence

"This time it vanished quite slowly, beginning with the end of the tail, and ending with the grin, which remained some time after the rest of it had gone."

Lewis Carroll, describing the Cheshire Cat in
Alice's Adventures in Wonderland

DISSOLVE is not a flashy program like WARP, but it is an important graphics effect and it serves to introduce you to the PC color nightmare.

The general command for the dissolve program is:

```
DISSOLVE <File1> <File2> [<Steps> [<OutFile>]]
```

<File1> is the first image and *<File2>* is the target of your dissolve.

<Steps>, the first option, is the number of frames in your sequence. If you don't include it, the program will produce the halfway picture and quit. You **must** enter a sequence number if you want to save a sequence.

<OutFile>, the second option, is the sequence root name of the numbered PCX files to save. You can have an output filename only if you first have declared *<Steps>*. The name length should be six characters or less.

If you don't provide a name, the program will preview the sequence on-screen without saving any files. In preview mode, the computer beeps after completing each frame and waits for you to press Enter. It's very patient. If you don't hit Enter, the computer will wait forever (or at least until the power goes out). If you suspect that's happening—and if it's inconvenient for you to wait forever—then by all means, press Enter.

As you might recall from the previous chapter, DISSOLVE creates pictures that look like double exposures. In that chapter, you created a dissolve that was halfway between the two given images. In order to create a sequence, however, you need to slowly increase the influence of the second image while decreasing the influence of the first.

A five-step dissolve has the starting frame, the ending frame and three in-between frames. The first in-between is one-quarter of the way, the second is halfway, and the last is three-quarters of the way to the target image.

Put it all together and you can make a sequence that mimics a Hollywood lap-dissolve, so called because one scene overlaps the other. Here's how you do it:

DISKETTE DEMO: Dissolve

To dissolve a baby into a grandmother in five steps, type:

>DISSOLVE BABY GRANDMA 5 BG

This will fade the baby out while fading the grandmother in. The sequence will be stored in the five files labeled BG1.PCX to BG5.PCX.

DISSOLVE saves each frame with the most popular 256 colors it finds. As discussed in Chapter 4, that means each frame has a unique palette.

This technique yields some pretty dissolves, but it has its problems. When these frames are played back with the LOAD program, there is a nasty flicker as the palettes change. To see what I mean, type:

>LOAD BG

This will load the five-step sequence you created and play it back. Notice the ugly color flashes as each image starts a new color palette.

Why does this happen? The problem is with the speed of graphics cards. It doesn't matter how fast your computer is, when it puts pixels on the screen, it slows down. Way down.

The part of memory that holds the graphics screen is called video RAM. Because of some peculiarities with the hardware, any access to video RAM is snail-paced. It turns out that you just can't fill the screen fast enough to beat the raster scan. The raster flies inexorably across the monitor and you have absolutely no control over it. It's a lot like life.

As your monitor scans at seventy frames per second, it plucks pixels out of video RAM and sticks them on the screen. That's when the raster is "looking" at the picture. Meanwhile, the software is updating those pixels, chugging away as fast as possible. Because the raster moves faster than the RAM can update, it overtakes it and you see part of the old image. But the palette has changed, so the old image doesn't display properly. That's when you see the flash.

This doesn't happen when you play back the WARP sequences. They are produced from a single image, so they all have the same palette. How nice.

The playback flicker is really distracting and annoying. If you watch it long enough, you could get a headache or have a seizure. So don't do it. There must be a way to fix this rotten state of affairs. And that leads me to the next program.

Fixing a sequence

"Physicians of the utmost fame,

Were called at once; but when they came

They answered, as they took their fees,

'There is no Cure for this Disease.'"

Hilaire Belloc

Well, it's not quite as bad as all that. In fact there is a program called FIX that does a pretty good job of healing the visual gashes left by the current crop of graphics cards.

FIX takes a sequence of frames with distinct palettes, and it produces another sequence with a single, best-fit palette. It loads all the frames of the sequence and examines the RGB components of each one. It then creates a new palette that represents the 256 most popular colors in the entire sequence. All the colors that aren't popular enough to make the grade are mapped to the nearest popular color.

The command looks like:

FIX <InFile> <OutFile>

Here <InFile> is the root name of the sequence to fix, and <OutFile> is the root name of the sequence to create. As you know by now, a root name can be only six characters long.

The sequences created by DISSOLVE or MORPH have a lot of different palettes, so they need to be fixed for the LOAD program. When you get your true-color graphics card, you can throw away this Band-Aid of a program.

 **DISKETTE DEMO: Fix**

Fix the sequence you just created, BG1.PCX–BG5.PCX, by typing:

>FIX BG FBG

This instructs the program to read the BG sequence in, collect the palette information and find the best-fit palette. Then, using that palette, it writes out the fixed sequence, FBG.

Did it work? Type:

>LOAD FBG

As you can see, the flicker is gone, yet the new colors are pretty close to the original colors. Certain sequences might become washed out. For these, you might want to keep the original files around on the off chance that graphics cards will improve in the near future and you can bid a fond farewell to flicker.

FOR PROGRAMMERS ONLY: The FIX program

FIX.C

The program parses the command line to get the input and the output sequence name. Then, like LOAD, it calls `rootSequence` to create a linked list of the input files.

It loads each picture of the sequence, merges its palette with the current big palette, and then frees the memory for that picture. Then it loads in the next file, and so on.

After all the files are read and their colors merged, the program collapses the big palette, producing a 256-color palette. It reads the files again from the disk. This time, it forces each picture to use the collapsed palette by calling `remapPicture` (in COLOR.C). It saves this new picture under the output sequence name. Then it clears the memory so it can load the next file in the sequence.

FIX.C—The Listing

```
/********************************************************************
* FILE: fix.c
* DESC: This program inputs a list of pictures, creates a best
*       fit palette, remaps the pictures, and writes them out.
*
* HISTORY:  Created  1/13/1993
* LAST CHANGED: 3/10/1993
*
```

continues

FIX.C—continued

```
*    Copyright (c) 1993 by Scott Anderson
*
*****************************************************************/

/* --------------------INCLUDES---------------------------- */

#include <conio.h>
#include <stdio.h>
#include <io.h>
#include <math.h>
#include <graph.h>
#include <malloc.h>
#include <memory.h>
#include <string.h>

#include "define.h"

/* ---------------------EXTERNALS-------------------------- */

extern LINKED_LIST  *rootSequence(int argc, char *argv[]);

/**** color routines ****/
extern int      closestColor(int r, int g, int b, PALETTE *pal);
extern void     collapseColors(PALETTE *palPtr);
extern int      mergePalette(PICTURE *pic);
extern int      remapPicture(PICTURE *picPtr, PALETTE *palPtr);

/**** line routines ****/
extern int      getLine(int *argx1, int *argy1,
                        int *argx2, int *argy2);
extern int      movePoint();
extern int      setLength(LINE *line);

/**** other variables ****/

extern char     *OutFilename;

/* set from last picture loaded */
extern int      Xmin, Ymin, Xmax, Ymax;

/* ---------------------GLOBAL DATA------------------------ */

PICTURE *Src;        /* source & destination picture pointers */

/***** variables used to compute intermediate images ****/
```

```c
/* number of colors in tweened image before reduction*/
extern int  Ncolors;
/* r, g, b frequency counter array */
extern unsigned int far Freq[MAX_COMP][MAX_COMP][MAX_COMP];

/* tweened images red, grn, and blu components*/
extern unsigned char far Red[MAX_WIDE][MAX_TALL];
extern unsigned char far Grn[MAX_WIDE][MAX_TALL];
extern unsigned char far Blu[MAX_WIDE][MAX_TALL];

extern PALETTE TweenPal;                /* resulting palette */

/****************************************************************
* FUNC: main (int argc, char *argv[])
*
* DESC: Read in a list of filenames to load, change their palettes
*       to the best-fit palette, and write them out.
****************************************************************/

main (int argc, char *argv[])
{
    int     file;
    LINKED_LIST *pcxList, *pcxListHead;

    /* load the pcx file if one is given */
    if (argc < 3) {
        printf("Usage: fix <infile> <outfile>\n\n");
        printf("Where: <infile>  is the input sequence name\n");
        printf("       <outfile> is the output sequence name\n");
        exit(0);
    }
    OutFilename = argv[argc-1];
    initFreq();
    pcxListHead =  rootSequence(argc-1, argv);
    for (pcxList = pcxListHead; pcxList; pcxList=pcxList->next) {
        printf("Loading the file %s\n", pcxList->str);
        Src = loadPicture(pcxList->str);
        if (Src == NULL)
            quit(MEMORY_ERR, "");

        mergePalette(Src);
        freePicture(Src);
    }
    collapseColors(&TweenPal);
    setGraphicsMode();
    setPalette(&TweenPal);
```

continues

FIX.C—continued

```
for (pcxList = pcxListHead; pcxList; pcxList=pcxList->next) {
    Src = loadPicture(pcxList->str);
    if (Src == NULL)
        quit(MEMORY_ERR, "");

    remapPicture(Src, &TweenPal);
    displayNoPal(Src);
    saveScreen(&TweenPal);
    freePicture(Src);
}
setTextMode();
}
```

Morphing a sequence

"Patience, n. A minor form of despair, disguised as a virtue."

Ambrose Bierce, *Devil's Dictionary*, 1911

You have been very patient so far. Here is your reward. After tweening, warping, and dissolving, you finally can create a morphing sequence.

Say you want five intermediate steps in the metamorphosis. You tween the control lines one-fifth of the way for each step. You warp the source image and the target image to those control lines, so they both have similar shapes.

Because this is the first tween, you display both images simultaneously with five parts of color from the source and one part from the target. On the next tween, you take four parts from the source and two from the target, etc.

The command format looks like:

```
MORPH <File1> <File2> [<Steps> [<OutFile>]]
```

> *<File1>* is the name of the source file and *<File2>* is the name of the target file. As before, these must be PCX files with 320 X 200 resolution in 256 colors. As usual, the program automatically appends .PCX to the end of the filename, so you don't need to add it.

<Steps> is the optional number of frames to generate for the sequence. The maximum number of steps is 99. If <Steps> is not specified, the program produces the halfway morph and stops. You did that in the last chapter, as you recall. Now you're ready for the good stuff.

<OutFile> is the optional root filename for the sequence files. You only can specify an output file if you have defined the number of steps. If you do supply a name, make sure it is six characters or less. As in WARP and DISSOLVE, the program tacks the sequence number onto the root name to make a new PCX filename.

For instance, if the output file name is OUT and the number of steps is three, the program will generate and save three PCX files with the names OUT1.PCX, OUT2.PCX, and OUT3.PCX. The first is just the source frame, the second is the center morph, and the third is the target frame. As before, if you don't specify an output name, no files are saved. Instead, the program lets you preview the sequence on-screen.

Is the suspense getting to you? Are you ready to see a demo? Well, finally, here it is:

DISKETTE DEMO: Morph

To morph an image named JACK.PCX into JILL.PCX in seven steps and save those seven frames to the files named JJ1.PCX through JJ7.PCX, type:

```
>MORPH JACK JILL 7 JJ
```

The seven steps include the starting and ending frame, leaving five frames in-between.

The program loads the two files, JACK.PCX and JILL.PCX. There should be some pre-defined control lines attached to JACK. You are asked if you want to use them. Say yes and take the shortcut. I don't want you to delay gratification any longer.

JACK is displayed and the lines are drawn on top of his face (see Figure 5.7). Press the Enter key to accept these control lines as they are.

Now the program wants to know if it can use JILL's control lines. Again, say yes. JILL shows up on the screen with her control lines (Figure 5.8). Press Enter to accept these lines.

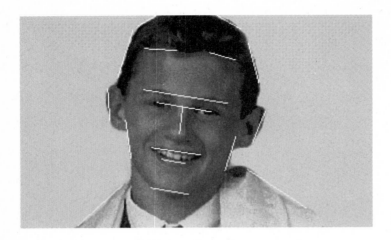

Figure 5.7.
The starting face for a sequential morph with the control lines superimposed.

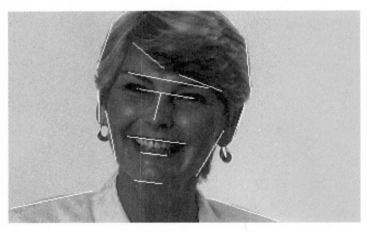

Figure 5.8.
The target face with its control lines.

Now the program can start your sequence. Because it takes about five minutes (on a 33MHz 486 PC) for each tweened image, expect to wait about half an hour for the sequence. The source image (JACK) is saved as the first file of the sequence, JJ1.PCX.

The program then tweens the control lines one-fifth of the way to the target. Both images are warped by this set of lines. These two images are then combined with five parts of color coming from the first and one part from the second. The computer beeps, and in a minute, the screen is updated.

This is your first morphed image. It has a lot of the first and a little of the second image in it. It is saved to the disk as JJ2.PCX (Figure 5.9).

Then the control lines are tweened again and the next morphing frames are created and saved until all five tweens are saved to the disk, from JJ2 to JJ6 (see Figures 5.9–5.13). Finally, the target image is saved as JJ7.PCX.

Figures 5.9-5.13.
The five morphed images in between Figures 5.7 and 5.8.

To look at a single frame from your sequence, say JJ3.PCX, type:

```
>LOAD JJ3
```

This loads and displays the desired picture. Or, to load the whole sequence of images and play them back quickly, use just the root name:

```
>LOAD JJ
```

As with the DISSOLVE program, MORPH creates nice pictures with carefully optimized palettes. These look great if you can output them to video with a frame-grabber. Without that hardware, however, you get that awful flashing as the palette switches. To correct the problem, run the sequence through the FIX program:

```
>FIX JJ FJJ
```

This creates the sequence FJJ1.PCX through FJJ7.PCX. When this group is viewed with the LOAD program, it displays without palette flicker:

```
>LOAD FJJ
```

Finally! You have created and played back a full-screen morphing sequence. Amazing, isn't it?

The starting and ending pictures you have used so far are all people. But they don't have to be. You could morph a human into a tiger:

```
>MORPH LEW TIGER 7 LT
```

Again, you can use the pre-defined lines and save yourself some time. The program creates a sequence of files named LT1.PCX through LT7.PCX.

The lines for LEW.PCX and TIGER.PCX should match up, unless someone has used them for other purposes. If the morphing looks totally bizarre, you might suspect this.

If you have corrupted your line files, you always can restore the originals from the subdirectory called LINES (see Appendix B).

"Fix" the sequence you have created and look at it with LOAD:

```
>FIX LT FLT
>LOAD FLT
```

Use the space bar to look at the individual frames. Notice how the tiger stripes show up on the man's face. These beastly morphs are fun to watch. Even though you know how the trick is done, it still seems a little magical.

The PCX files on the disk have the same set of control lines: eyes, nose, mouth, etc. Since they all match up, you can morph any pair of them. You can use the technique I've used above: take the first letter of each file to make a two-letter root name. When you fix it, add F in front.

If your disk gets cluttered, you can delete the original sequence and just keep the fixed sequence around. To delete the LT sequence, you would type:

```
>DEL LT*.PCX
```

This can be a dangerous command. Make sure you don't have any other PCX files that start with LT. A safer method is:

```
>DEL LT?.PCX
```

This method will delete only the first nine files in a sequence, however. It is a good idea to type a directory command before you delete. That way you can see how DOS will interpret the command before you commit yourself:

```
>DIR LT?.PCX
```

Be careful. I don't want you to delete all the PCX files on your hard disk. By the way, when was the last time you backed everything up?

You have seen that morphing is a mixture of warping and cross-dissolving. Although morphing is what this book is about—and it is a mesmerizing effect—these other programs are important tools in their own right. WARP can produce animation from a single image, and DISSOLVE is a standard of movie-making. Now you know how the masters of movie magic accomplish some of their best tricks.

So, start some projects. Morph your cat into your analyst (catalyst?), a cantaloupe into Lassie (melancholy?), or your congressman into a crook (redundant?).

Use the WARP program to make people talk. Draw control lines to define the mouth and then warp it around. You can get some great expressions, along with some very unusual ones.

Draw control lines on the top and bottom of an eye and make someone wink.

Interesting things happen when you morph a photograph into artwork. In the middle you get something that is photographic, yet painterly. Morph yourself into a portrait of the Mona Lisa or Van Gogh.

Often it is not the sequence, but an individual frame that you want. If you are thinking about starting a family, morph yourself into your spouse to see what your child might look like (but probably won't).

There are endless variations on the theme, so what are you waiting for? Grab that mouse and get to work!

Special Effects and Morphing in the Movies

6

"Artists haven't yet taken animation seriously enough. When they do, they will make some marvelous pictures."

**Winsor McCay,
circa 1920**

"Sleepwalkers" images courtesy of Columbia Pictures.

The Beginning

Since the early 1800s there existed several clever animation devices with terrific names, such as the phenakistiscope, the zoetrope, the phantasmatrope, and the praxinoscope.

Animation for these gizmos was all tediously hand-drawn. Natural motion was difficult to depict, so these first studies were sometimes stilted. Oblivious to these technical problems, audiences were fascinated.

Then Eadweard Muybridge's sequential photographs of animal and human motion lit a fuse in the art world. For the first time, artists saw real, live action frozen into key frames, and it explained motion as never before. They exploded with ideas.

Scientific American published the pictures, along with suggestions on how to cut them out and paste them into a zoetrope. The zoetrope was just a rotating drum with a dozen vertical slots cut into its top half. Around the inside of the bottom half you pasted the picture sequence to be animated.

As the drum rotated, you looked into it through the slots. As each slot swept by, it exposed the picture opposite it. The rapidly changing sequence became animated.

Spurred by the interest the world took in his work, Muybridge worked out an arrangement to project his pictures on a screen. Although his device—which he called the zoopraxiscope—is lost to history, it must have been a modification of the phenakistiscope. Whatever it was based on, historians are sure of one thing: it had a pretentious greek name.

The phenakistiscope is far simpler than its name would suggest. Although there are several versions of this device, the one Muybridge most likely used had two disks. One disk had radial slots around its edge to serve as shutters, and the other had the pictures to be animated. These two disks rotated in opposite directions. You could view a frame at a time through the rotating slots.

By mounting this device in front of a bright light and a lens, the animation could be projected. Audiences were thrilled.

Scientific American attended a showing in San Francisco and claimed that the projector "threw upon the screen apparently the living, moving animals. Nothing was wanting but the clatter of the hoofs upon the turf." That, of course, was soon to come.

It is worth noting that these early movies were shown before the movie camera was invented. And if you needed 24 high-quality cameras to capture one second of action, movies didn't seem to have much of a future.

In 1881, Muybridge packed up his zoopraxiscope and headed for France and England to show his movies. An obvious stopover was the studio of the French equestrian painter Meissonier, who was understandably enthused by the horse sequences. He invited all of his friends to see the show. One of those lucky attendees was the French scientist Etienne Jules Marey.

Within a year, Marey had produced the first movie camera. With the phenakistiscope as his inspiration, his camera looked very much like a modified machine gun. The fat barrel of the gun housed the lens, which focused an image onto a rotating photographic disk. With a pull on the trigger, he could expose twelve pictures in one second.

When the disk was developed, the twelve pictures were ready to be viewed in the phenakistiscope. Incredibly, Marey was interested in analyzing stopped motion only. He had no use for a projector. So, as strange as it seems, the first movie camera wasn't used to take movies.

So far we have Muybridge's projector without a camera, and Marey's camera without a projector. If there was an unseen hand guiding the development of the movies, it was shaky—to say the least.

Thomas Edison and William K.L. Dickson heard about Muybridge's projections, and set about to make their own movies. Edison figured he could wrap the pictures around his talking cylinders. He would have sound with the first movies. But it just wouldn't work, so he gave up and told Dickson to play with it.

Dickson was unleashed. The creative constraints of the phonograph cylinder no longer applied. He cast around for new ideas.

George Eastman had just released the Kodak box camera to the public in 1888. It used a film strip, and Dickson saw his opportunity. He worked with Eastman to develop reels of 35-millimeter film. Then Dickson made a camera and a viewer—your typical weekend project. To make Edison happy, Dickson included sound. He made a movie of himself talking. Thus, the very first film was a talkie. I bet you didn't know that.

Edison took the credit with great modesty as he patented the Kinetograph (the camera) and the Kinetoscope (the viewer). A few years later, Kinetoscope peep shows were spread around the world. However, they were not the only peep-show machines. In fact, the inevitability of film wasn't apparent at all in those days. A year after the Kinetoscope was introduced, Herman Casler invented the Mutoscope. It didn't use film at all. In fact, it was a throwback to flip-books, and it used about 800 pictures, pasted on cards and mounted on an axle like a rollodex.

Because the images were bigger and the machine was hardier than the Kinetoscope, the Mutoscope gained in popularity. In fact, the first Mutoscopes were built like tanks. While the Kinetoscope films disintegrated, the Mutoscope cards kept flipping. There are functioning Mutoscopes around today, still in great condition.

The Kinetoscope steadily improved and held its own, but the victor in this battle was hard to pick for a long time.

Edison was happy for the success of the Kinetoscope, even if it didn't use the phonograph cylinder. At least he made sure the Kinetograph cameras and the Kinetoscope viewers used electric motors. That way, they would return an additional royalty in motor sales and electricity fees.

Unfortunately, the motors made the cameras heavy and bulky. They were as discreet and portable as an upright piano. There was another tiny bug. You couldn't single-frame. So much for animation.

The only way to make use of this machine was to build a well-lit studio around it, which Dickson did. It was a charming building, completely covered with tar-paper to make it light-tight. It was nicknamed "The Black Maria" after the black paddy-wagons of the era. Its roof was removable for day scenes, and the whole structure could be turned on a track to chase the sun.

To make a movie, Dickson would cajole theatrical performers to ply their trade in front of his cyclopean audience of one. Thus began the Edison movie legacy of filmed dance, vaudeville, and circus acts. The rather lame concept of using a new technology to reiterate old art still plagues modern film.

Edison made three mistakes that cost him dearly. The first, already mentioned, was to force every camera to have a bulky, balky electric motor. The second mistake was ignoring the projector. Although the Kinetoscope was spread around the world, it was not a projector! Rather, the Kinetoscope was a personal viewing machine (with an electric motor, of course). The movies they played were called peep-shows. Put a nickel in the slot and watch a movie.

When someone suggested to Edison that he should create a projector, he thought the idea was absurd. Obviously one person per machine was better business than a hundred people per machine. It only made sense. He calculated that it would take just ten projectors to satisfy the entire country, whereas he could sell millions of Kinetoscopes.

This was an interesting lapse in Edison's judgment. As an inventor, he usually was interested in creating whatever was needed and whatever was possible. But here he acted like many a modern businessman, thinking he could reap a profit by stopping progress.

Not even Edison could stop progress, although he might have tried harder. Being somewhat of an unreasonable skinflint, he refused to spend an extra $150 to secure the foreign rights to the Kinetoscope. That was his third mistake.

In France, the birthplace of Liberty, people dissected Edison's machine—and made some changes.

The Lumière brothers, Louis and Auguste, dispensed with the electric motors and substituted a hand crank. Cut from its umbilical cord, the movie camera entered the world at large. Finally anyone, anywhere, could make a movie.

And the Lumière's camera could single-frame.

Around the world, in France, Germany, England, and America, there was a flurry of creative activity. All the pieces were finally available and people were trying every permutation possible.

In America, the predominant theme was big bucks, big companies, and big cameras. Extravaganzas were being filmed, but all on a stage—and from a single immobilized eye.

The Europeans, possessing portable equipment, took to the streets to capture real life. In those days, it wasn't hard to make a silent film. The cost was not prohibitive, and creativity was encouraged.

You would approach a wealthy patron or gallery owner, and sweet-talk them out of the price of film and development. While you were at it, you would ask to use their castle for the weekend. You would borrow a camera, buy a bottle of burgundy, and invite some of your theatrical friends over to the castle for the shoot.

After developing your magnum opus, you would show it at one of the little ciné-clubs in the artistic part of town. You might even make a little money.

The chronology of film is difficult to document. Sadly, the materials used for the first films were unstable and many have long ago crumbled away. There also was the odious studio practice of destroying every existing print of a movie before filming the remake. So rather than pick a single inventor, I will just point out that there were dozens of geniuses, artists, and entrepreneurs that contributed to the final form of cinema.

Even Edison came around. With no time to invent his own projector, he bought one—the Vitascope, invented by Thomas Armat of Washington, D.C.

By the end of the nineteenth century, movie theaters were spread around the world, and Milk-Dud sales have never been the same.

Georges Méliès

"A veritable alchemist of light."

Charlie Chaplin, describing Georges Méliès

Georges Méliès was a French showman who had his own little theater in Paris. He entertained his audience with dramatic sketches and magic, using the trusty tools of the trade: trap doors, smoke, and mirrors.

One day, desirous of a croissant and a café latte, he strolled down the avenue to his favorite bistro. The Lumière brothers were there, setting up a strange device. The lights were killed, and their freshly invented projector flickered to life.

Méliès was astonished. His mind raced with the possibilities of incorporating this amazing machine into his act. Before the lights had come back up, Méliès was talking to the Lumières about buying a camera (which also was the projector—very clever, these Lumières).

They refused. In fact, they tried to talk him out of getting into movies at all. "Movies are a novelty," they said. "Save your time and money." Strange advice from two of the few entrepreneurs who actually managed to make a living from the cinema. Perhaps they thought there were already too many people at this picnic.

At any rate, it didn't stop Méliès. He found the English to be more receptive to his proposal, and he obtained the equipment he needed from Robert Paul. For the first time the Lumières had a little competition.

By 1896, Méliès started showing his movies in his theater. A born thespian, it was only natural for him to film stage acts, including his own.

One day, while filming in front of the opera house, his camera jammed. Frustrated, he played with the crank a little and managed to fix it. Disappointed that he lost the shot, he nevertheless picked up filming where he had left off.

Méliès knew the shot was ruined, but on a whim, he developed the reel anyway. When he played it back, he almost fell out of his chair. There, on the screen, a horse-tram was metamorphosing into a hearse.

Méliès immediately understood what had happened. By a wonderful circumstance, a hearse was in exactly the same spot the tram had been when the camera jammed. Going the same speed, the hearse just continued from where the tram left off. Amazingly, the first special effect in the movies was a morph!

The effect was never to be accidental again.

Méliès starting making what came to be called "trick films." He made people disappear, sawed people in half, and even had exploding heads. Cinema was still a young brat and Méliès already had the first special-effects studio. He used double exposures, sleight-of-hand, and a lot of editing to invent almost every trick used today.

He discovered that in film, it is almost as easy to represent a dream as it is to represent a reality. His explorations of fantasy broke ground for the avant-garde artists of the 1920s and beyond.

Like any good magician, he carefully guarded the secrets of his trade. He did such a good job that today we still don't know exactly how he did his effects.

One of his most successful films was *Le Voyage dans la Lune* or *A Trip To The Moon*, made in 1902. It was a remarkable achievement on many fronts. In a time when most movies were one or two minutes long, Méliès stunned the public with a twenty-one–minute epic. Although it wasn't the first science-fiction movie, it was the first to have a real plot.

The story was based on Jules Verne's *From the Earth to the Moon*, published thirty years earlier, and H.G. Wells' *The First Men in the Moon*, published only the year before. It was partly homage and partly a parody on those works (and science in general).

Méliès designed and helped create the sets, wrote the screenplay, did all the special effects, directed, produced, and starred in the movie. He had the lead, of course.

Méliès plays Professor Barbenfouillis (a name that doesn't really travel well), who proposes going to the moon in a most uncomfortable way: fired from a huge cannon, à la Jules Verne. He puts his plan before the Scientific Congress of the Astronomic Club. In an act uncharacteristic of the current American Congress, they decide to fund the project.

The cannon is cast in a huge foundry. Finally it is T-minus zero and our heroes are blasted to the moon in their space shell. In a rather disgusting scene, they hit the Man in the Moon smack in the eye.

As they leave the space shell, the astronauts look up at the earth in the sky. The scene is eerily similar to the real thing, which occurred some fifty years later. As Oscar Wilde noted, life imitates art.

In the middle of their revelry, a snowstorm kicks up, forcing the group to seek shelter in a crater. There they find their way underground—where the lobster-like Selenites live.

The Selenites capture our intrepid crew and take them to their King. But our heroes don't go down that easily. They slug it out with the Selenites, who turn out to be pathetic antagonists—they blow up when they are punched.

The adventurers make it back to the surface and escape from the moon in their space shell (without a gun, yet). Their naval re-entry predates NASA by some sixty years. It also gives the explorers a chance to admire underwater life. They are picked up by a ship and taken back to Paris, where they are the toast of the town. The mayor decorates them and dedicates a statue to their bravery.

This amazing movie combined animation, optical effects, double exposures, wipes, fades, dissolves, and almost every visual trick ever used in film.

By 1912, Méliès had made more than five hundred films. He sold the rights by the film-foot to any movie house he could. Unfortunately, anyone who cared to could copy the movie as many times as they wanted.

That wasn't the worst. An American producer named Sigmund Lubin simply brought the films to America, put his name on them, and copyrighted them as his own. This continued even after Méliès started plastering copyright notices over all the props in his movies.

This brazen act of piracy was well-rewarded. Lubin went on to rake in the big bucks while Méliès—due to money troubles—was forced back to the stage, doing his magic act. When he died, he was an impoverished vendor in a tawdry Paris newsstand.

He wasn't the first, and he won't be the last, creative genius to be ruined by an unscrupulous businessman. Then, as now, the rewards go to the rapacious, not the sagacious.

James Stuart Blackton

Meanwhile, back in America, the cartoonist James Stuart Blackton was using a different kind of trick. While Blackton stood in front of a blackboard drawing a face, a movie camera was cranked once, taking a single frame. Blackton erased parts of the drawing and redrew them to make the characters move slightly. The camera was cranked again.

When the movie was viewed, it looked like the characters had come to life under Blackton's hand. The effect was quite a crowd-pleaser. His 1906 film *Humorous Phases of Funny Faces* is considered to be the first stop-frame animation film. Now you know what it means to crank out a film.

Blackton was a partner in Vitagraph, an early American movie studio. His trick films were designed as short teasers for the live-action films that were the studio's bread and butter.

It is interesting that the first filmed animations were presented as a special effect, usually with live actors in the scene. Animation that could stand on its own had yet to come. Nevertheless, these short animations captured the public's fancy. People were astonished to see inanimate objects and chalk drawings spring to life. The impossible happened right in front of their eyes, and they couldn't get enough.

The wild success of these "trick" movies convinced animators to switch from their mechanical animation methods to film. The movie projector allowed a large audience to view the animation, and it was a photographic medium, allowing live action and special optical effects. Cinema was here to stay.

Emile Cohl

One of the first to make the switch to film was Emile Cohl, yet another Frenchman. Between 1908 and 1918, the prolific Cohl produced over 200 animated shorts. A few frames from one of his earlier films is shown in Figure 6.1. Wouldn't you know that among the first filmed animations there would be a morph?

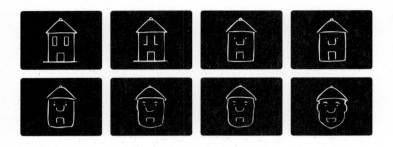

Figure 6.1.
An early animation, circa 1910, shows a house metamorphosing into a face. And you thought morphing was new.

Cohl put animation on a new footing. No longer a special-effects prop for a human actor, animation stood on its own as a new artistic medium. Cohl developed a dreamy style, with an emphasis on metamorphosing shapes.

Like Méliès, Cohl kept his methods secret. He worked alone to create his cartoons. Cohl created the first regular animated character, named Fantoche.

By 1909, his movies had made their way to New York. In 1912, Cohl followed suit. New York's budding animation scene was starting to bloom. The world center of animation was shifting from France to America.

Winsor McCay

"Any idiot that wants to make a couple of thousand drawings for a hundred feet of film is welcome to join the club."

> Winsor McCay, to an associate who pleaded with him to patent his animation process

One of the New York greats that attracted Emile Cohl to America was Winsor McCay. As you might recall from Chapter 3, McCay was a well-known comic-strip artist working for William Randolf Hearst. He also toured the vaudeville circuit with the likes of W.C. Fields. McCay had a great act: was a "lightning sketcher." By quickly drawing and erasing pictures on a chalkboard, he would gradually age a boy and a girl through the "Seven Ages of Man" as the orchestra played "Ah, Sweet Mystery of Life."

McCay wasn't the only lightning sketcher. Bud Fisher of *Mutt and Jeff* fame, Richard Felton Outcault, creator of the *Yellow Kid* and *Buster Brown*, and James Blackton were also masters of the chalkboard. Believe it or not, this was a popular form of entertainment left over from the Victorian age. For a long time, it was as close as most people got to animation.

After five years of being a human zoetrope, McCay discovered real animation. His reaction must have been wonderful to behold. Finally, he could give his arms a rest.

McCay credited his son Robert for his first exposure to animation. Robert, he said, had brought home some advertising flip-books that hooked him on cartoon motion.

Perhaps not coincidentally, Emile Cohl's movies were imported to the United States at the same time. It is possible that Cohl made a bigger impact than the flip-books. McCay does mention Cohl as being influential in his move to film.

McCay immediately transferred his most popular comic-strip character, Little Nemo, into an animated short that he added to his act. Audiences were enchanted. This movie, the first comic strip converted to animation, marked a great departure from previous animation. The drawings were superb and the motion was impressively smooth.

McCay single-handedly set a standard that couldn't be touched for another twenty years, and then it was by a *team* of Disney animators.

Being incredibly inventive, he introduced audiences to warping—the "squash" and "stretch" so beloved by later animators. Little Nemo compresses and then stretches his two companions with just a wave of his hand.

McCay had noticed that characters could easily seem flat in an animation, so he paid special attention to "weight" in his films. Weight is a combination of careful drawing (artists talk about the "quality of line") and attention to the effects of gravity on a body. McCay's characters, although standing on a completely blank background, had weight.

Earlier animators, such as Emile Cohl, started with a picture and then made small changes to get to the next picture. A lot of interesting things popped up this way. Cohl pounced on these fortuitous images and took the animation in a new direction. That is one reason for the dreamy quality of his work. Like stream-of-consciousness, the pictures just flow from one into the next, with no apparent plan. This would come to be called "straight-ahead animation."

McCay had a story to tell. He didn't want to depend on a happy coincidence of lines. That made things much more difficult. With straight-ahead animation, it is tough to make two characters synchronize their actions. The animation takes on a life of its own. Once a motion is started, it must continue with the same pacing or it will be jerky. So if the first increment is wrong, your destination is way off.

McCay invented a method he called the "McCay Split System." Instead of simply going forward in the animation, McCay would draw just a few key frames to pace the action. Then (you guessed it!) he split the difference between key frames and drew an in-between frame. Winsor McCay invented tweening around 1914.

He also invented what later would be called "slow-in slow-out." To keep the motion smooth, McCay would start a motion slowly, accelerate it, and then slow it down.

McCay seems to have been the first to "cycle-animate." This refers to the simple process of repeating a cyclic action by rephotographing the same pictures. Audiences got a chance to examine the motion better, and the animator got a big break as well.

McCay's methods tamed animation for the storytellers. His insights were not ignored by later animators—especially Walt Disney.

The next year, McCay created one of the first "splatter" films with "How a Mosquito Operates," a disgusting but humorous look at that blood-sucking insect. There is more than a little influence of surrealism in McCay's work.

In 1914, McCay startled audiences with a new movie starring a scenery-chewing dinosaur named Gertie. The film was inspired by McCay's interest in using animation for education as well as entertainment. He consulted with scientists and practically lived in the dinosaur exhibits at the New York museums.

This movie had an important addition: a background. Previous animators despaired at all the work a background implied. Backgrounds were either spartan or nonexistent. McCay wanted a hilly background with rocks, shrubs and a lake. Even a lightning-fast artist like McCay didn't want this job. He hired his neighbor, a young art student named John Fitzsimmons, to help.

McCay drew a master background scene, and then he animated Gertie on sheets of translucent rice paper. Fitzsimmons' job was to take the pictures of Gertie and trace the background onto them from the master. Over and over again. What fun.

Thousands of frames later, the movie was photographed in the studios of Vitagraph, James Blackton's movie studio. Because every background frame is hand-drawn, there is a pleasant, shimmering quality to it. The lake sparkles and the leaves rustle slightly, suggesting a gentle breeze. But what a lot of work!

On February 2, 1914, Winsor McCay showed Gertie to the public. Every cartoonist in New York was in the theater that night, including Emile Cohl. But Gertie the Dinosaur wasn't just a film. Someone like McCay wouldn't be content to simply show a movie. Instead, he created a performance multimedia event!

As the curtain was raised, McCay walked out into the spotlight and cracked his bullwhip. That cued the projectionist to start the movie. As the audience watched in astonishment, a thirty-ton diplodocus first peeked, then leaped out from behind a pile of rocks. As she ambled toward the viewer, she ate a rock and a tree and slaked her thirst by drinking the lake dry. The real McCay gave the cartoon Gertie commands—which she obeyed when she felt like it.

Here's how Emile Cohl described it: "On the stage, in front of the screen, McCay stood, in evening dress, whip in hand. He started a little speech; then, going back to the screen, like a lion tamer he gave an order to the beast, which came out from behind the rocks. Always under the command of the tamer, it gave an exhibition of acrobatic skill; the dinosaur jumped, danced, uprooted trees, and finally took a bow in front of the wildly applauding audience."

At the end of the act, McCay left the stage only to "reappear" in the cartoon. The French call this a "trompe l'oeil," and it was a favorite device of Marcel Duchamp and the surrealists. Gertie gently lifted the cartoon McCay onto her back and then ambled off into the distance.

For a change, the critics raved. The *Chicago Examiner* proclaimed "Thus the camera, that George Washington of mechanisms, at last is proved a liar…You are flabbergasted to see the way the reel minds its master."

This expert blending of fact and fantasy is truly a classic of animation. Not until 1934, with *Snow White*, did Disney match the technical prowess of this film. By then, McCay was dead.

While producing *Gertie*, a young man named John Randolph Bray visited McCay. He said he was writing a magazine article on animation. McCay was more than accommodating. He showed the fellow every trick he used to bring drawings to life—from the registration pegs and punched rice paper to the Mutoscope machine he used to preview his work.

Bray never wrote an article. But he did start the largest cartoon factory of his day, using everything he learned from McCay. Bray, the "Henry Ford of animation," patented what McCay would not. One dark day, Bray served McCay with a citation of patent infringement.

In time, McCay apparently beat the bum rap, but the old saw still cuts: you can recognize the pioneers by the arrows in their backs.

Bray's studios were churning out a cartoon a week. Bray not only purloined McCay's methods, he pirated McCay's movies. Bray even copied *Gertie*. It was a poor imitation. Bray eventually made more money off of his patents than he did from his lifeless animations. There is no good evidence that McCay saw a penny of it.

Before the computer age

Throughout the twentieth century, morphing has remained an important tool for the cinematographer. Besides the obvious special effect—Wolfman, Dracula, and so on—there is a milder use for it. It makes an effective cut: fade out on one subject, fade in on another. Done effectively, there is a curious, mystical quality to it.

But the real draw is the magical metamorphosis—an impossible transformation, realized on-screen. The effect is so hypnotizing that it was worth spending days to get a few seconds of film.

For the Wolfman transformations, they would strap down the hapless actor (usually Lon Chaney Jr.), and immobilize his head. For the next few hours, the makeup man would apply a few hairs, then the cameraman would shoot a few frames. A little putty here and there, a few more hairs, and shoot more frames. It was agony for everyone involved, it was easy to screw up, and it was fantastically popular.

Of course, you could see slight movements in the dissolves, and if you knew anything about photography you could figure out how it was done, but it was fun nevertheless.

Other types of metamorphosing were dealt with differently. The bat turning into Count Dracula was usually animated. There were many ways of doing this, but the basic methods were pioneered by Méliès, around the turn of the century.

With modern cameras, it turns out to be delightfully simple to create your own special effects—even morphing.

At the risk of exposing family skeletons, I will tell you a story about my own childhood brush with morphing.

My father (who is a little strange) used to put special effects in our home movies. He had a 16-mm camera that could single frame, and he made great use of it. Dad didn't just make home movies, though—he scripted, acted, and directed family *epics*.

For these spectacles, the whole family's participation was necessary. In one hilariously gruesome movie titled *Slaughter on Smith Avenue*, circa 1960, everyone in the family (almost) is hideously murdered. Dad used a different special effect for each murder.

For my Aunt Mary, the masked murderer chooses strangulation by nylon stocking. After she overacts her way to death, Dad decided to turn her face green. We protested, but he was the director, and he prevailed. He appointed me as special-effects supervisor for the greening of Aunt Mary.

For the next four hours, cousin Spike and I took turns applying green makeup to poor Aunt Mary, who was remarkably sporting about the whole thing. Of course, she is just as weird as my dad, and that explains a lot.

For each layer of green, I clicked off a few more frames. More and more green makeup was laid on until we hit the precise color I wanted. Actually, we got tired, so we quit.

When the film came back, the effect was perfect. Aunt Mary, nylon wrapped around her neck and tongue sticking out, turns a deep green in about 10 seconds. We didn't brace her, so she slumped a bit through the shoot. That added a nice bit of unexpected movement to the scene that I promptly took credit for.

This story is told to illustrate the appeal of the technique. How many other strange (but lovable) families are out there playing with special effects? There must be some reason for manufacturers to put single-framing on a camera.

Of course, once everybody can do it at home, Hollywood has to up the ante. Audiences get educated quickly. They demand more.

The Modern Age of Television

Television, that great wasteland, really does have a purpose. It is to sell you things. And if you have to sit through an occasional boring melodrama, it's worth it to see the best of television—the commercials.

The commercials have pioneered many morphing effects. If you have only thirty or even fifteen seconds to sell your product, you go for the best impact you can get. Hang the expense. You're going to get killed by the airtime costs anyway, so get the best bang for your buck.

In the beginning were the traditional dissolves and optical effects, where kitchens would magically become spotless, and food would evaporate from the plates. Some of these effects are perfect illusions. At first they were startling, but viewers quickly gained sophistication. The effect was assimilated into the expanding vocabulary of visual phrases.

Then came analog effects. Torsos were twisted by stomach-aches and foreheads were warped by headaches. These effects are very realistic, and they racheted expectations up even higher.

Ultimately, computers started contributing to the visual lexicon. The first break-through was digital video. Once the image was in the digital realm, computers could work their magic.

One of the first tricks was *compositing*. Although compositing (which means mixing two strips of film together to make a third—the composite) is available with optical printers, there is a problem. If you want to combine more than two scenes, you need to go through the optical printer again. You lose a little bit of resolution with every pass, so you have to keep the layers to a minimum.

With digital compositing, you can stack up as many images as you desire with absolutely no degradation of the quality. This led to the Cola commercials, which combined moons, cityscapes, cola bottles, cars, and teenagers in a multi-layered, continuous pan.

It was animated montage. Technology was nudging the arts again.

Then came the warping effects, stimulated, as you recall from Chapter 3, by certain scientific problems with imaging. Out of this came some intriguing commercials.

The first warping for commercials was done by Pacific Data Images (PDI, Los Angeles). They wanted the Plymouth account, so they ran down to their local Plymouth dealer and picked up some brochures. They scanned different models into the computer and morphed between them. Plymouth was sold and PDI made a commercial that shows different parts of a Voyager warping as the voiceover comments on them.

A later PDI spot also involved cars. In a commercial for Exxon, PDI made a car morph into a running tiger. The effect is made even more dynamic by warping the car to match the tiger's stripes (see Figures 6.2-6.4 and the full-color insert).

**Figures
6.2-6.4.**
A few frames from
a Pacific Data
Images commercial
for Exxon. Notice
how the tiger's
stripes are reflected
in the wrinkling of
the car.

Kool-Aid has created a dazzling series of commercials where everyone and everything gets morphed to pieces. Schick commercials feature blockheads that metamorphose into normal faces (that need a shave, of course). Sega commercials have people's eyes bug out, and Nintendo warps kids flat with their G-Force commercial.

Although commercials lead the pack of morphing converts, regular television programs have incorporated the technology also—most notably the two *Star Trek* series.

These handsomely produced, expensive shows are peppered with morphing. Typically, as in *Star Trek: Deep Space Nine*, the method used is 3D metamorphosing. In particular the character of Odo, played by Rene Aberjonois, gets a lot of computer assistance. Odo is a shape-shifter, and has the ability to change into anything and go anywhere. His metamorphoses are created as 3D shapes in the computer that are then tweened to provide smoothness.

Besides commercials and the occasional series, the only other place to find morphing on television is in a music video. Music videos are closer to commercials than features, both in terms of length and visual intensity. It is no surprise then, to find commercial directors crossing over to music videos.

One video in particular, Michael Jackson's *Black or White*, put a spotlight on morphing. In a scene considered long by morphing standards, actors dancing in front of the camera are morphed, one after another. Faces of all nationalities are blended so well it's hard to tell where one begins and another leaves off.

This is a terrific use of morphing—not just as a special effect, but as a startling, visual renunciation of racism. The sequence makes it obvious that although humans come in many varieties, we are all closely related. We just occupy different places in the spectrum. Thousands of years of written arguments are bested by this little video with its profound visual impact. This is art and technology at its best.

Strangely, the rest of the video lapses into the worst of art and technology, glorifying pointless violence. After its much ballyhooed premier, this part of the video was excised. With it went another morphing sequence with Michael Jackson and a black panther. It is competently done, but lacks the punch of the dance sequence.

Because of the expense of the method, morphing is used sparingly outside of commercials. Except, of course, for big-budget blockbuster movies. And who better to start the ball rolling than George Lucas?

Ron Howard—Willow

In 1988, Ron Howard wanted some magical effects for his movie *Willow*. Written by George Lucas, the mythological story involves the evil queen Bavmorda, played to the hilt by Jean Marsh. She discovers that a baby has been born in her realm who is destined to bring her downfall. She wants to kill the baby—but only after a ritual exorcism.

The baby girl is narrowly spirited away and floated down the river to the land of the little Nelwins. They decide to return her to the big people where she belongs. The Nelwins choose Willow, the man who found the baby, to undertake the arduous journey.

Willow sets out with some assistance from the local wizard, whose magic is just a little rusty. After much trial and travail, they are captured by the evil queen. It is up to Willow to use the magic wand and save the day.

But Willow is not too experienced in these matters, being but a humble farmer. To fight Bavmorda, he must metamorphose the good sorceress Raziel back into a woman. His first attempts don't work out so well, and he succeeds only in turning her into a crow, then into a goat.

Finally, putting everything into it, he tries again. Raziel's goat-neck stretches out to an impossible length, then she turns into an ostrich. Peacock feathers appear, then shrivel away. Willow keeps trying. Raziel shrinks down to a turtle, whose long neck pulls back into its shell.

She exhorts Willow to try harder, which he does. The turtle sprouts paws which grow into a tiger. Finally, the tiger metamorphoses into the exhausted sorceress, played by Patricia Hayes (see the full-color insert for five stills from this scene).

This amazing sequence was the first to expose an audience to computer morphing. Later in the movie, Willow tries to turn the nasty queen to stone. Another morphing sequence ensues where Bavmorda's hand turns to marble. But her magic is stronger than Willow's, and she metamorphoses back.

In fact, the queen seems quite unbeatable until Willow uses a simple stage-magic trick to make the baby disappear. Distracted, the queen is destroyed by the forces of good in a whirl of red smoke.

When director Howard told the special effects people what he wanted, they first toyed with the idea of cross-dissolving puppets, a time-honored tradition in the business. But Doug Smythe at Industrial Light and Magic (ILM, a division of LucasArts), remembered the short movie that Tom Brigham had made a few years earlier, and decided to give the computer a try.

He wrote a new version of the warping and morphing software. It was decided, after a few trials, that the software couldn't do everything. Some of the stretches were so exaggerated that the image became pixillated—the pixels themselves were stretched to the limit. So a compromise was devised.

Models were created that could do part of the warping, then the computer would take over and finish the job.

For the goat, a clever puppet was made that could stretch its neck and do some of the metamorphosing on its own. That was accomplished by building a foam goat head around a fiberglass cast of an ostrich skull. When a vacuum inside the skull was turned on, it sucked the foam into the shape of an ostrich head. At the same time, the neck was elongated.

The models were filmed and then the programmers and animators went to work. They further stretched and warped the images, and finally pieced them together with the morphing algorithm.

The movie was a hit, and audiences begged for more morphing. They were soon to get it.

The audiences weren't the only ones to be impressed by this tour-de-force of special effects. ILM's technique garnered them a well-deserved Academy Award.

Steven Spielberg—Indiana Jones and the Last Crusade

The next director to pick up the morphing baton was Steven Spielberg. He called on the now-experienced morphing team at ILM to craft the dramatic demise of the villain of the piece.

After chasing around the world to find the Holy Grail, Indiana Jones and his evil rival converge on the prize at the same time. Confronted with a choice of goblets, the scoundrel grabs what he takes to be the Grail.

Drinking from the Grail is supposed to confer immortality, so he chugs down the contents of the goblet. Whoops, wrong goblet. The blackguard is sent to his just reward as the poison quickly ages him—then it kills him and dries him out for good (see the full-color insert for four stills from this scene).

The sequence involved lots of makeup and three progressively mummified latex masks. Then the computer folks massaged the images to smoothly morph each face into the next.

The result could make a person give up drinking entirely.

James Cameron—The Abyss

After some films that he probably would like to forget, in 1989 James Cameron made a movie called *The Abyss.* One of the key players was a computer-generated water "pseudopod." A lot of computer power was thrown into this movie.

The movie concerns the rescue of a Navy submarine from its precarious perch on the brink of a bottomless trough (of course). Fortunately for the Navy, there is a manned, underwater drilling rig nearby.

After the requisite string of disasters and strange happenings, the crew of the Deepcore drilling rig works toward the precipice. Along the way they confront the pseudopod, which is a beautiful, computer-generated tentacle of water that undulates through their underwater habitat.

The pseudopod seems to inspect one of the crew, played by actor Ed Harris. In a startling transformation, it takes on Harris's face. This terrific morphing effect is the highlight of the movie.

The computer work was done at ILM, of course. The graphics supervisor was Jay Riddle, working with Scott Anderson (no relation), Lincoln Hu, Mark Dippé, Steve Williams, and John Knoll.

Using Silicon Graphics workstations, they spent six months designing the watery creature. They used a software animation system from Alias Research in Toronto, Canada. It was chosen because it uses spline- or curve-based shapes. Water just doesn't look right modeled with polygons.

ILM also used Renderman, from Pixar in San Rafael, to create the final images. The feature that attracted them to Renderman was it capacity for "motion-blur." This useful effect corrects a problem with all previous animation: jerkiness. When you animate, you create crisp, clean images. But real motion sometimes leaves a blur on even the fast exposures used in film.

Renderman mimics this effect, blurring the action when the motion is faster than a certain threshold. The effect also is used to match computer animation with the rest of the scene. In a quick pan, for instance, it won't look right if the computerized parts are crystal sharp while everything else is a blur.

As is often the case, success is in the details. The computer animators took it to the limit, even mapping reflections of hidden ceiling beams onto the watery form as it tweened from one shape into another.

This kind of metamorphosing is three-dimensional, using carefully designed models. To make the pod imitate Ed Harris, the actor had to be scanned with a 3D laser digitizer from Cyberware. Because the pod mimics his motions, Harris had to be scanned while making different faces, as well.

The Cyberware scanning information can be used to directly create a 3D object in the computer. It turns out, however, that it is very difficult to deal with realistic facial animation in 3D. Instead, the data was "unwrapped" to create a 2D-representation of the face. That image was manipulated by warping algorithms similar to the ones included with this book.

Each of Harris's expressions became a keyframe. Then warping was used to smoothly tween from one expression to the next. When the art directors were satisfied with the motion, the 2D model was rendered as a 3D surface for filming.

The folks at ILM had a great time on the project. It appeals to the Dr. Frankenstein in us to create impossible beings. Director Cameron was pleased, as well. The pod had made the leap from his imagination to the screen completely intact. That is one of the beauties of working with computer rendering systems. They can present anything, even dreams, with startling reality.

Terminator 2

If Cameron was happy with the effects in *The Abyss*, he was even happier that they were brought in under budget and on time. It convinced him to give computers a bigger role in the movies. In 1991, he made the most technologically advanced movie to date. He wrote the script and directed the movie. He called it *Terminator 2*.

Starring Arnold Schwarzenegger, the movie was a guaranteed box-office hit. Industrial Light and Magic was again picked to provide the computerized effects.

The story picks up more or less where the first *Terminator* left off. Schwarzenegger, as the Terminator, comes from the future again, but this time as a good guy. Again, Linda Hamilton is recruited to save the world.

She has her work cut out for her. The bad guys from the future have created a new, improved villain, the T-1000. He is a gleaming liquid-metal, quick-change artist. The role is sometimes played by actor Robert Patrick, but just as often it is the computer that you see on the screen.

For this magnificent antagonist, the wizards at ILM created a complete three-dimensional model of Patrick. They analyzed his gait and gestures. All of this went into the computer. What they cranked out seemed to be a living, breathing human, but it was as evanescent as the bits that made it up.

Finally, here was an actor that was not bound by the rules of the screen-actors guild. He could walk through fire and steel bars and not break a sweat. For director Cameron it was literally a dream come true.

Tweening, of course, gave this computer actor his smooth motions. Metamorphosing was used to produce the creature's changes—such as the one where he disguises himself as a linoleum floor, only to rise up and kill an unwary policeman. (See Figures 6.5 and 6.6.)

At ILM, they distinguish between morphing and metamorphosing, preferring the first term for 2D and the second for 3D. The distinction might be useful to them, but since the included software is 2D only, I won't worry about it here.

Besides the 3D creature, there is a lot of 2D morphing happening in this movie. At one point in the story, the T-1000 impersonates Linda Hamilton. In the climactic steel-mill scene, he changes back to his normal shape as Robert Patrick.

The metamorphosis is perfectly executed, with Hamilton's hair pulling in then growing short as the morph unwinds. First one sleeve of the T-1000's uniform appears, then the next. All the while the features of her face slowly change into Patrick's.

One of the interesting features of computerized morphing is how transparent it seems. The effect is compelling even under the scrutiny of slow motion. In this video age, an effect like that can translate into big bucks.

It is one thing to morph Hamilton into Patrick. At least they had obvious points in common to map to. But there is another scene that has to be seen to be appreciated.

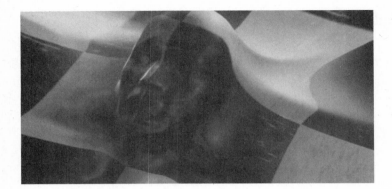

Figures 6.5 and 6.6.

Terminator 2: Judgement Day stills courtesy of Carolco © 1991.

In a knock-down, drag-out fight with Schwarzenegger, Patrick gets thrown against a wall, face first. Instead of turning around to continue the brawl, the T-1000 simply mutates to face backward.

The job of the animator here was to make Patrick's face sprout out of the back of his head. Not having anything but hair to go on, they gave it a little punch by starting his features small, in the middle of his head. As the features grew to normal size, the hair faded out and the transformation was complete.

To keep the eye busy (and for those people with an itchy slo-mo finger) they even morphed his shirt. Two seams down his back smoothly shift in to the middle and become the seams around his front buttons. It is the only morph in the movie that isn't seamless (yes, that was a pun—I apologize).

The grand finale of the movie has our battered hero finally dispatching the T-1000 in a vat of molten steel. Steve Williams and Andrew Schmidt threw themselves, and everything else, into the task of animating the monster's swan song.

As he writhes and twists in burning agony, the T-1000 goes through all the forms it adopted in the movie. Heads and hands intertwine and fold into each other. In its final death spasm, the screaming creature turns inside-out and is gone.

Other Works

This could be one of the last books to list all the movies that use morphing. Soon the list will be too long to print. Since the seminal *Willow*, morphing in the movies has grown exponentially.

In 1992, the Steven King movie *Sleepwalkers* (directed by Mick Garris) made good use of the morphing technique. The sleepwalkers of the title are "shape-shifters"— some sort of unholy cross between humans and cats. To live, they need human flesh—from pretty young virgins, of course.

There is a lot of metamorphosing in this movie. The monsters change from beautiful people to nasty gargoyles before they attack the unwary (see the color plates). Some of the morphing was done in a more traditional way, with latex models that swell and shrink. But the majority of the morphing was done on the computer. The special effects were created by Apogee Productions.

Another recent movie to feature morphing is *Freddy's Dead: The Final Nightmare*. Here morphing is used to transport a house into outer space. With the house stationary, the backyard zooms away, morphing into the earth as it grows distant.

Finally, there were several morphing sequences in *Death Becomes Her*. Some pretty grusome things were done to Meryl Streep and Goldie Hawn with morphing and warping. Streep's head gets twisted backward and Hawn's mid-section gets blasted out. Of course they have taken a potion that makes them immortal, so they can suffer these indignities with something approaching aplomb. The potion provides another morphing situation as Streep grows younger in front of a mirror.

That pretty much wraps up the morphing movies to date. But dozens of new projects are already in the works. In Hollywood, if somethings works, it gets milked for all it's worth.

Epilogue

"It is the spectators that make the pictures."

Marcel Duchamp

Duchamp wanted to reach his audience directly. Like Ernest Hemingway, he wanted his work to be transparent—to let the story shine through, unimpeded. He was interested in the spectator, not the painting.

He didn't create in a vacuum. All good filmmakers want the same thing. They talk about suspending disbelief, which just means they want to suck in an audience and never give them a reason to doubt the reality of what they see.

Morphing satisfies those requirements, even in the details.

Where are we today with morphing? Has it been done to death? Perhaps. It didn't help *Death Becomes Her*, which used morphing to great effect, but was critically panned and performed anemically in distribution.

Nevertheless, people have always been in love with the idea of metamorphosing. As a literary or film device, it will always be popular.

The real legacy of morphing, however, is more subtle. It can be used to fix makeup or slightly modify some part of an actor. It can alter backgrounds and hide the wires supporting a stuntman.

It can be used to cover up glitches. Say you have just shot two takes of a scene. You hate the beginning of one and you hate the ending of the other. The solution: take the good parts and splice them together with an invisible morph.

That's where morphing becomes an indispensable tool—it ensures the continuity needed to fool the eye. And that's what Hollywood is all about.

Hollywood is also about money. It takes vast resources to make a movie. Unfortunately, that puts the power into the hands of the bean-counters. They want accountability, and in Hollywood, there are a lot of evanescent qualities, such as star power or location shooting, that are hard to pin down. Not so with special effects. There is a known amount of bang for your effects buck. This totally mercenary philosophy will ensure a steady stream of novel effects.

Morphing is here to stay, and now that it's here, watch out! Just remember, you can no longer believe what you see—at least in the movies.

Software

First, make a backup of the disk. There are line files (with the extensions .LN1 and .LN2) that are automatically created by MORPH.EXE and WARP.EXE. If you change the control lines for an image, its corresponding line files are overwritten. The line files are saved whether or not the tweening sequence is saved. If you corrupt the line files and you want to get the originals back, just copy them from the subdirectory LINES. From the DOS command line, type:

```
>COPY LINES\*.*
```

Or just copy them one-by-one as you need them. For instance, to restore the original control lines for the picture TIM.PCX, you would type:

```
>COPY LINES\TIM.LN?
```

The first line set, LN1, is used to describe the general outline of the head and shoulders, as well as the hairline, eyebrows, eyes, nose, nostrils, upper and lower lips, and the chin. There are 22 lines in all. The second line set, LN2, is a warped version of the first. Both line sets are used by WARP. MORPH, on the other hand, uses only the LN1 set from each image.

With 22 lines it takes my 33 MHz 486 about three to five minutes to create each tween. For faster morphing, you can reduce the number of lines. You can make surprisingly good morphs with just three lines: an eye, a nose, and a mouth line.

The lines are similar for the animals, with the exception of the ears. The animals on the disk, like the lion and zebra, have their ears located high on their heads. Instead of stretching the human ears up, I make them part of the head outline and blend them away. Meanwhile the animal ears sprout from the hair.

The Programs

All the following programs work with PCX files having 256 colors and 320 x 200 resolution. When specifying a PCX file, you don't need to type in the file extension. The programs automatically append ".PCX" to the end of each filename, saving you the trouble.

Some of these programs produce a numbered sequence of output files. These are also PCX files. The maximum sequence size is 99. The sequence number, from 1 to 99, is appended to the root name of the file sequence. This takes two characters away from the generous DOS allotment of eight. Therefore, the `<OutFile>` name can be, at most, six characters long.

WARP

WARP `<File>` [`<Steps>` [`<OutFile>`]]

> `<File>` is the name of the PCX file to warp.

> `<Steps>` is the optional number of tweening steps in the warping sequence. If you don't specify the number of steps in your sequence, the program produces one warp. You *must* specify `<Steps>` if you want WARP to create output files.

> `<OutFile>` is the root name of the optional output files. The value of `<Steps>` determines the number of files to output. The step number is appended to the root name, so the `<OutFile>` name must be six characters or less.

> WARP reads the indicated PCX file. It warps the image in the given number of steps to make a sequence of files. The files are numbered and can be displayed by the LOAD program.

Examples:

```
WARP JIM
```

This command will cause WARP to load the file JIM.PCX. It will warp the image as directed, then display it. No files are created.

```
WARP JIM 7
```

This command will cause WARP to load the file JIM.PCX. It will warp the image in a sequence of seven frames and display them. No files are created.

```
WARP JIM 7 WJIM
```

This command will cause WARP to load the file JIM.PCX. It will warp the image in a sequence of seven frames. Each frame is displayed while it is saved to the disk. The files will be named WJIM1.PCX, WJIM2.PCX,…WJIM7.PCX.

DISSOLVE

```
DISSOLVE <File1> <File2> [<Steps> [<OutFile>]]
```

> *<File1>* is the name of the source PCX file to dissolve.
>
> *<File2>* is the name of the target PCX file.
>
> *<Steps>* is the optional number of output files. If you don't specify the number of steps in your sequence, the program produces one in-between dissolve. You *must* specify *<Steps>* if you want to output files.
>
> *<OutFile>* is the root name of the optional output files. The value of *<Steps>* determines the number of files to output. The step number is appended to the root name, so the *<OutFile>* name must be six characters or less.

DISSOLVE reads two input files: the source and target PCX images. It dissolves between the two in the given number of steps, making a sequence of files. The files are numbered and can be displayed by the LOAD program.

Examples:

```
DISSOLVE JIM BOB
```

This command will cause DISSOLVE to load the files JIM.PCX and BOB.PCX. It will create a balanced double-exposure and display it. No files are created.

```
DISSOLVE JIM BOB 7
```

This command will load the files JIM.PCX and BOB.PCX. It will create a sequence of seven frames and display them. No files are created.

```
DISSOLVE JIM BOB 7 JIMBOB
```

This command will load the files JIM.PCX and BOB.PCX. It will create a sequence of seven frames. Each frame is displayed while it is saved to the disk. The files will be named JIMBOB1.PCX, JIMBOB2.PCX,…JIMBOB7.PCX.

MORPH

MORPH *<File1>* *<File2>* [*<Steps>* [*<OutFile>*]]

> *<File1>* is the name of the source PCX file to morph.

> *<File2>* is the name of the target PCX file.

> *<Steps>* is the optional number of output files. If you don't specify the number of steps in your sequence, the program produces one in-between morph. You *must* specify *<Steps>* if you want to output files.

> *<OutFile>* is the root name of the optional output files. The value of *<Steps>* determines the number of files to output. The step number is appended to the root name, so the *<OutFile>* name must be six characters or less.

MORPH reads two input files: the source and target PCX images. It metamorphoses between the two in the given number of steps, to make a sequence of files. The files are numbered and can be displayed by the LOAD program.

Examples:

```
MORPH JIM BOB
```

This command will cause MORPH to load the files JIM.PCX and BOB.PCX. It will create the middle tween and display it. No files are created.

```
MORPH JIM BOB 7
```

This command will load the files JIM.PCX and BOB.PCX. It will create a sequence of seven frames and display them. No files are created.

```
MORPH JIM BOB 7 JIMBOB
```

This command will load the files JIM.PCX and BOB.PCX. It will create a sequence of seven frames. Each frame is displayed while it is saved to the disk. The files will be named JIMBOB1.PCX, JIMBOB2.PCX,…JIMBOB7.PCX.

LOAD

```
LOAD <File>
```

> `<File>` is the root name of a PCX sequence to display.

LOAD reads a sequence of PCX files indicated by the given name. It reads as many as it can fit into memory, then it displays them sequentially. You can control the playback rate by pressing a number from 1 (slow) to 9 (fast). To single-step through the pictures, press the space bar. To continue playback, press Enter. To quit, press ESC.

Example:

```
LOAD JIM
```

This command will cause the program to load a numbered sequence of PCX files with the root name of JIM, such as JIM1.PCX, JIM2.PCX, and so on.

FIX

```
FIX <InFile> <OutFile>
```

> `<InFile>` is the root name of the PCX sequence to fix.

> `<OutFile>` is the root name of the fixed PCX sequence.

FIX takes a sequence created by DISSOLVE or MORPH and forces each picture in the sequence to have the same palette. Then it writes the sequence out under the new name.

Examples:

```
FIX JIM FXJIM
```

This command would read the sequence JIM1.PCX, JIM2.PCX, and so on. It would output the same number of files named FXJIM1.PCX, FXJIM2.PCX, and so on.

```
FIX JIM JIM
```

This command would read the JIM sequence and write over the original files. Be careful! Make sure you don't need the originals before you do this.

Hints for Programmers

Compiling instructions

These programs were all compiled with the Microsoft compiler. When you installed the compiler, you were asked if you wanted to include the graphics library. If you didn't, you will need to link that library in at compile time. Use a command like:

```
cl program.c /link graphics.lib
```

You say you don't remember if you included it? No problem, just try it both with and without the graphics library—only one way will work.

For the morphing routines, I have included a makefile. It is set up assuming that you *haven't* installed the graphics library. Examine it to see how to compile the various modules. If you *have* installed the graphics library, then delete all instances of:

```
/link graphics.lib
```

To make the programs work with other compilers, you will need to make some changes. In particular, any non-ANSI standard commands will need to be revised. In Microsoft, these commands have an underline as the first character in their name. Thus, one way to correct them is to search for the underline, check your compiler for the corresponding command, and make the change.

Changes and Additions to the Programs

The programs on the included disk are a good way to learn about morphing and warping. But the curious programmer will want to take this material and go further. To help you, here are some of the things that might bring large rewards quickly:

If you have expanded memory, you might be able to devise a method of swapping that memory in and out to handle much longer animation sequences. If you have eight megabytes of expanded memory, you could hold 16 extra frames in memory. Not everyone has expanded memory.

Don't confuse it with extended memory. (How can you not?) You probably have a lot of extended memory, but you can't use it without Windows to give you access to it. Expanded memory, on the other hand, is almost obsolete, but it can be swapped in and out of normal memory space by a DOS program. Consult the manuals that came with your expanded memory.

If you can work with smaller images—say quarter-screen, 160 x 100 resolution—you should be able to quadruple the number of frames and speed up the animation. The routines to change are in IO.C, the display picture routines. Currently, they slam a continuous string of bytes into memory. To fix it for smaller screens, you need to move the image one line at a time.

If you have a true-color card, you don't need the agonizing color-collapsing routines. Just yank them all out. You will need to save the files in 24-bit color mode, which can present some data problems, so look at the drivers and documentation for your particular graphics card.

To capture PCX images for use in these programs, you need to find 320 x 200 images and use a TSR program such as *Snap*, from Inner Media. Or you can find GIF images on CompuServe and convert them with a program like *Paint Shop* from ZSoft. Remember to convert the number of colors to 256.

To tweak the algorithm, you might want to play with the weighting function of the warping routine. The code is in `sumLines` in the file LINECALC.C. You also might wish to convert some of the slow floating-point math to fixed point. It would certainly speed things up, but is there enough accuracy?

For good ideas, pictures and algorithms, you should get a subscription to *IEEE Computer Graphics and Applications* (714-821-8380), the premier magazine for computer graphics.

Also, you need the *Siggraph* journal from the Association for Computing Machinery (1-800-447-2226). The algorithms for this book were inspired by Siggraph articles.

Also of great use is *Dr. Dobb's Journal* (1-800-456-1215), which regularly carries articles on computer graphics.

Finally, although it doesn't discuss algorithms, there are lots of pretty pictures and insider news in *Computer Graphics World* (918-831-9400).

Glossary

Algorithm: An algorithm is a recipe for a computer. Donning its chef's hat, your computer executes each step of the recipe—to the letter. It can do it over and over again, perfectly. Programming is like creating a new dish. It can take a long time to learn how to keep a souffle from falling or an algorithm from crashing. Practice, practice.

Bit: The smallest unit of a computer's memory. Believe it or not, everything a computer does is based on transistors that can be either "on" or "off." Because they have only two states, they are called binary. A light switch is binary, so this is just a fancy way of talking about something exceptionally simple. Bit is short for <u>bi</u>nary di<u>git</u>. Don't pay any attention to the fact that digit means ten, not two. The people who created this term sure didn't.

Byte: This colorful word usually means eight **bits**. I say usually because sometimes it means three or nine or sixteen. That makes this a very useful word if you want to confuse someone. It really refers to a basic unit of memory storage, which was eight bits in the 70s and 80s, but is often sixteen bits in the 90s. Nevertheless, nine times out of ten, someone who is talking about bytes is talking about eight bits. A byte is good enough to represent a number from zero to 255. The alphabet (uppercase and lowercase with special symbols), fits nicely into a byte. So does an index into a 256-entry color table, and that's one of the tricks VGA cards exploit.

CMY or CMYK: Cyan, Magenta, Yellow, and Black are the primary colors used in printing. Of course, they just happen to be the opposite of the colors used on the computer: Red, Green, and Blue (see **RGB**). That is because the printing colors are subtractive, meaning that each successive application of colored ink subtracts from the overall brightness. If you pile up all three primary colors, you should get black. In fact, you get mud. Rats. Usually black is added to the mix to fix it. That pushes you into the four color world of CMYK. (The K stands for blacK because Blue had already absconded with B.)

Color: On a computer monitor, color is an additive combination of three components: red, green, and blue (see **RGB**). These three components do a fine job of creating most of the colors you might be interested in. In printing, these three colors are translated into the subtractive colors: cyan, magenta, and yellow (see **CMY**). There are algorithms for converting from RGB colors to CMY colors, but not all colors translate with perfect fidelity. Life is tough.

Dissolve, cross-dissolve, or lap-dissolve: This is Hollywood-speak for fading out one image while fading in another. Because the fades overlap, the screen intensity doesn't change and the effect is very smooth. It is distinct from the straight fade, where the screen goes to black. The computerized version uses the following method: for the first **tween** of a ten-frame sequence, take ten percent of the source image and ninety percent of the target image and combine them. For the second tween, add twenty percent of the source with eighty percent of the target, and so on.

DOS: The Disk Operating System is the "old" operating system for the IBM. The "new" operating system is called Windows. But Windows still uses DOS, underneath everything, to deal with the disk drives. To accommodate the largest audience, the included programs work under DOS. If you have Windows, click on the *DOS Prompt* icon to start DOS up.

Extension: With **DOS** (the Disk Operating System), everything is saved to the disk in files that have eight-character names, a period, and then a three-character "extension" such as TXT or **PCX**. Check out your DOS manual for further information.

Extrapolation: Like **interpolation**, this provides new data based on a given set. Extrapolation extends the general direction of the data *past* the last known point.

Fade-In or Fade-Out: A Hollywoodism that instructs the cameraman to slowly change the diaphragm (f-stop for you camera buffs). If it is a fade-in, the diaphragm is opened and the sequence goes from black to the fully-lit scene. For a fade-out, the diaphragm is closed and the screen goes to black. If you rewind the film after a fade-*out* and shoot a new sequence while fading *in*, you get a **cross-dissolve**.

Frame: A single frame in a film, video, or computer movie. To qualify as animation, new frames should be displayed at least ten to thirty times per second. Sixty times a second would probably be best, but it will take a few years to get there. Film is twenty-four frames per second, video is thirty, and computers go as fast as the hardware allows.

ILM: Industrial Light and Magic, a division of LucasArts in San Rafael, California. This is the computer graphics studio that started it all. Look at the end of any recent movie with great special effects and you will see a credit for ILM. These guys are the champs.

Interpolation: A mathematical term for evenly filling-in between two end positions. Intermediate positions are generated to provide the desired continuity. This is the basis of the **tweening** algorithm.

Key Frame: In **tweened** animation, the **key frames** are the ones you draw. The rest—the tweens—are created by the computer. To save time, the key frames represent just the extremes of motion. For instance a waving hand can be animated with just the left and right positions of the wave. Everything in-between can be **interpolated**.

Morph: A vaguely sinister term. When you play with the included programs, don't tell someone over the phone that you are doing morphing. They are likely to think you are a junkie and gossip about you. Actually this word is a shortened version of metamorphosing, and it refers to a sequence of smooth changes between two different images, such as a man and a werewolf, or a bat and a vampire. Technically, morphing combines a **warp** and a **dissolve**, as discussed elsewhere.

Palette: A group of colors. In the best of all possible worlds, we would have millions of colors available on our computers. In fact, there are wonderful things called "true" or "24-bit" color cards that you can put in your IBM and really get those millions of colors. But most of us have VGA cards and 256 colors at best. These 256 are culled from the possible millions and represented in a table called the palette. Each **pixel** on the screen is just an index into this table. The actual color is in the palette in the form of its constituent red, green and blue components.

PDI: Pacific Data Images, Los Angeles, California. This company is the primary competitor to **ILM** (Industrial Light and Magic) in the computer special effects department. The warping program on the included disk is based loosely on the algorithm developed at PDI to do the Michael Jackson video, among others. Very clever people.

Pixel: A picture element—in lay terms, a dot on the screen. I know, there is no "X" in picture element. I think someone must have been hitting the Jolt Cola a little too hard when they came up with that one.

PCX: This is one of the standard graphics formats on the IBM. The version of PCX file used for the programs in this book is the 256-color mode with 320 x 200 resolution. This resolution requires 64,000 bytes. The files are "packed" or run-length encoded, so they are usually smaller than that, to save you some disk space.

RGB: This is a dreaded **TLA**. It stands for Red, Green, and Blue. These three colors are the basis of the additive color you have on your computer screen. These colors are complementary to the **CMY** colors used in printing.

TLA: Three-Letter Acronym.

Tween: This is a somewhat silly shorthand for in-be*tween*ing. It refers to a series of images that smoothly connect two other images. If the images are similar—say a horse in two different poses—the result is regular animation. If the images are different, tweening creates a smooth metamorphosis called **morphing**.

Warp: This is a technique for stretching and squashing an image. Think of the image as printed on a sheet of rubber. Pick parts of it to push and pull around. If you combine warping with tweening, you can get animation from a single image.

Wild Card: When referring to files, DOS provides special characters that are like wild cards in games—they stand for anything. There are two of them, the question mark and the asterisk. The question mark stands for a single character only, whereas the asterisk stands for multiple characters. For example, FILE?.PCX would find FILE1.PCX through FILE9.PCX, but not FILECAB.PCX; whereas FILE*.PCX would find FILE1.PCX through FILE99.PCX, not to mention FILET.PCX, if such a file existed.

Zoetrope: An early machine for displaying animation. Also a company founded by Francis Ford Coppola. And it gives me an entry for Z.

Bibliography

Edward Angel, *Computer Graphics,* 1990, Addison-Wesley Publishing Company: Reading, Massachusetts. ISBN 0-201-13548-5.

Bruce A. Artwick, *Applied Concepts in Microcomputer Graphics,* 1984, Prentice Hall, Inc.: Englewood Cliffs, New Jersey 07632. ISBN 0-13-039322-3.

Jean-Christophe Bailly, *Duchamp,* 1986, Universe Books: New York. ISBN 0-87663-887-6.

Craig F. Bohren, *Clouds in a Glass of Beer,* 1987, John Wiley & Sons, Inc.: New York. ISBN 0-471-62482-9.

Thomas Bulfinch, *Myths of Greece and Rome,* 1981, Viking Penguin Inc.: New York. ISBN 0-1400-5643-2.

Robert Burton, *Bird Flight,* 1990, Facts On File: New York. ISBN 0-8160-2410-3.

John L. Casti, *Alternate Realities,* 1989, John Wiley & Sons, Inc.: New York. ISBN 0-471-61842-X.

Geoffrey M. Cooper, *Oncogenes,* 1990, Jones and Bartlett Publishers, Inc.: 20 Park Plaza, Boston, MA 02116. ISBN 0-86720-136-3.

John Culhane, *Walt Disney's Fantasia,* 1983, Abradale Press, Harry Abrams, Inc.: New York. ISBN 0-8109-8078-9.

Joseph Deken, *Computer Images—State of the Art,* 1983, Stewart, Tabori & Chang: New York. ISBN 0-941434-37-0.

Marshall Deutelbaum, *Image, on the Art and Evolution of the Film,* 1979, Dover Publications: New York. ISBN 0-486-23777-X.

Gerald M. Edelman, *Topobiology,* 1988, Basic Books, Inc.: New York ISBN 0-465-08634-9.

Jack C. Ellis, *A History of Film,* 1985, Prentice Hall, Inc.: Englewood Cliffs, New Jersey. ISBN 0-13-389479-7.

M.C. Escher, *Escher on Escher, Exploring the Infinite,* 1986, Harry N. Abrams, Inc.: New York. ISBN 0-8109-2414-5.

Anthony Esler, *The Human Venture, the Great Enterprise,* 1986, Prentice Hall, Inc.: Englewood Cliffs, New Jersey. ISBN 0-13-447830-4.

James D. Foley and Andries Van Dam, *Fundamentals of Interactive Computer Graphics,* 1984, Addison-Wesley Publishing Company, Inc.: Reading, Mass. ISBN 0-201-14468-9.

Richard Mark Friedhoff, *The Second Computer Revolution—Visualization,* 1989, Harry N. Abrams, Inc.: New York. ISBN 0-8109-1709-2.

Howard Gardner, *Frames of Mind,* 1983, Basic Books, Inc.: New York. ISBN 0-465-02508-0.

Martin Gardner, *Penrose Tiles to Trapdoor Ciphers …and the Return of Dr. Matrix,* 1989, W.H. Freeman and Company: New York. ISBN 0-7167-1986-X.

D.M. Glover & B.D. Hames, *Genes and Embryos,* 1989, IRL Press at Oxford University Press: Oxford. ISBN 0-19-963028-3.

Rafael C. Gonzalez and Paul Wintz, *Digital Image Processing,* 1987, Addison-Wesley Publishing Company, Inc.: Reading, Massachusetts. ISBN 0-201-11026-1.

Bernard Grun, *Timetables of History,* 1982, Simon & Schuster, Inc.: New York. ISBN 0-671-24987-8.

Phil Hardy, *Science Fiction, the Complete Film Sourcebook,* 1984, William Morrow and Company: New York. ISBN 0-688-00842-9.

Steven Harrington, *Computer Graphics, A Programming Approach,* 1987, McGraw Hill, Inc.: New York. ISBN 0-07-026753-7.

Donald Hearn and M. Pauline Baker, *Computer Graphics,* 1986, Prentice Hall, Inc.: Englewood Cliffs, New Jersey 07632. ISBN 0-13-165382-2.

Douglas R. Hofstadter, *Gödel, Escher, Bach: an Eternal Golden Braid,* 1979, Basic Books, Inc.: New York. ISBN 0-465-02685-0.

Maurice Horn, *The World Encyclopedia of Cartoons,* 1980, Chelsea House Publishers: 133 Christopher Street, New York, NY 10014. ISBN 0-87754-088-8.

Bradley Dyck Kliewer, *EGA/VGA A Programmer's Reference Guide,* 1988, Intertext Publications, McGraw Hill Book Company: 11 West 19th Street, New York, NY 10011. ISBN 0-07-035089-2.

Craig A. Lindley, *Practical Image Processing In C,* 1991, John Wiley & Sons, Inc.: New York. ISBN 0-471-53062-X.

C.J. Pennycuick, *Newton Rules Biology,* 1992, Oxford University Press: Walton Street, Oxford OX2 6DP. ISBN 0-19-854020-5.

Clifford A. Pickover, *Computers and the Imagination,* 1991, St. Martin's Press, Inc.: 175 Fifth Avenue, New York, NY 10010. ISBN 0-312-06131-5.

G. Polya, *How To Solve It,* 1973, Princeton University Press: Princeton, New Jersey. ISBN 0-691-08097-6.

Roger T. Stevens, *Graphics Programming in C,* 1988, M&T Books: 501 Galveston Drive, Redwood City, CA 94063. ISBN 1-558-51018-4.

George Sutty and Steve Blair, *Advanced Programmer's Guide to the EGA/VGA,* 1988, Brady Books, a division of Simon & Schuster, Inc., distributed by Prentice Hall Trade. ISBN 0-13-729039-X.

Bob Thomas, *Art of Animation from Mickey Mouse to Beauty and the Beast,* 1991, Welcome Enterprises, Inc: 164 East 95th Street, New York, NY 10128. ISBN: 1-56282-899-1.

Frank Thomas & Ollie Johnston, *Disney Animation, the Illusion of Life,* 1984, Abbeville Press: New York and Walt Disney Productions: Burbank, CA. ISBN 0-89659-498-X.

Steven Vogel, *Life's Devices,* 1988, Princeton University Press: 41 William Street, Princeton, New Jersey 08540. ISBN 0-691-08504-8.

Steven Vogel, *Vital Circuits,* 1992, Oxford University Press: 200 Madison Ave, New York, NY 10016. ISBN 0-19-507155-7.

Neal Weinstock, *Computer Animation,* 1986, Addison-Wesley Publishing Company, Inc: New York. ISBN 0-201-09438-X.

Tony White, *The Animator's Workbook,* 1986, Watson-Guptill Publications: 1515 Broadway, New York, NY 10036. ISNB 0-8230-0228-4.

Richard Wilton, *The Programmer's Guide to PC & PS/2 Video Systems,* 1987, Microsoft Press, 16011 NE 36th Way, Box 97017, Redmond, WA 98073-9717. ISBN 1-55615-103-9.

George Wolberg, *Digital Image Warping,* 1990, IEEE Computer Society Press: 10662 Los Vaqueros Circle, PO Box 3014, Los Alamitos, CA 90720-1264. ISBN 0-8186-8944-7.

I Index

To Order Fantavision:

- Complete this form and return it with your check or money order in U.S. dollars, drawn on a U.S. bank, payable to Wild Duck, **or**
- Fax your Purchase Order to Wild Duck at (707) 586-0728, **or**
- Call Wild Duck at (707) 586-0728 Monday through Friday between 10:00 A.M. and 5:00 P.M. PST.
- For special rates on site licenses, call Wild Duck at (707) 586-0728.

Name _____

Title _____

Organization/School _____

Address _____

City/State/Zip_____

Phone: (_____)_____   Fax: (_____)_____

	End User	**School Ed**	**Lab Pack**
IBM	☐ $79.95	☐ $99.50*	☐ $195.00*
Apple IIGS	☐ $79.95	☐ $99.50*	☐ $195.00*
Amiga	☐ $79.95	☐ $89.50	☐ $185.00

*Price includes the Teacher's Guide to Fantavision

Subtotal (please check a box, above)	
CA residents add Sales Tax (7.5%)	
Shipping**	
TOTAL	

**Shipping: U.S. orders $4.00, Canada and Mexico $9.00, Overseas orders $22.00

Wild Duck

mail to: 979 Golf Course Drive
Suite 256
Rohnert Park, CA 94928

Add to Your Sams Library Today with the Best Books for Programming, Operating Systems, and New Technologies

The easiest way to order is to pick up the phone and call

1-800-428-5331

between 9:00 a.m. and 5:00 p.m. EST.
For faster service please have your credit card available.

ISBN	Quantity	Description of Item	Unit Cost	Total Cost
0-672-30318-3		Windows Sound FunPack (Book/Disk)	$19.95	
0-672-30309-4		Programming Sound for DOS and Windows (Book/Disk)	$39.95	
0-672-30240-3		OS/2 2.1 Unleashed (Book/Disk)	$34.95	
0-672-30288-8		DOS Secrets Unleashed (Book/Disk)	$39.95	
0-672-30298-5		Windows NT: The Next Generation	$22.95	
0-672-30269-1		Absolute Beginner's Guide to Programming	$19.95	
0-672-30326-4		Absolute Beginner's Guide to Networking	$19.95	
0-672-30341-8		Absolute Beginner's Guide to C	$16.95	
0-672-27366-7		Memory Management for All of Us	$29.95	
0-672-30249-7		Multimedia Madness (Book/Disk-CD-ROM)	$44.95	
0-672-30248-9		FractalVision (Book/Disk)	$39.95	
0-672-30315-9		The Magic of Image Processing (Book/Disk)	$39.95	
0-672-30310-8		Windows Graphics FunPack	$19.95	
0-672-30040-0		Teach Yourself C in 21 Days	$24.95	
0-672-30372-8		Teach Yourself QBasic in 21 Days	$24.95	
❏ 3 ½" disk		Shipping and Handling: See information below.		
❏ 5 ¼" disk		TOTAL		

Shipping and Handling: $4.00 for the first book, and $1.75 for each additional book. Floppy disk: add $1.75 for shipping and handling. If you need to have it NOW, we can ship product to you in 24 hours for an additional charge of approximately $18.00, and you will receive your item overnight or in two days. Overseas shipping and handling, add $2.00 per book and $8.00 for up to three disks. Prices subject to change. Call for availability and pricing information on latest editions.

11711 N. College Avenue, Suite 140, Carmel, Indiana 46032

1-800-428-5331 — Orders   1-800-835-3202 — FAX   1-800-858-7674 — Customer Service

Book ISBN 0-672-30320-5